Great Christian Thinkers

Great Christian Thinkers

Hans Küng

Continuum · New York

1996

The Continuum Publishing Company
370 Lexington Avenue, New York, NY 10017

Translated by John Bowden from the German *Grosse
Christliche Denker* copyright © R. Piper GmbH &
Co. KG 1994
Translation copyright © John Bowden 1994

Library of Congress Cataloging-in-Publication Data
Küng, Hans, 1928–
    [Grosse christliche Denker.   English]
    Great Christian thinkers / Hans Küng.
        p.   cm.
    Includes bibliographical references.
    Contents: Paul—Origen—Augustine—
    Thomas Aquinas—Martin
    Luther—Friedrich Schleiermacher—Karl Barth.
ISBN 0-8264-0643-2 (hbd.)   ISBN 0-8264-0848-6 (pbk.)
        1. Theology—Introductions.   2. Theologians.
    I. Title.
    BT77.K79   1994   94-883
    230'.092'2—dc20   CIP

Printed in the United States of America

Contents

For Eberhard Jüngel and Jürgen Moltmann,
my theological companions in Tübingen,
in gratitude for many intimate ecumenical discussions,
always inspiring, sometimes passionate.

A Brief Introduction to Theology

This short book offers a somewhat unusual but, I hope, relatively simple **introduction to Christian theology,** what it is focussed on and how it is done. There are many introductions to theology; most have a thematic approach, using abstract methodological or hermeneutical principles. With some satisfaction, here I have adopted another course. Here is theology in the doing, theology in the living, theology as reflected by paradigmatic figures of the history of Christianity – great Christian thinkers who are representative of whole eras.

Can Christians, may Christians, call **Christian thinkers 'great'**? May some Christians say of others that they are 'great' theologians? We need to be careful: someone who regards others as great theologians, indeed who even regards himself as the greatest theologian, may well be the greatest – ass! That, at any rate is the view of one of the seven 'greats' that we have to discuss here: 'If, however, you feel and are inclined to think that you have made it, flattering yourself with your own little books, teaching, or writing, because you have done it beautifully and preached excellently; if you are highly pleased when someone praises you in the presence of others; if you perhaps look for praise, and would sulk or quit what you are doing if you did not get it – if you are of that stripe, dear friend, then take yourself by the ears, and if you do this in the right way you will find a beautiful pair of big, long, shaggy, ass's ears. Then do not spare any expense! Decorate them with golden bells, so that people will be able to hear you wherever you go, point their fingers at you, and say, "See, see, there goes that clever beast, who can write such exquisite things and even so remarkably well." That very moment you will be blessed and blessed beyond measure in the kingdom of heaven. Yes, in that heaven where hellfire is ready for the devil and his angels.' Thus Martin Luther, when at a late stage in his career, in 1539, he had to compose a preface to the first volume of his German writings ('Preface to the Wittenberg Edition of Luther's German Writings', in *Martin Luther's Basic Theological Writings*, ed. Timothy F.Lull, Minneapolis 1989, 67f.).

So we have been warned: those who think that they can measure the 'greatness' of a theologian by the extent of his or her work, the influence of his or her words or popular admiration are doing the work of the devil! The greatness of at least a Christian theologian is measured only by whether **the Christian message**, Holy Scripture, God's very Word, comes to light through his or her work. The theologian is to be the first servant of the Logos, the Word. Not the theologian's ideas but God's Word is to be translated for the men and women of a time. Through their indefatigable questioning and research, theologians have to understand God's cause anew and make it understandable to each new age – in season, out of season; whether it pleases the spirit of an age or not.

So in these seven brief portraits we shall always have two concerns, **description** and **criticism,** not least because of the influence exerted by these great thinkers, which has lasted down to the present day. By their work they have not only understood the world in different ways but also changed it. It will not be easy to condense into a few pages thinkers who (apart from the first) have all written small libraries and (without exception) have had a large library written about them, to describe their basic views against the background of their lives and at the same time to make a critical evaluation of them. Specialists in the history of theology (listed in the bibliographical surveys), to whom I owe so much, in particular will understand this. Not everything can be mentioned in such an undertaking. A broad perspective has to be combined with concentration on what is central for these great figures. My little book cannot and should not be a substitute for reading their works. On the contrary, the greatest reward would be if sometimes it could lead readers to immerse themselves personally in the world and work of these great figures.

This short book is a **forerunner** to the second volume of my trilogy 'The Religious Situation of Our Time', which is to be devoted to **Christianity.** In that book I shall be returning in a wider historical context to the theologians discussed here. As already in *Credo*, which preceded the present book on the Christian thinkers, I am deeply grateful to my team for their intensive collaboration, above all to Dr Karl-Josef Kuschel, Privat-dozent in the Catholic Theological Faculty and Deputy Director of the Institute for Ecumenical Research, and to my colleague Frau Marianne Saur. Once again the overall design of the book and checking of notes was in the hands of Stephan Schlensog, and the manuscript was prepared by Frau Eleonore Henn and Frau Franziska Heller-Manthey; the proofs were read by my doctoral student Matthias Schnell and Michel Hofmann. Once again I would like to thank the Robert Bosch Jubilee Foundation for its generous support of our research project 'No world peace without peace among the religions', within the overall framework of which it also proved possible to write this short book.

I warmly invite readers to enter with me into the world of these seven great Christian thinkers, which at first is very strange, not only for their own sakes, but also in order to have a better understanding of today's reality.

Tübingen, September 1993   Hans Küng

Paul
Christianity becomes a World Religion

Chronology (following Helmut Koester)

35	Conversion.
35-38	Missionary activity in Arabia (Gal.1.17f.).
38	Visits Peter in Jerusalem (Gal.1.18).
38-48	Activity in Cilicia and Syria (Gal.1.21).
48	Apostolic Council in Jerusalem (Gal.2.1ff.; Acts 15).
48-49	Episode in Antioch (Gal.2.11ff.).
49	Mission in Galatia (against Acts 16.6).
50	Mission in Philippi, Thessalonica and Beroea (Acts 16.11-17.14).
50	Autumn: via Athens to Corinth (Acts 17.15; 18.1); composition of I Thessalonians.
50	Autumn to 52 spring: mission in Corinth (Acts 18.11).
52	Summer: journey to Antioch, then through Asia Minor to Ephesus, including second visit to Galatia (Acts 18.18-23; cf. Gal.4.13).
54	Intermediate visit to Corinth (presupposed in II Cor.13.1, etc.).
54-55	Winter: Imprisonment in Ephesus; composition of correspondence with Philippi and the letter to Philemon.
55	Summer: journey through Macedonia to Corinth.
55-56	Winter: stay in Corinth; composition of Romans.
56	Journey to Jerusalem (Acts 20); preparations for handing over the collection (Acts 21.15ff.); arrest.
56-58	Imprisonment in Caesarea.
58	Felix replaced by Festus; Paul sent to Rome.
58-60	Imprisonment in Rome (Acts 28.30).
60	Martyrdom.

1. The most controversial figure for Christians and Jews

A word in advance: Paul the Jew, the first Christian author and theologian, who came from the city of Tarsus in Cilicia (now Turkey), which at that time was a significant trading city on the through route from Anatolia to Syria, is the most controversial figure for Jews and Christians – to the present day. For many Jews this rabbinic scholar has remained **the** Jewish apostate. For most Christians he is **the** apostle, to be mentioned in the same breath as Peter (they are often both patrons of the same church) – not least because according to the Roman calendar the two rivals are celebrated together every year on 29 June!

Paul is a controversial man. Did he ever give up his Jewish faith? That is the question for Jews. And did he really understand Jesus of Nazareth rightly, or did he make something else of him? That is the question for Christians.

Nietzsche already put this decisive question. In his late work *The Antichrist*, he portrayed Paul as the real founder of Christianity, who was at the same time its great falsifier. It was Nietzsche who focussed modern criticism of Paul by playing off Jesus against Paul. Nietzsche could say of Jesus: 'Basically there was only one Christian, and he **died** on the cross. The "gospel" died on the cross.'[1] By contrast Paul is abused by Nietzsche as the 'dysangelist' and 'counterfeiter out of hatred': 'the opposite type to the "bringer of joyful news", the genius in hatred, in the vision of hatred, in the inexorable logic of hatred'.[2] But even Christian theologians were superficial and foolish enough to call for a 'repudiation of Pauline Christianity' with the cry 'back to Jesus!'.

However, Paul was controversial from the beginning. His case disturbed the young Christian community more than any comparable one. For here a man had appeared who was **not a direct disciple of Jesus**, who knew Jesus at best by hearsay, and yet who claimed – on the basis of a quite personal and therefore unverifiable call – to be an apostle of Jesus Christ. Here moreover a man had appeared who had at first come into prominence as a **persecutor of Christians**. Both the sources for Paul's life at our disposal – the authentic Pauline letters and the Acts of the Apostles – agree on one point, that the name of Paul was feared in the young community: 'But Saul laid waste the church, and entering

17

house after house, he dragged off men and women and committed them to prison' – thus the Acts of the Apostles.[3] And the authenticity of this report is endorsed by Paul's own confession: 'Circumcised on the eighth day, of the people of Israel, of the tribe of Benjamin, a Hebrew born of Hebrews; as to the law a Pharisee, as to zeal a persecutor of the church, as to righteousness under the law blameless.'[4]

This very text from Philippians gives us important **basic biographical information**. Here we have sure biographical ground under our feet. For the picture that Acts draws of Paul is strongly influenced by the intentions of its author Luke and the ideas of the communities in the post-apostolic period; it is not always confirmed by the authentic letters of Paul. So restraint is called for: we should not simply take over the accounts of Paul in Acts. However, Tarsus as his birthplace can hardly have been invented, and the original name of the Jew Paul may have been 'Saul' (after the Israelite king of that name), as Acts tells us, even if Paul himself always uses only his Roman name 'Paul' in his letters. The proverbial change of name from Saul to Paul as a result of a conversion experience is, however, less probable, as 'Paul' may well have been a Hellenistic parallel name to Saul from the beginning, chosen (as was customary at the time) because of the similar sound. It is also uncertain whether Paul, who still earned his living as a craftsman (probably a tent-maker) on his missionary journeys, had inherited Roman citizenship from his father, since as a Roman citizen he could more easily have avoided the manifold punishments that he had to endure in the course of his missionary activity, as Acts also in fact reports.[5] Finally, it is uncertain whether Paul grew up in Jerusalem and studied there under the famous rabbi Gamaliel I.

So the authentic letters of Paul have priority for his biography (cf. the chronological table); all the later sources must be checked, and sometimes corrected, by them. On the basis of his own testimony[6] we may certainly assume that Paul came from a Jewish family of the tribe of Benjamin, had been circumcised on the eighth day according to Jewish tradition, after that had had a strict Jewish upbringing, and joined the sect of the Pharisees. This included a formal training in the exegesis of the law and the Hebrew Bible, which presupposed a knowledge of Hebrew (and probably also of Aramaic). So we must imagine the young Paul as a reflective, deeply serious Pharisee of strict observance, influenced by contemporary Jewish apocalyptic, zealous for the law and the preservation of the traditions of the fathers. He was probably born at almost the same time as Jesus, but he grew up in a Hellenistic environment in which Greek was the everyday language and therefore was his mother tongue. His letters bear witness to some command of Greek and a knowledge of popular philosophical views and rhetoric, which can indicate a Greek education.

But this Pharisaic zealot for God and the law saw himself challenged by the emergence of the Jewish Christianity of the Hellenists (probably outside Jerusalem), which was free of the law.[7] Fanatic that he was, he resolved to combat it actively, 'beyond measure', as he writes in Galatians.[8] The scandal presented to every Jew by the assertion of a Messiah who had been crucified under the curse of the law evidently strengthened him further in his boundless zeal for persecution.[9] However, he now arrived at a surprising turning point.

2. A change in life at the end of an age

Paul is virtually the archetypal figure for a great **change in life**, from persecuting Christians to proclaiming Christ – however difficult this may be for us to explain in our day either historically or psychologically. At any rate, Paul himself does not attribute this radical turning point - presumably around 35 near Damascus – to human instruction, a new self-understanding or a heroic effort. Rather, he attributes it to an experience of the living Christ on which he does not elaborate, a 'revelation' (a 'vision') of the risen Crucified One. Paul himself understood this visionary experience - Acts[10] turns it into a legendary story of an appearance of Jesus – less as an individual conversion than as a **call to be an apostle**, a plenipotentiary – **to missionize the Gentiles**.[11] And if we do not doubt an authentic nucleus in the stories of the calls of Hebrew prophets like Isaiah, Jeremiah and Ezekiel, we may not *a priori* doubt an authentic nucleus in the story of the calling of Paul the Pharisee either.

At any rate, it is now the former persecutor of Christians himself who manifests a different attitude to the law and therefore must endure discrimination, persecution, imprisonment and physical punishment from the Jewish establishment and probably also from Jewish Christian agitators. Acts is full of this, and here too Paul himself confirms the authenticity of such accounts – above all when he has to defend himself: 'Three times I have been beaten with rods; once I was stoned. Three times I have been shipwrecked; a night and a day I have been adrift at sea; on frequent journeys, in danger from rivers, danger from robbers, danger from my own people, danger from Gentiles, danger in the city, danger in the wilderness, danger at sea, danger from false brethren.'[12] It is all the more astonishing that this constant **pressure of suffering** did not quench the confidence, hope and joy of the apostle which keeps breaking through.

The inner conversion of Paul from persecuting Christians to proclaiming Christ ultimately remains a mystery which we cannot decipher. However, its consequences were manifest: an **epoch-making shift** in early Christianity, indeed in the ancient world generally. For no matter what is controversial about Paul, **the significance of the apostle and his theology for world history** is indisputable.

But it is quite wrong to depict Paul as the real founder of Christianity, as Nietzsche already did. For long before Paul's personal conversion there was a faith in Christ: in other words, Jewish followers of Jesus experienced the Crucified Jesus as the Messiah (Christ) now elevated to God. So Paul is not responsible for the fundamental shift from Jesus' faith to the community's faith in Christ. What is 'responsible' for that is the Easter experience of the Jesus who was raised to life; from then on it was impossible for a certain group of Jews to believe in the God of Israel apart from the Messiah Jesus.[13]

But what is Paul responsible for? He is responsible for the fact that despite its universal monotheism, it was not Hellenistic Judaism, which was already carrying on an intensive mission among the Gentiles before Paul, but Christianity which became a universal religion of humankind. Paul succeeded in doing what neither prophets nor rabbis had been able to do: to disseminate belief in the one God of Israel all over the world. Paul, who was far and away the best-known and most influential figure of early Christianity, was quite justified in saying in his own defence that he had done more than other apostles. From the most important centres of trade, industry and administration like Antioch, Ephesus, Thessalonika and Corinth, with a whole network of colleagues and intensive correspondence, in a few years he had organized missionary work in Syria, Asia Minor, Macedonia and Greece as far as Illyria.[14]

So that is the significance of the apostle Paul for world history. The one who primarily preached everywhere to Jews, but was mostly rejected by them, opened up access to Jewish belief in God for non-Jews and thus **initiated the first paradigm shift in Christianity** – from Jewish Christianity to Hellenistic Gentile Christianity. To what extent? To the extent that at the Apostolic Council in Jerusalem in 48 he pushed through the decision, in the face of the early Christian circles in Jerusalem, that **Gentiles too can have access to the universal God of Israel,** and can do so **without** first having to accept **circumcision** and the Jewish laws of cleanness, the regulations about food and the sabbath – the 'works of the law' – that they found so alien. Paul recognizes the historical priority of the Jerusalem community and supports it effectively with a large-scale collection in the new Gentile Christian communities, but only when he has gained recognition of his mission to the Gentiles apart from the law from the people in Jerusalem.

In practice all this means that a Gentile can become a Christian without having to become a Jew first. The **consequences** of this basic decision **for the whole Western world** (and not only the Western world) are incalculable:

– Only through Paul did the Christian mission to the Gentiles (which already existed before and alongside Paul) become a resounding success, in contrast to the Jewish-Hellenistic mission.

– Only through Paul did Christianity find a new language of original freshness, direct force and passionate sensitivity.

– Only through Paul did the community of Palestinian and Hellenistic Jews become a community of Jews and Gentiles.

– Only through Paul did the small Jewish 'sect' eventually develop into a 'world religion' in which West and East became more closely bound together even than through Alexander the Great.

– So, without Paul there would have been no Catholic church, without Paul there would have been no Greek and Latin patristic theology, without Paul there would have been no Hellenistic Christian culture, and finally without Paul the change under Constantine would never have taken place. Indeed, later paradigm shifts in Christian theology associated with the names of Augustine, Luther and Barth are also unthinkable without Paul.

However, now we cannot put off an answer to our initial question any longer: did Paul really understand Jesus correctly, or did he make out of him something that Jesus did not want?

3. Uninterested in Jesus?

This question has not been plucked out of thin air. For is it not striking that Paul, who did not know Jesus personally, **hardly refers to the person and preaching of the historical Jesus** in his letters either? Is it not striking that nothing either of the parables of Jesus or the Sermon on the Mount or Jesus's miracles seems to occur in Paul's letters, nor anything at all of the content of Jesus' message? My reply is that it is indeed striking, but that must not lead us to false conclusions. Of course one could go on at great length about the differences between the 'rustic' Jesus of Nazareth, who spoke in the language of fishermen, shepherds and peasants, and Paul the city-dweller and Diaspora Jew, who draws his imagery from city life, from athletics and wrestling, from military service, the theatre and seafaring. But that does not contribute very much. We do not even know whether Paul was tall or short, handsome or ugly, nor what the 'thorn' in his flesh means and what his mystical experiences were. Here above all we must reflect on two important perspectives:

1. The centre of Pauline theology is not human beings generally or the church, or even the history of salvation, but **Jesus Christ himself, crucified and risen.** One must be either blind to what Jesus himself quite radically sought, lived out and endured, or fail to recognize under the Jewish Hellenistic presentation the elemental driving force in Paul, if one cannot see that the letters of Paul in particular keep crying out, 'Back to Jesus, God's Christ!' The crucified Jesus Christ who has been raised to life by God

stands in the centre of Paul's view of God and man. So in favour of human beings there is a christocentricity which is grounded and comes to a climax in a theocentricity. 'God through Jesus Christ' – 'through Jesus Christ to God': this is a basic formula of Pauline theology.

2. Paul is more interested in the **historical Jesus** than the theologians who followed Karl Barth and Rudolf Bultmann were inclined to accept. Certainly, Paul did not want to know about a 'Christ after the flesh'. But that did not mean that he wanted to play the historical or even crucified Jesus off against the risen, exalted Christ, as the representatives of dialectical theology in the twentieth century did. For when Paul says that he wants to know nothing of a 'Christ after the flesh', he is referring to a Jesus Christ who at that time (when he was a persecutor) was known – or better, misunderstood – in a natural human, unbelieving, i.e., 'fleshly' way. This Jesus Christ was contrary to the Jesus Christ whom he now knew (after his conversion) in a pneumatic and believing, 'spiritual' way. So Paul is not concerned to devalue the historical Jesus but with a fundamentally changed relation to him – a relation to Jesus Christ in the Spirit.

Paul was no enlightened sage like Confucius, nor an inward-looking mystic like Buddha. He was a **prophetic figure** through and through, who was stamped by an intense spirituality. He was a great thinker in his own way! He was a completely coherent theologian, but like the prophets of Israel he was not a balanced systematic theologian who has left us a closed system of faith with no contradictions in it. He did not develop an abstract theological problematic of law and gospel, faith and works, like a scholar in an ivory tower; later Lutheran theologians did that. But in the midst of his restless activity as a missionary and a 'worker priest' he reflected on the consequences of his conversion from Pharisaism to belief in Christ and on all the implications of this faith for the Jewish Christian and especially the Gentile Christian communities.

In doing so, this **pioneer thinker of early Christianity** refers relatively rarely to the Gospel tradition about Jesus. But beyond doubt he is positive towards it. At any rate, at least twenty important passages can be cited from the authentic Pauline writings – mostly occasional works, some of which (like Philippians and II Corinthians) consist of several fragments of letters put together afterwards and in any case are not preserved in their completeness – in which Paul is clearly basing himself on the Gospel tradition of Jesus.[15] We can conclude from this that over and above what has been preserved in a highly fortuitous way, Paul could tell his communities a good deal more of what he had heard about the message, conduct and fate of the earthly, historical Jesus in Jerusalem, Damascus, Antioch or elsewhere. Or should we perhaps assume that, say, in Corinth, where he lived for a good eighteen months, in his preaching and catechesis Paul constantly repeated and varied only an abstract 'kerygma' of the crucified and risen Jesus? That he told his hearers nothing about Jesus himself? Did not hand on anything of what he must have heard in his contacts with Peter and other eyewitnesses in Jerusalem, and then again later at the Apostolic Council and elsewhere? That would be to think unhistorically. But in that case where does the continuity between Jesus and Paul lie?

4. *The connection between Paul and Jesus*

It has already become abundantly clear that early Christianity changed decisively through Paul and his restless missionary activity. But this did not happen in contradiction to Jesus. It happened **in connection with Jesus**. For if we look closer, we recognize that in Paul, who always modestly and proudly called himself simply a fully authorized 'messenger', an 'apostle of Jesus Christ' for the Gentiles, very much more of the preaching of Jesus is preserved than individual 'words of the Lord' indicate. Indeed, the 'substance' of the preaching of Jesus has quite smoothly been transformed through the paradigm change into the preaching of Paul. We might reflect on the following seven key words.

   1. **Kingdom of God**. Paul, too, lived quite intensely in the expectation of an imminent kingdom of God, which was expected by many Jews. If Jesus had looked to the future here, Paul at the same time now looks back on the kingdom of God that has already dawned through the death and resurrection of Jesus. Now already the name of Jesus Christ stands for God's kingdom.

   2. **Sin**. Paul, too, begins from actual human sinfulness (but not

sexually transmitted original sin as with Augustine), particularly the sinfulness of righteous, pious people who are loyal to the law but nevertheless lost. But he develops this insight theologically, using biblical, rabbinic and Hellenistic material, and above all by contrasting Adam-Christ as the types of the old and the new.

3. **Conversion**. Paul, too, sees human beings in crisis, calls for faith and requires repentance. However, for him the message of the kingdom of God is concentrated in the word of Christ's cross, which in a scandalous way causes a crisis for Jewish or Hellenistic sages who 'boast of themselves' before God. On the one hand Paul criticizes the legalistic obedience of Jewish Christians to the law (e.g. in Galatians), and on the other hand he criticizes the arrogant wisdom speculation of the Gentile Christians (for example in I Corinthians).

4. **Revelation**. Paul, too, claims God for his activity. But he does so in the light of the death and resurrection of Jesus, where for him the activity of God, a God of the living and not of the dead, has manifestly broken through in a definitive way. After his death and resurrection, Jesus's own *de facto* christology became the explicit, express christology of the community already before Paul and then through Paul.

5. **Universalism**. Paul, too, caused offence to many of his contemporaries. He turned in a quite practical way, beyond the limits of the law, to the poor, the lost, the oppressed, the outsiders, the lawless, the law-breakers, and advocated a universalism in word and deed. But now, in Paul, Jesus' universalism in principle in respect of Israel and his *de facto* or virtual universalism in respect of the Gentile world has become – in the light of the crucified and risen Jesus – a direct universalism in respect of **the world of Israel and the Gentiles**, which virtually requires the preaching of the good news among the Gentiles.

6. **Justification**. Paul, too, presents the forgiveness of sins from sheer grace, the acquittal, vindication, justification of the sinner not on the basis of the works of the law (Jesus' parable of the Pharisee in the temple) but on the basis of an unconditional trust (faith) in the gracious and merciful God. But his message of the justification of the sinner without the works of the law (without circumcision and other ritual actions) presupposes Jesus' death on the cross, where the Messiah was executed by the guardians

of law and order in the name of the law as an accursed criminal, but then appears justified over against the law as the one who is raised by the God who gives life, so that for Paul the negative side of the law has now also been made manifest.

7. **Love.** Paul, too, proclaimed the **love of God and neighbour** as the actual fulfilment of the law and lived it out in the most radical way in unconditional obedience to God and in selfless existence for fellow men and women, including enemies. But precisely in the death of Jesus Paul recognized the deepest revelation of this love of God and of Jesus himself, which may now be a ground and an example for human love towards God and neighbours. So it has now become clear that both have:

5. The same cause

In Paul we certainly find high emotionalism and powerful rhetoric, which also includes irony and sarcasm; there are some highly polemical statements and harsh quarrels with his opponents. But this man of passion for the cause he represents is never a man of personal hatred and resentment. Rather he is a man of service, of love, of joy even in suffering, a real 'messenger of good news' who neither wanted to found a new religion nor in fact invented one.

No, Paul did not create a new system, a new 'substance of faith'. As a Jew – albeit in a completely new paradigmatic constellation – he built on that foundation which according to his own words has been laid once for all: Jesus Christ.[16] Christ is the origin, content and critical norm of Paul's preaching, and that distinguishes Paul from the majority of his contemporaries. So, in the light of a fundamentally different situation after the death and resurrection of Jesus, Paul did not advocate another cause, but the same cause. And this – to put it in a phrase – is the cause of Jesus, which is none other than God's cause and the human cause – but which now, sealed by death and resurrection, is summed up briefly by Paul in the formula **'the things of Jesus Christ'**.[17]

So Paul's preaching is ultimately about a **radicalized understanding of God in the light of Jesus Christ**! Since then Jews and Christians have struggled over it, each in their different ways –

and the distinguished New Testament scholar Ernst Käsemann has recently spelt this out in a response to the Jewish scholar Pinchas Lapide. In fact, if we regard the history of Israel from the wandering in the wilderness through the history of the prophets and the Qumran sect to the present, the people of Israel always faced the need to depart from false worship. Indeed the writings of the Hebrew Bible are full of this: God is not only not known properly among the heathen; he is not even known properly by the people of God themselves. And this people constantly experienced dramatic and tragic tensions and splits, constantly struggled with apostates and rebels over the true God and correct, perfect worship. Precisely this, too, was the deepest, the ultimate concern of Jesus: 'Where and when and how is the God who is hidden in heaven rightly known and appropriately worshipped on earth? The Jew Paul also asks this question, and he answers it by giving belief in God a christological orientation... Today we perhaps honour the rabbi of Nazareth on both sides, whether as teacher, as prophet or as brother. For Paul, the crucified Christ alone is the sole image of the divine will, the countenance of the God who seeks out the godless, who scandalizes the pious and moral, those faithful to the law and bound by norms at all times, and blesses the fallen and lost world as his creation. From there we can and must understand the whole of his theology.'[18]

So Paul did no more and no less than to draw out consistently and translate into Hellenistic language that line which had been drawn first in the proclamation, conduct and fate of Jesus. In so doing he attempted to make the Christian message understandable beyond Israel to the whole inhabited world of his time. And the one who as a disciple of his master, after the tremendous commitment of the whole of his life, suffered the violent death of a martyr in Rome under the emperor Nero (probably around 60), has continued to give constant new impetus all down to the centuries to Christianity, in a way second only to Jesus, through the few letters and fragments of his letters that have been preserved: impetus to rediscover and follow the true Christ in Christianity, which is by no means an obvious matter. For since his time it has become clear that the difference between the 'essence' of Christianity and Judaism, for the old world religions and the modern humanisms, is this **Christ Jesus himself**. Precisely as the crucified one he is distinct from the many risen, exalted, living gods and divinized founders of religion, Caesars, geniuses, lords and heroes of world history.

All this makes it clear why Christianity is now **no longer a different paradigm within Judaism but** finally and really **a different religion** (though with Jewish roots which it cannot give up) – since Jesus had now been rejected by the majority of the people of Israel as the Messiah of Israel. And that Christianity could become a world religion, but a world religion inconceivable without its Jewish roots, can be demonstrated in particular by that great struggle which burdened early Christianity and which Paul fought to a conclusion at the Apostolic Council and then in the quarrel with Peter: the dispute over the Jewish law.

6. Paul against the Jewish law?

It is clear to anyone confronted with Orthodox Judaism that the Pauline problem of the law was not only a Jewish problem of the time but is also a Jewish problem for today. As the Jewish theologian Shalom Ben-Chorin remarks, Paul can be rightly understood today by those who have made the attempt 'to put their lives under the law of Israel, to observe and practise the customs and precepts of the rabbinic tradition'. And he adds: 'I have attempted to take upon myself the law in its Orthodox interpretation without finding in it the satisfaction, that peace which Paul calls justification before God.'[19] What he is referring to here are **experiences of zeal for the law** and **falling short of the law**: 'Nowadays in Jerusalem we know this type of fanatical Yeshiva pupil from the Diaspora, though of course he no longer comes from Tarsus, but from New York or London. In demonstrations against those who are peacefully driving their automobiles on the Sabbath he is very often to be found among the zealots for the law who throw stones at cars and drivers – those Talmudic students from abroad. Presumably they would not react in this way to a formal desecration of the Sabbath in New York or London, but in Jerusalem they want to legitimate themselves as one-hundred-and-fifty-per-cent Jews. This is precisely how we must imagine the young Saul from Tarsus, who emphasizes that he surpassed many in Judaism in his conduct, that he was zealous for the law and that he delighted in the stoning of heretics (how similar it all is, how topical!). – However, we must now understand what it is to experience the iron discipline of the law, the halakhah, the *mizvot*, day after day, without experiencing any real proximity of God from it, without getting rid of the burdensome feeling of transgression, *averah*, sin... Does not the multiplicity of human commandments and precepts ensnare people?'[20]

That makes the question all the more pressing: did not Paul definitively 'abolish' the Jewish law, usher in its 'end' – and justifiably so? For centuries this was something that was regarded as settled in Christian exegesis. And particularly if one reads Paul through the spectacles of German exegesis, especially the exegesis inspired by Luther and impressively given systematic form by Bultmann in his *Theology of the New Testament*, then one's conviction is hardened that:

– With the death and resurrection of Jesus Christ, for Paul the Jewish law is finished once and for all. Now the gospel prevails instead of the law.

– For Christians, the Jewish law is insignificant, and all that matters is belief in Jesus Christ; instead of the law, faith is now what counts.

– Together with the Jewish law, in the end Judaism itself is now also superseded: the new people of God, the church, is now taking the place of the old people of God.

But can we be content with such exegesis and the totally antagonistic Lutheran scheme of 'law and gospel'? We cannot avoid some brief comments on this controversy over the validity of the law. Today it polarizes more than any other issue both Jewish and Christian exegetes of Paul, and also brings about a polarization among Christian exegetes. It is so complicated, not because Paul was a man of inconsistencies and contradictions, but because in his correspondence, which was written in Greek, he does not use the Hebrew word 'Torah' (even as a Hebrew loanword) but the Greek word 'nomos/law', which had been used generally for the word 'Torah' ('teaching', 'instruction') since the Greek translation of the Hebrew Bible, the Septuagint. But this has the disadvantage that we can never know whether in a particular passage in his correspondence Paul is using 'nomos' in the wider or narrower sense: in the **wider** sense as Torah, which in fact means the whole corpus of the five books of Moses, or in the **narrower** sense as halakhah ('Law'), the religious law of the rabbis, already grounded in the Torah and now increasingly permeating the whole of life, though at that time it was still not codified.

The disputed question is: may we say that for Paul the **Jewish law has ongoing validity**? Does the law still apply, or has it been abrogated? To be specific:

– According to Paul, have the Jews who are zealous for the law really perverted the law?

– May the Jewish law really no longer be observed by Jews who follow Christ? So is Jewish Christianity no longer a legitimate possibility alongside Gentile Christianity?

– Is Judaism, then, wrong not only because it rejects Jesus as the Messiah but also because and in so far as it still holds to the law?

It is important to differentiate in our answer.

7. *The Torah is still valid*

There is still widespread prejudice about Paul and his attitude to the Jewish law, not only among Jewish but also among Christian theologians. However, if we read the numerous Pauline texts on the law as far as possible without traditional schemes, whether Christian ('law and gospel') or Jewish ('abolition of the law'), it cannot be disputed that Paul takes it for granted that in so far as 'law' denotes the **Torah,** the law is and remains **God's** law, i.e. an expression of the will of God. Paul emphatically stresses that 'The law is holy and the commandment is holy and just and good.'[21] The law is to lead people 'to life'.[22] It is 'the embodiment of knowledge and truth',[23] it is 'spiritual'.[24] The 'giving of the law' is one of Israel's privileges.[25] Here 'law' for Paul clearly means the Torah in the sense of the five books of Moses, to which human beings have to be obedient as a demand of God.[26]

It follows from this that according to Paul, God's holy law, the Torah, is in no way abolished even after the Christ event, but remains relevant as the 'Torah of faith'.[27] Indeed, Paul explicitly says that it is **not 'overthrown'** (far from it!), but is 'upheld', 'established',[28] by faith. So it is clear that Paul's polemic is not directed against the law in itself, the Mosaic Torah, but against the **works** of the law, against a **righteousness** from the law. His slogan is not justification by faith 'without the law' (as though faith were something arbitrary and random and without any practical consequences), but 'without works of the law'. Paul does not oppose faith and law but faith and works. It remains the case that human beings are not justified before God here and now by what they do. God himself justifies human beings, and only one thing is expected from them: faith, unconditional trust. For both Jews and Christians it is true that 'no flesh will be justified before God on the basis of works of the law!'[29] If one were to want to use the law for one's own justification before God, this would be a 'dispensation of death', a 'dispensation of condemnation';[30] since 'the letter kills'.[31] But if the Torah stil holds, what does the freedom of which Paul boasts so much mean?

8. The most famous dispute in the early church

'Has Christ made us free for **freedom**'?[32] We can now reply that what Paul means is not simply freedom from the Torah and its ethical demands, but freedom from the works of the law. That is the freedom to which Christians are 'called',[33] which they 'have in Christ Jesus'.[34] To this degree those who now believe in Christ are 'no longer under the law, but under grace'.[35]

What follows from this for the question of the Torah? After all that we have heard, the answer can only be that when Paul speaks of freedom from the 'law' he is **by no means against the Torah in principle;** indeed, according to Abraham's example the Torah teaches justification by faith, and in his view its ethical commands even apply to the Gentiles. But what he is in fact doing – without already using this later terminology – is to speak **against the halakhah,** to the degree that this does not make ethical demands in general but calls for doing the '**works of the law**'. This means - as Jewish scholars also recognize today – those **works of the Jewish ritual law** (circumcision and the commands relating to cleanness, food and the sabbath) which are still an oppressive burden for many Jews even now and which according to Paul may not be laid upon the Gentiles. So what has lost its fundamental significance is not the Torah in the general sense of God's teaching or instruction but the Torah in the narrower sense. Paul rejects this ritual halakhah for Gentile Christians and makes it a fundamentally relative matter for Jewish Christians: for it is now to be understood according to the spirit that makes alive and not the letter which kills.[36]

So what does this now mean in practice for Christians? It means one thing for Jewish Christians and another for Gentile Christians:
– Christians of Jewish origin can observe the halakhah, but need not necessarily do so: what is decisive for salvation is no longer the doing of such 'works of the law' but faith in Jesus Christ; the works of the law are no longer to be understood literally, but according to the Spirit: **a life in the Spirit.**
– Christians of **Gentile origin** may have **only the ethical commands of the Torah** laid upon them (though Paul does not make a terminological distinction nor develop the question theoretically), and not the cultic and ritual commandments, which are developed in such breadth in the halakhah for the whole life of Jews. In other words they must not be compelled to adopt **the Jewish way of life:** circumcision, festivals, sabbath, commandments about purity and the sabbath.

The most famous **dispute in the early church,** in **Antioch,** the second great centre of Christian mission outside Jerusalem, was specifically on this last point, and particularly about kosher food (still an important question – who eats with whom?). It was a dispute between Paul, who was responsible for the mission to the Gentiles, and Peter, who was responsible for the mission to the Jews, as had been resolved at the Apostolic Council in Jerusalem.[37]

Peter was personally open to the Gentile mission. He had at first practised table-fellowship with the Gentiles in Antioch in the same way as Paul, but gave this up – out of toleration or cowardice? – after the arrival of followers of James from Jerusalem, who now stipulated kosher food and kept their own company.

Paul defends the freedom of the Gentile Christians passionately, specifically on this point of eating together. The account which he gives in Galatians is probably unintentionally biassed. But one thing is certain: Paul 'opposed Peter to his face'![38] From his perspective this was understandable: he had passionately to oppose the break in table-fellowship and eucharistic fellowship which had indeed destroyed the reconciliation of Jews and Gentiles in the one community of Jesus Christ. And what was more central for him than that? Even if Paul never denied his Jewishness and never forbade Jewish Christians to live in accordance with the halakhah, but affirmed it for his own sphere, this Jewish lifestyle was not to become a divisive factor over against the Gentile Christians. For the sake of a community made up of Jews and Gentiles, while he did not expect the Jewish Christians to deny the Torah of Moses, in this particular instance (not generally) he did expect them to deny the halakhah – which prohibited such table-fellowship by its ritual precepts – since those who believed in Christ were not to interpret it according to the letter but according to the spirit. For this is what the freedom brought by Christ has freed men and women for. Faith in Christ must also be fundamental for Jewish Christians.

In all this, it cannot be overlooked that in his criticism of the law Paul also reflects **the attitude of Jesus**. In quite specific instances – the sabbath, laws about food and cleanness – Jesus too spoke out for 'God's commandment' and against the application of the halakhah, the 'tradition of men' or 'the tradition of the fathers',[39] calling for an ethically determined cleanness of the heart in place of cultic and ritual purity (washing of the hands)![40]

Now is it true, as is often asserted, that with this decision of Paul's the fate of the Jewish Christians in the growing Diaspora church was really already sealed and that therefore the premature split into a Jewish-Christian and a Gentile-Christian church was preprogrammed? Was this an unavoidable conflict with a tragic outcome? No! An understanding would have been possible, indeed necessary, in the spirit of Jesus. For as Paul explicitly says, true freedom is never heedless: 'See that this freedom of yours does not become a stumbling-block for the weak.'[41] One is to serve others,[42] but without giving up one's own freedom: 'Do not become slaves of men.'[43]

Being open to others, being there for others, unselfish love: for Paul that is the supreme realization of freedom: 'For you were called to freedom, brethren; only do not use your freedom as an opportunity for the flesh, but through love be servants of one another. For the whole law is fulfilled in **one** word, "You shall love your neighbour as yourself."'[44]

These fundamental statements by the apostle Paul all still apply today. Nevertheless we face the question: can Paul still be a practical model for Christianity over and above such fundamental statements?

9. A man of his time

Paul's remarks cannot simply be repeated and applied in a fundamentalistic way as an infallible word in our time, any more than any other texts of the Bible. They are all to be understood in terms of a time and translated into our time.

Take what Paul says about **women**. That woman was only a 'reflection of the man'[45] was a prejudice widespread in the Hellenistic world of his time. That while being married is good, being unmarried is better (though not to be insisted on)[46] is a statement made against the background of the Jewish expectation of an imminent end to the world, which Paul shared. The two cannot simply be taken over into our time. That 'women must be silent in church' and should 'submit'[47] is in any case according to present-day exegesis a subsequent insertion, since it contradicts the practice attested many times in Paul of the complete participation of women in liturgical life and in holding office in the communities. Paul even knows and praises women apostles like Junia, 'outstanding among the apostles'[48] (a later tradition, which can no longer imagine women apostles, has turned her into a male 'Junias'). And the list of greetings in Romans shows a whole series of women as collaborators, including Phoebe from Cenchreae, the missionary and community leader.[49]

What Paul says about the **state** is just as time-conditioned as what he says about women: the **state authority** which comes from God and to which everyone has to show 'due obedience'.[50] Christians today will naturally also affirm the right to resist a tyrannical state authority, and in extreme cases may even have to join the resistance.

Remarks about eating **meat offered to idols**[51] also seem to us out of date today. Nevertheless, this example in particular shows

34

how much the principles developed in this instance about the strong in faith not despising the weaker ones and the weak in faith not censuring the stronger ones are still of significance. In other questions, too, Paul gives abiding stimuli for today: stimuli for individuals and their basic attitude to reality, stimuli to questions about the fate of Israel, and stimuli towards the structure of the Christian community.

10. The abiding stimuli for the individual, the people, the community

(a) What does Paul say about the secular **everyday life of Christians**? Paul is not an eccentric ascetic who despises all the good things in the world. On all occasions men and women are 'to test what the will of God is: the good and well-pleasing and perfect'.[52]

However, those who believe in Jesus Christ do not need a world of personal perfection or even to escape into a community of the perfect. Such people may and should do the will of God in the midst of the secular world. They need in no way give up all the good things of the world. But they must not devote themselves to them. The believer can give himself, herself away only to God. Paul had already recognized that no Christian need leave the world, but Christians must not fall victim to it. What is called for is not external, physical distance from the things of this world, but internal, personal distance. For those who are freed from the law the great saying is: 'All things are permissible for me.'[53] But at the same time: 'I must not allow myself to be dominated by anything.'[54] In the world 'nothing is of and in itself unclean'.[55] But I can lose my freedom to something in the world and allow myself to be dominated by it as if it were an idol. Then, while it is still the case that 'All things are permissible for me', it is also true that 'not everything is healthy'.[56]

And finally, at the same time one must ask: can what is both permissible and healthy for me nevertheless harm my fellow human beings? What then? Then, too, it is still the case that 'All things are permissible.' But at the same time, 'Not everything is edifying.' Therefore, 'Let no one seek his own, but that of the other.'[57] So freedom can become renunciation, renunciation above

35

all of domination: 'Although I am free towards others, I have made myself the servant of all.'[58] Here the freedom of the believer is not denied; on the contrary, it is claimed to the full. In the last instance the believer is never bound by the opinions and judgments, traditions and values of the other: 'For why should my freedom be judged by another's conscience?'[59] My own conscience, which knows the difference between good and evil, binds me.[60]

(b) What does the Jew Paul think of the greater part of the **Jewish people** which has not accepted Jesus as the Messiah? This is anything but a theoretical question for Paul. It is prompted by a wound which the one who had been brought up a Pharisee did not want to close in his lifetime. But despite all his sorrow and disappointment, Paul maintains that the election of Israel, the people of God, is binding, indispensable, irrevocable. God has not changed his promises, though after Christ their validity must be seen in a different light. The Jews are and **remain God's elect people, indeed his favourites**.[61] For, according to Paul, to the Jews – his 'brothers' by common descent[62] – still belong:

– the 'sonship': the appointment of the people of Israel as God's 'firstborn son' which already took place in Egypt;

– the 'glory': the glory of the presence of God ('Shekhinah') among his people;

– the 'covenants': the covenant of God with his people, constantly threatened and renewed;

– the 'giving of the law': the good ordinances of life given by God to his people as a sign of his covenant;

– the 'worship': the true worship of the priestly people;

– the 'promises': the abiding promises of God's grace and salvation;

– the 'fathers': the fathers of the former time in the community of the one true faith;

– the 'messiah': Jesus the Christ, born of Israel's flesh and blood, who in the first place does not belong to the Gentiles but to the people of Israel.[63]

How much the Jewish people and Christianity would have been spared had this theology of the apostle Paul, as it is presented above all in Romans 9-11, not been suppressed, indeed completely forgotten! Paul's 'great sorrow' and 'incessant grief'[64] about the attitude of 'Israel' were transformed in the course of history into the unimaginable sorrow and cruel grief of Israel itself! In the name of the Jew Jesus and the Jew Paul, the people of the Jews was discriminated against beyond all bounds, persecuted and indeed exterminated.

Here it was not Paul who detached Christianity from Judaism: others did that after his death and the destruction of the Second Temple. Paul, the Jew who gave up being a Pharisee, **as a Christian in no way gave up his Jewishness**. Whatever one may say about him, though he was constantly attacked, misunderstood and defamed, he in no way felt that he was a transgressor of the law, an apostate, a heretic. The Christian Jew and apostle was simply fulfilling his Jewishness in a new, more comprehensive spirit, and in so doing thought that he had the Torah on his side: in the light of the God who had already beforehand acted in constantly new, unexpected ways and still did so, and of his Messiah. And Paul also believes in the salvation of the Jews, when Christ returns from Zion to judgment.

(c) How does Paul understand the **Christian community**? Were he to come again and see in particular the structure of the Catholic church, this church law worked out to the smallest detail, this monstrous hierarchy, above all the service of Peter endowed with a claim to infallibility and primacy, he would go to the barricades and once again resist 'to the face' anyone who 'deviates from the truth of the gospel'.[65] For 'holy rule', '*hier-archia*', was quite alien to Paul. He did not commend a hierarchical structure to his communities or build them up, but trusted in the charisma of all those who wanted to work together for the good of the community.[66] He was concerned with the 'democratic' interplay brought about by God. In his view, every member of the community has a particular task, a particular service, a particular charisma – and by this we should not just understand extra-ordinary phenomena like speaking with tongues and healing the sick. One cannot talk of enthusiasm in Paul any more than one can talk about clericalism. On the contrary, according to Paul **any** ministry which in fact is performed for the building up of the community (whether it is permanent or not, private or public) is charisma, **church** service, and as concrete service it deserves recognition and subordination. So **any** ministry, whether or not it is official, has authority in its own way if it is performed in love for the benefit of the community.

But can one keep **unity and order** in this way? Indeed, were not the Pauline communities in particular put in serious danger by rival groups, chaotic behaviour and morally dubious practices? Paul's correspondence with his communities is clear here: Paul did not want to produce unity and order by levelling out differences, by producing uniformity, hierarchy, centralization. Rather, he saw unity and order guaranteed by the **working of the one Spirit** which does not give all charismas to each person but gives each person his or her own charisma (the rule is: to each his or her own!), a charisma which is not to be used egocentrically, but for the benefit of the other (the rule is: with one another for one another); indeed it is to be used in submission to the one Lord (the rule is: obedience to the Lord!). Anyone who has not confessed Jesus and used his or her gifts for the benefit of the community does not have the Spirit of God. That is how spirits are to be discerned. The signs in the community of the Spirit of God which is identical with the Spirit of Jesus Christ are not clerical supervision and spiritual dictatorship, but consideration, recognition, behaviour in solidarity, collegial harmony, discussion, communication and dialogue in partnership.

(*d*) But in this perspective, is there still **authority in the church**? Could Paul exercise authority? Here too the answer is: Yes! Paul has an amazing authority, and he was not afraid in certain circumstances to use this apostolic authority forcefully. But Paul's practice of authority never became authoritarianism. The apostle never built up his authority - for example with a view to exercising a sacral jurisdiction. Rather, he constantly limited his authority voluntarily in the conviction that the apostles are not lords of faith but those who contribute to the joy of community members; that his churches do not belong to him but to the Lord, and therefore are free in the spirit: called to freedom and not to be slaves of others.

Certainly where Christ and his gospel are to be abandoned in favour of another gospel, in some circumstances Paul can even threaten the curse and exclusion. But whatever he may have done to an individual, temporary exclusion for betterment, he never did to a community even in the most serious cases of deviation. Rather, instead of issuing a prohibition he appealed to people's own judgment and responsibility; instead of exerting pressure he wooed them; instead of ordering them about he encouraged them; instead of talking about 'you' he talked about 'I'; instead of inflicting punishment he offered forgiveness; instead of oppressing freedom he challenged people to be free. That is apostolic ministry in concrete according to Paul! In moral questions, too, where it was not a matter of the Lord and his word, Paul wanted to give his communities freedom and not put a rope around their necks. And how many in our churches who think that they have Paul behind them in fact still have him before them, have still not really, have still not yet, understood what is really the nucleus of Christian freedom with which he was concerned!

To conclude: in all that I have said I have not grasped Paul, but simply come nearer to him. If one is to get to know all his themes – the preaching of the cross and the hope of resurrection, spirit and letter, the two wisdoms, the dialectic of weakness and power, the body of Christ and the sighing of the whole creation for redemption – then one must read Paul oneself. Then it is possible to understand why Paul, tested by suffering and militant, weak yet strong, was a great theologian, a great Christian thinker. It was because with body and soul, in pride and humility, he was utterly devoted to the cause, the Christian cause, the cause of Jesus Christ. His theology constantly admonishes us that it is not the apostle, whether Peter or Paul, who is the Lord. Jesus is the Lord: 'Jesus Kyrios'[67] – that is also Paul's confession of faith. And this Lord lays down the norm for his churches and for individuals, in whatever function.

No one knew better than Paul that he was no superman. No one was more aware of his humanity and his fragility, which mocks all claims to infallibility. He was an apostle who was always clear how far he came short of the cause of Jesus Christ himself without ever falling victim to despair or resignation, and without ever giving up hope: 'Not that I have already obtained this,' he writes to his favourite community in Philippi. And it is with a passage from his letter to that community that I would like to end: 'or am already perfect; but I press on to make it my own, because Christ Jesus has made me his own. Brethren, I do not consider that I have made it my own; but one thing I do, forgetting what lies behind and straining forward to what lies ahead, I press on toward the goal for the prize of the upward call in Christ Jesus.'[68]

Origen
The Great Synthesis of Antiquity and the Christian Spirit

Chronology (following P.Nautin)

185	Born, probably in Alexandria.
201	Martyrdom of his father under Septimius Severus.
203-5	Continues his studies.
206-10	Time of persecution; instruction of those seeking baptism.
211	Emperor Caracalla: end of persecution; Origen opens a private school for grammar. 'Conversion': sells his library of profane literature and studies the Bible.
c.215	Travels to Rome for several months.
217-29	Returns to Alexandria; conversion of Ambrose, which makes it possible for Origen to have stenographers and copyists; beginning of his work on the 'Hexapla', the first commentary on the Bible; first minor works.
c.229	Travels to Arabia.
229-30	Alexandria: main systematic work, *De principiis*. Beginning of polemic against Origen; sermons in Caesarea and Jerusalem; return to Alexandria.
231-2	Journey to Antioch to the empress's mother Mammaea.
232	Short stay in Alexandria, travels to Greece via Palestine where he is ordained priest; protest actions from Bishop Demetrius of Alexandria.
233	Athens. Origen, informed of Demetrius's actions, responds with an autobiographical letter.
234	Returns to Caesarea.
235-8	Emperor Maximin the Thracian: renewed persecution of Christians; writes 'On martyrdom'.
239-45	Countless homilies and Bible commentaries.
245	Second journey to Athens.
245-7	Caesarea.
248	Stays with Ambrose in Nicomedia; letters of defence to Pope Fabian and Emperor Philip the Arab (murdered 249).
249	Caesarea: the apologetic work *Contra Celsum*; last Bible commentaries.
249-51	Emperor Decius: first general persecution of Christians; Origen arrested and tortured.
after June 251	Death of Origen.

1. The new challenge

When Origen was born around 185 CE, Christianity was still a small minority in the Roman empire. No one at that time could have guessed that around 150 years later it would already become an imperial church. For the imperial government which had initiated a local and temporary persecution of Christianity in the first century under Nero (to which Paul had fallen victim) was now to enter into a life and death struggle with the Christian community. Who would win? Around the end of the second century only a few doubted whether it would be the empire.

However, we should not be deceived: just because Christianity was a minority at that time does not mean that it was without influence. The English church historian Henry Chadwick has rightly pointed out that it was the Alexandrian philosopher **Celsus,** the one who still attempted to justify the traditional polytheistic Roman state religion once more in a comprehensive philosophical and theological tractate, who also seems to have been the first to recognize the strength of young Christianity: 'that this unpolitical, quietistic and pacifist community had the power to change the social and political order of the Roman empire'.[1]

Christianity as a subversive, revolutionary force? But at that time it took the most capable brain in the church to react adequately to the challenge of this renewed pagan philosophy. At that time the church had such a brain in the person of **Origen,** from Alexandria in Egypt, the city of learning. Origen – a brilliant, much-praised but also highly controversial theologian.

For centuries he was given only a secondary place in the history of theology. He was too much branded a heretic, he was condemned too much in the East, and in the West he was overshadowed by Augustine and Thomas Aquinas. In the German-speaking world it was Hans Urs von Balthasar who made an energetic plea that Origen should be set alongside Augustine and Thomas Aquinas and thus accorded his due place in history. And quite rightly so. Others, like the Protestant theologian Adolf von Harnack, had already long given him this place.

But why did Origen prove so fascinating for a Catholic theologian like Balthasar (who in the 1970s and 1980s unfortunately promoted a conservative, anti-conciliar Roman policy)? Because with this theology Balthasar, Henri de Lubac and their friends at the Jesuit College of La Fourvière in Lyons could undermine the almost complete domination of the Catholic church by Roman neo-scholasticism. None of the great figures, from the Cappadocians to Augustine, to Dionysius, Maximus, Scotus Eriugena and Eckhart, says Balthasar, could escape 'the almost magical attraction of the "man of steel", as they called him', and some had fallen completely under his spell. 'If we take the Origenistic shine from Eusebius, all that is left is a dubious semi-Arian theologian and a prolific historian. Jerome simply writes him off when he comments on scripture, still even when externally he had broken the chains harshly and angrily and denied the bonds which tie him to the master. Basil and Gregory of Nazianzus in enthusiastic admiration collected the most misleading passages from the innumerable works of one to whom they returned during their life, in the moments when they had some respite from the everyday struggle; Gregory of Nyssa fell victim to him even more deeply. The Cappadocian writings hand him on almost intact. Ambrose, who knows him at first hand, writes him off; yet some of his breviary readings (like those of Jerome and Bede) are barely altered texts of Origen.'[2]

Alexandria, city of learning, city of philosophy. When Origen was growing up there and beginning to think as a Christian, the **last great Greek philosophy** was beginning to develop: the Neoplatonism of **Plotinus**. Both the Christian Origen and Plotinus, a pagan who was around twenty years younger (c.205-70), had been disciples of the Platonist (or Pythagorean) Ammonius Saccas. But as far as we know, they never made each other's acquaintance. When Plotinus opened his Neoplatonic school of philosophy in Rome in 244, Origen had already been living for a good decade in Caesarea, the provincial capital of Palestine. How he would have liked also to work in Rome, where we know that he spent several months around 215, or in Athens, to which he travelled in 232 and 245!

What do we know about his person and work? We are better informed about Origen than about any other theologian before Augustine. Not only from autobiographical sources, from the evidence that Origen himself left behind, but also through theologians like Pamphilos, the Panegyric of Gregory (Theodore?)

and the church historian Eusebius[3] – though there are problems of chronology. However, for these one can confidently refer to the fundamental new work by Pierre Nautin.[4]

2. The thwarted martyr

The intellectual ground had already been prepared in Alexandria by Titus Flavius **Clemens**, who may have taught there since around 180. A much travelled man, with a classical education, already before Origen this free Christian thinker had found a way between Gnostic heresy and sterile orthodoxy. Clement was convinced that despite all their distance from paganism, despite all criticism of its philosophy and literature, Christians could learn much truth from Greek thought, especially from Plato and also from individual poets, despite all their frivolity.[5] Faith and knowledge, Christianity and Greek culture, need not be opposites. Rather, the 'Christian Gnostics' bound the two into a rational synthesis. Greek philosophy must not be rejected or simply commandeered, as by the apologists Irenaeus and Tertullian, to defend the Christian position. Rather, it was useful for clarifying thought and deepening Christian faith. Indeed, like the law for the Jews, for the Greeks **philosophy was the tutor to Christ**. Christian faith, which always remains the foundation, could go along with an illumination of the Christian message in the light of the Greek philosophical tradition.

But Clement of Alexandria wanted even more. He did not just want to write apologetic – like the Christian philosopher and martyr Justin at the beginning of the second century. He wanted to provide a positive theological elucidation of the Christian message, and he set this out in his book *Paidagogos*, which soon became a handbook of Christian ethics, highly prized by the laity, with practical instructions for a Christian attitude in all possible situations in life. **Christ** is the **great tutor of all the redeemed**. That is the basic thought of this book, which does not require an extreme ascetic ideal of Christians, but expresses a fundamentally affirmative attitude to creation and its gifts, including sexuality. At any rate, in the light of the Christian message everything can be put in the right proportion. But Clement soon had to leave

Alexandria. Perhaps he had to avoid a persecution of Christians under Septimius Severus in 202/3; perhaps he also had difficulties with his bishop. Be this as it may, Clement was compelled to emigrate to Jerusalem and Asia Minor, where he died before 215 – no one knows precisely where.

Clement's basic notions now also appear in **Origen,** who despite his Egyptian name ('son of Horus') came from a fairly well-to-do Christian family in Alexandria. But the basic mood of Origen is very much more serious than that of Clement. Why? Because at the age of seventeen Origen, the oldest of seven children, was traumatized by an event which was to determine his life once and for all. His father, who had made it possible for him to be trained in the sciences and had handed down to him a firm Christian conviction, was imprisoned for his faith. Indeed, he was tortured and publicly beheaded, and the family possessions were confiscated.

But Origen's misfortune had a silver lining. He was taken into the house of a rich Christian woman (whose orthodoxy was suspected by some) and was able to continue his education. After completing his literary studies, and with his mother and the rest of his family to feed, he opened a private school for grammar and studied philosophy again, now probably with the famous Ammonius. Between 206 and 210 there was another persecution, during which Bishop Demetrius and the greater part of the clergy of Alexandria made themselves scarce.

But not the young Origen: instead of also creeping away in fear, as 'the son of a martyr' he continued to teach undeterred. His pupils – candidates for baptism – were inspired by the martyrs to accept Christian faith. Origen kept up their morale, and cared for those arrested and condemned to death – he mentions them by name – so intensely that finally he himself had to go into hiding. Such decisive experiences shape a man for life: already in his early years Origen grew into not only a brilliant teacher but also a spiritual leader.

After the persecution Origen resumed teaching grammar and instructing in the faith in Alexandria, and the bishop on his return formally approved Origen's activity. However, after a kind of religious 'conversion' Origen closed his school of grammar and sold his library of *belles lettres*. Why? To devote himself wholly to teaching Christian philosophy and to the study of scripture. In his **Catechetical School**, which soon became famous, he reorganized teaching by dividing it into an elementary and an advanced course. All the human sciences, including logic, mathematics, geometry, astronomy and then ethics and metaphysics, were to be put at the service of theology and a more comprehensive understanding of the word of God. This was a truly ecumenical enterprise, which showed the breadth of Origen's thought and was open to Christians, non-Christians and Gnostics.

However, we must imagine Origen, stamped by his father's martyrdom, as what Hans von Campenhasuen has called a '**thwarted martyr**'.[6] This is manifested in his rigorous asceticism: celibacy, fasting, prayer, a spartan home, little sleep – in all this he differed completely from Clement. It is also manifested in his passionate theological commitment, which he probably saw as the only appropriate substitute for the martyrdom that he had escaped and now sublimated. How radically this Adamantius ('the man of steel') understood his Christian discipleship is clear from the way in which he followed Jesus' praise of those who are 'eunuchs for the sake of the kingdom of heaven'[7] by having himself secretly castrated by a doctor (already at that time a routine operation). Later this was to be used against him, even when he had gently distanced himself from such a literal interpretation of scripture.

Who was he, this Origen, whose heart burned with the hidden fire of scripture? An ecstatic? He never reported ecstatic experiences. A mystic? From all that we know, he was not a mystic in the strict sense, a man with a mystic experience of unity. But one thing is certain: he was a spiritualized, spiritual tutor to Christ – a theological 'spiritual director', as one might say. Through his life and his teaching of the inner, gradual ascent of the soul to God, he doubtless prepared the way for deep spiritual experiences. Here, since Origen, continence is no longer a post-marital matter for people of 'mature' age, but the ideal for a radical rethinking in youth. So Origen became the **model for ascetical monasticism**, which, as we know, did not begin with the earliest community in Palestine but only in the third and fourth centuries in the Egyptian desert with Antony and Pachomius. However, Origen is not hostile to science, like some monks after him. On the contrary.

3. The first model of a scientific theology

Origen also became the model for a scientific theology. His work was not 'academic', but pastoral, and aimed at the believer. He was not primarily interested in a method or a system, but in basic human attitudes before God and in life in the Christian spirit. Origen was a man with an insatiable thirst for learning, a comprehensive education and a tremendous creative drive. The bibliography made by Eusebius is said to have contained two thousand 'books'. His whole work had a clear aim: from the beginning he did theology passionately with the aim of achieving a definitive reconciliation between Christianity and the Greek world or, better, a **'sublation' of the Greek world into Christianity**, though a Christianization of Hellenism was the inevitable consequence of a Hellenization of Christianity. And so while Origen's theology does not represent a paradigm shift, **the Gentile Christian/Hellenistic paradigm already initiated by Paul achieves theological completion** in him. But what does completion mean?

Origen was a convinced Christian, but he remained a Greek through and through, as Porphyry, Plotinus's biographer, admiringly and bitterly confirms: Greek and Christian, Christian and Greek. He was a pacifist who rejected military service for Christians, but he was loyal to the state authorities (except in matters of faith). He now created, indeed embodied, **the first model of a scientific theology**, which moreover was to have tremendous effects throughout the old ecumene, in the East and also in the West. Indeed, we are fully justified in saying that Origen was the only real genius among the Greek church fathers. Professor and confessor at the same time, he was the admired model of a highly-cultivated Christian life and a spiritual leader. Critically yet constructively, this universalist who found value in everything worked through all previous theological approaches and materials, including those from Gnosticism.

So Origen proved to be a cultural mediator *par excellence*. He was not, as his predecessor Clement had ultimately been, still a brilliant dilettante, but the first scholar in Christianity to engage in methodical research; indeed he was the greatest scholar of Christian antiquity, and by the unanimous verdict of patrologists the inventor of theology as a science. So the French patrologist

Charles Kannengiesser rightly also says: 'He invented the appropriate **praxis** for this kind of theology, and the methodological **theory** which it needed. One wonders only if inventing a new paradigm need always entail as much innovation as Origen's creativity required.'[8]

Be this as it may, completely at home in the church community and yet at the same time in ongoing dialogue with Gentile and Jewish scholars of his time, Origen was able to open up a variety of new ways and express them in language which could be understood; he did so at a very early stage, and very boldly, in particular by an innovative way of **steeping the biblical message in systematic theology**. Presumably in response to criticism which had been expressed, he broke off work on a powerful commentary on Genesis to sum up his theological views in a major theological scheme: its idealism was inspired by Plato and its evolutionary character by the Stoa.

The work is called *On the Principles* (Greek *Peri archon*, Latin *De principiis*), and it deals with the basic principles of being, knowledge, Christian doctrine. However, because of some peculiar theses (for example on the pre-existence of souls) it made Origen an even more controversial theologian. Right up to his death it brought him the charge of heresy and ultimately condemnation – with devastating effects on his work as a whole, so that we have it only in fragments (his *Peri archon* above all in Rufinus's Latin translation). But Origen himself distinguished precisely between the *dogmata* of the church tradition which were to be maintained and the *problemata* which were to be discussed, i.e. the open questions in answering which already at that time he claimed and practised freedom of theological thought in the face of the bishops.[9] However, viewed historically, *Peri archon* is the impressive documentation of the completion of the Gentile-Christian/Hellenistic paradigm, a reconciliation of Christianity and the Greek world, which Origen embodies in a way unlike any before him. What does this reconciliation look like?

4. Reconciliation between Christianity and Greek culture: A vision of the whole

Loyal to the programme of his predecessor Clement, Origen attempted to reconcile Christian faith and Hellenistic education in such a way that **Christianity appears the consummation of all religions**. What is the foundation of his doctrinal system? It is Holy Scripture, but this is interpreted according to the tradition of faith of the apostles and the church. The result is less a first Dogmatics than a first 'Christian Doctrine',[10] in which the coherence of the discussion of various themes was for Origen a sign of truth. Precisely what is 'On the Principles' about? Here it is possible to mention only a few basic ideas.

The presupposition of Origen's theology is the Platonic-Gnostic scheme of fall and subsequent ascent and the thoroughgoing separation of eternal idea and temporal manifestation. We understand Origen only when we become clear that for him the question of the **origin** (and thus being) of Logos, spirit, spiritual being – one could call this the 'alpha' question – is in the foreground of his theological interest – as with the Gnostics, but without Gnostic sexual symbolism, mythologies and fantasies. That explains the four parts ('books') of his work, in which Origen presents the **whole of Christianity** in three great arguments: God and his unfoldings; the fall of the creaturely spirits; the redemption and restoration of the whole (Part 4 deals with the allegorical understanding of scripture). From the central 'elements and foundations' of Christianity Origen works out a 'coherent and organic whole':[11] a great synthesis which is not disowned but confirmed by Greek thought. Here are just the most important basic concepts.

1. **God**. Clearly the centre of theology, God is not understood anthropomorphically as a superman, but as the primal living One, the pure, absolutely transcendent, incomprehensible Spirit which can only be named in negatives or superlatives. He is the only One (against all polytheism), and he is the good creator God who directs everything through his providence (against Gnosticism and Marcion, who accept an independent demiurge below or even alongside the supreme God).

2. **Logos**. The Logos is God himself and at the same time a

separate 'hypo-stasis' (the Latin *sub-stantia* is open to misunderstanding). From eternity he is begotten constantly by God, the Father (Godself = *autotheos*), as Son, is his perfect image and at the same time the embodiment of the ideas and of all truth. However, the Logos remains clearly subordinate to Godself as 'second God' (*deuteros theos*), although 'of one being' (*homoousios*) with him; the Logos is not 'simply good' but the 'image of goodness'.[12]

3. **Holy Spirit.** The Holy Spirit proceeds from the Son, is less than him and remains subordinate to him: a third stage or hypostasis. So here in Origen for the first time we find talk of 'three hypostases' (in the West at the same time Tertullian was speaking of three 'persons') in the Godhead itself: the beginning of the doctrine of the Trinity proper.

4. **Spiritual being.** All the 'spiritual beings', called *logikoi*, are created by God in freedom, but they have all fallen from the primal light in a primal fall and are banished into material bodies for punishment and education. Those beings who only sinned slightly are banished to an ethereal body: they are the angels. Those who sinned gravely are banished to the densest body of all, the devils. Those in between are banished to an earthly body, as human beings. So it is not a lower divine being who is responsible for all the evil and wickedness in the world, as in some mythologies; the cause of this evil and wickedness is the misuse of freedom by creatures themselves.

5. **Redemption.** The redemption of all these spiritual beings, all of which are striving for the pure light world above, which is perpetually the same, comes about through the Logos made man, the 'God-man': he functions as a mediator for the return of beings to God; for the angels he is an angel and for human beings a human being.

6. **Soul.** The believing human soul, if it is inwardly united with Christ, may ascend stage by stage in freedom to perfection. Accordingly, the inner life is understood as a process of spiritual ascent from this earthly-material life, until the soul finally becomes one with the Godhead in the vision of God, indeed is divinized and becomes immortal.

7. **Apokatastasis.** Right at the end – Origen can imagine further periods and redemptions of the world – there takes place the

restoration of all things' (*apokatastasis ton panton*). Then God will finally be 'all in all'[13]: even the evil spirits will be redeemed, evil will disappear altogether, and everything (*ta panta*) will be restored to its original pure and identical spiritual state. The great cosmic circle between pre-existence, creation, fall, incarnation of all, ascent and reconciliation of all is closed. And is that not a grandiose solution to the problem of theodicy for Origen? God has triumphantly justified himself beyond all that is negative.

This is certainly a tremendous vision of the whole; many aspects of it may be alien to us today, but at the time it was fascinating for many people. In this way, along the lines of Clement, the history of humankind itself can be understood as a great **process of education** leading continually upwards through all breaks: **as God's pedagogy (*paideia*) with human beings!** In other words, the image of God in human beings, overlaid with guilt and sin, is restored by the providence and educational skill of God himself in Christ. So human beings are brought to perfection in accordance with a quite definite plan of salvation = an *oikonomia*, the word used by theologians more than a thousand years before it came to be used by economists. In Christ 'the union of the divine nature with the human took its beginning, so that the human nature itself might become divine through close union with the divine'.[14] According to this '*oikonomia*' the **incarnation of God** is itself the presupposition of the divinization of human beings.

Was it the idea of the reconciliation of all things, and thus the rejection of eternal punishment in hell and the redemption even of the devil, that now entangled Origen in a serious **dispute with his bishop Demetrius**? That is quite questionable. It is, though, certain that this scholar who meanwhile had become world-famous, who in 231 had even been invited to Antioch by the emperor's mother Julia Mammaea to give a lecture, was a burden for the Bishop of Alexandria. Probably Origen had too often criticized the ritualistic and hierarchical church in his interpretation of scripture and censured the all too worldly lifestyle of churchmen. In the meantime, in the Hellenistic-Roman metropolis of Alexandria the office of bishop had in fact changed from being a charismatic function of service into an institution of power and control which was often lacking in spirit and in love. Evidently the bishop preferred Origen's more pliant pupil and colleague

Heraclas to his spirited master: he ordained Heraclas presbyter, but refused ordination to Origen – allegedly because he had castrated himself (which was an impediment to ordination).

Origen did not accept this discrimination. On a journey to Greece in 232 he had himself ordained in Caesarea in Palestine by his friends the bishops of Caesarea and Jerusalem, without involving the Bishop of Alexandria. Demetrius reacted promptly: at two synods of presbyters the pioneer thinker of the Greek church was banished by his bishop, deprived of his office and at the same time denounced to the Bishop of Rome and other bishops: Heraclas became head of the school (and later even succeeded Demetrius). Origen was also condemned without a hearing by the Bishop of Rome – who was always concerned to have good relations with Alexandria. An evil omen! The first great conflict in church history was between a monarchical bishop and a free Christian teacher, between church power and spiritual authority, between an institutional church leadership and professional theology. It was a conflict in which the one attacked is criticized but cannot defend himself – and yet does not give way! But new possibilities of work opened up for the versatile Origen outside Alexandria and Rome.

5. How Origen read scripture

Origen continued his work, now supported by the bishops in Jerusalem and Caesarea. At the age of about forty-eight he founded a new school with a large library in Caesarea, the provincial capital of Palestine. Here he was able to do extremely fruitful work for almost two more decades. He had an enormous programme: extensive correspondence, various journeys, and numerous lectures and disputations before bishops and congregations, and at the same time the instruction of significant pupils who became theologians, men of prayer, saints, martyrs. He was a *homo spiritualis* who could speak in a simple style without rhetorical pomp, to educated and uneducated people alike. In his last decades, time and again Origen indefatigably expounded Holy Scripture book by book: for him this was the soul of any theology and spirituality. But in this intellectualy highly-developed

Hellenistic milieu, how could an often primitive and unphilosophical scripture be understood?

Here Origen opened up new ways in **biblical textual criticism and exegesis.** As one who always understood himself to be primarily a scriptural interpreter and theologian he sees the exegesis of Holy Scripture as his central task. His Bible commentaries do not fall far short of modern Bible commentaries in extent and density. But his method is fundamentally different. Like the Greek philosophers before him who interpreted the myths of, say, Homer, and like the Jew Philo, who later, at the beginning of the Common Era, interpreted the Five Books of Moses, now Origen expounded the Old and New Testaments essentially not in a historical way, but **allegorically,** in other words symbolically, in different senses, spiritually, pneumatically. He did this not only because a fundamentalist and literal exposition of scripture would have produced something unworthy of God, immoral and contradictory – a criticism which the Gnostic and heretic Marcion had already advanced especially against the Old Testament. No, Origen believed that only in this pneumatic way could the Bible be plumbed in all its depth and mystery, as an inspired, spiritual word of God, as the place of the presence of God. According to him everything in Holy Scripture has a 'spiritual' meaning, but by no means always a historical meaning. Just as the cosmos and human beings themselves have three levels, body, soul and spirit, so too in principle scripture has a **threefold meaning:**[15]

– the somatic-literal-historical sense: the somatic can see Christ only as a human being;

– the psychical-moral sense: the psychical person sees Jesus only as the historical redeemer of his world-age;

– the pneumatic-allegorical-theological sense: the pneumatic sees in Christ the eternal Logos, who is already in God at the beginning.

Now already at that time, as still of course today, Origen was accused of arbitrariness and fantasy because of his virtuoso allegorical interpretation of scripture, since at many points he only keeps to a pneumatic sense and rejects the literal sense. This criticism is certainly not unjustified. But we should not forget that Origen is also the greatest **philologist of Christian antiquity!** He had learned Hebrew from a Jew, and his exegesis contains numerous explanations of the literal meaning of the text, grammatical references and attempts at concordance. And because he wanted to have the authentic Greek text, particularly in discussions with rabbis, in a work which took him more than twenty years he produced the monumental five-volume *Hexapla*, the sixfold (= in six columns) Bible. In six columns he set out the Hebrew text: 1. in Hebrew writing and 2. in Greek transcription; then 3. the translations of Aquila, 4. Symmachus, 5. the Septuagint (here above all the important text-critical signs) and 6. Theodoret (in the meantime three further translations of Jewish origin had appeared). It was an unprecedented work. Existentially interested in the wording and literal meaning of the biblical texts, Origen himself even investigated Hebrew etymologies; indeed he attempted to identify the geography, and even carried out excavations in the river caves of the Jordan. So Origen was a systematic theologian and a biblical scholar in a comprehensive sense. And even more:

6. Christian universalism

For Origen, who so often preached, his commentaries and homilies (sermons) were even more important than all this scientific effort. However, he himself wrote hardly anything down; his rich pupil and convert Ambrose had made it financially possible for him to have everything (the homilies, though, only towards the end of his life) written out by six stenographers, who were supported by copyists and calligraphers. Through the spoken word, this philosophical theologian, who was always also a missionary and preacher, perceptively and with a good knowledge of people attempted to explain the spiritual meaning of scripture to his hearers and thus at the same time to communicate a Christian spirituality – in the face of widespread pagan criticism of Christianity. So Origen the systematic theologian and exegete proved also to be a perceptive apologist.

Indeed, Origen also opened up new ways for Christian apologetics: the one who attempted to integrate the values of Greece into his Christianity and was at the same time well aware of the weaknesses of paganism was a man of dialogue. As a clear-sighted, intrepid dialogue partner he disputed in a modest and superlative way simultaneously wth rabbis, pagan philosophers, and orthodox and heretical Christian theologians. Precisely on the basis of his theory of the divine Logos, who is at work everywhere, he advocates a **Christian universalism**, but does not exclude a discerning of the spirits – on the basis of the Christian message, which is and remains the decisive criterion for him.

So it should not surprise us that Origen – presumably just a few years before his death, wrote the most learned and perceptive **apologetic work** of Christian antiquity, *Contra Celsum*, against that philosopher Celsus about whom we heard at the beginning. Origen quotes him sentence by sentence (that is the only way we know about Celsus's work *The True Doctrine* at all), and then gently refutes it sentence by sentence. Jesus and the apostles are defended against the charge of deliberate deception, and Christianity generally is defended against the rationalistic charge that it calls only for blind faith and is opposed to any rational investigation. Nor does Origen fail to give a survey of Christian doctrines, beginning with the person and divinity of Christ and moving through creation and the nature of good and evil to the end of the world. Comparisons of statements by Plato with words from the Gospels, remarks about Satan, the Holy Spirit, the prophecies, the resurrection and the knowledge of God conclude the discourse.

What a life of ever new toil that was: sermons, dialogues, letters, journeys, literary production! And constantly this utterly pure man attempts to defend his orthodoxy to bishops, only towards the end of his life to have to resign himself to the fact that one should not rely on bishops. In particular in the great cities like Alexandria, they often behaved like autocrats. And as the persecutions of Christians had become increasingly rare by the middle of the third century, both the episcopate and the Christian communities could develop well in a period of peace. But this was a lull before the great storm.

7. New persecutions and the success of Christianity

In the middle of the third century – at a time of economic and political decline – there was an unexpected reversal. In particular, the millennary celebrations of the city of Rome in 248 became another occasion for loading frustration and hatred on to Christians and taking action against a church which, we must grant, had increasingly become a state within the state. On top of all this, the next year (249), the emperor Philip the Arab, who was well-disposed towards the Christians, was murdered. Under his successor Decius (249-251) there followed the **first general persecution of Christians,** which was continued by his successor Valerian (253-260). Specifically, that meant that a state law commanded all Christians in all provinces of the Roman empire, even women and children, to report to the authorities, perform a state sacrifice and obtain an official permit. The aim of these compulsory measures was not to execute as many Christians as possible but to persuade as many as possible to become apostates and thus break up the communities.

In 250 **Origen,** too, did not escape his fate. He was **imprisoned** and put in irons; in the torture chamber his feet were stretched all day long 'to the fourth hole'. But the threatened fiery death was not inflicted on this famous man: Origen was an unbroken confessor, but again a thwarted martyr. Had he died as a martyr at this time, this honourable death would presumably have spared him a number of charges of defective orthodoxy over the following centuries. But the martyr's son, who had himself longed for martyrdom at such an early age and had written an 'Admonition to Martyrdom', survived, and died – we do not know precisely where – between 251 and 254. He must have been approaching seventy.

When Origen died, Christianity – which so far had spread primarily in the eastern half of the empire and was Greek-speaking even in Rome – still formed a relatively small minority. In the third century, the most widespread religion was the cult of Mithras, which derived from the Indo-Iranian sphere; it was a sun cult which was compatible with the emperor cult, but not with Hellenism. Here Christianity had a quite different and ultimately successful capacity for adaptation: the forces and methods of Hellenistic philosophy were integrated. Many ideas from syncretistic Hellenistic piety were adopted – for example the understanding of baptism (now increasingly widely disseminated as infant baptism) and the eucharist (understood as a sacrifice).

And also borrowing from the empire, had not the church increasingly developed a strict discipline and compact organization?

Origen did not strive in practice for that kind of Christian theocracy in which the church would take over the political tasks of the state, as is claimed in our century. His allegory of, for example, Christ as the sun and the church as the moon is not focussed on the present church but on the future, eschatological church. But at a time of sun worship and the emperor cult, such an allegory could easily be understood by the Christian masses as the foundation for a new, Christian theocracy.[16] In fact for an increasing number of people the question increasingly arose whether Christianity was not perhaps the religion of the future, permeating the empire and binding it together. There is no doubt that with his combination of faith and science, theology and philosophy, Origen had attained that **theological turning point** which made possible the **cultural** turning point (the combination of Christianity and culture) which in turn made possible the **political** turning point (the alliance of church and state). It is in fact amazing that this should have been achieved just over fifty years after Origen's death – despite all the reactions of the pagan state.

However, first of all the persecutions by the emperors Decius and Valerian brought a decade of terror for Christianity. Valerian, too, had recognized the danger for the pagan state and attempted to exterminate Christianity with measures extending throughout the empire. Indeed his edict of 258 even intensified earlier decrees: immediate death penalty for bishops, presbyters and deacons; the death penalty also for Christian senators and *equites* if loss of rank and confiscation of possessions did not make them see the light; loss of possessions and perhaps banishment for well-to-do women; loss of possessions and forced labour on the imperial estates for imperial officials; confiscation of all church buildings and burial places. Much blood was shed over these years, involving figures like Bishop Cyprian of Carthage, the great defender of episcopal rights against the Bishop of Rome, who was claiming more and more power...

However, despite all the compulsory measures, the **persecutions** were a **fiasco** for the state, and Valerian's son Gallienus already found himself compelled in 260/1 to repeal the anti-Christian decrees. There followed round about forty years of peace, so that Christianity, which was tolerated in fact, if not by law, was able to spread more and more through Mesopotamia, Persia and Armenia, in North Africa and Gaul, even in Germany and Britain. It increasingly found access to educated and well-to-do people (even at the imperial court and in the army), as a more philosophical and spiritual form of worship – because it had no bloody sacrifices, statues of gods, incense and temples.

And this relative time of peace was one of the presuppositions for the coming hey-day of church theology, without which a broad discussion and a developed theology could hardly have come about. In particular at the centre, in christology, the momentous paradigm shift which had long been heralded was now to take place. Here Origen played a key role. But even now there is much discussion as to how his theology is to be evaluated. The question is:

8. Development or apostasy from the gospel?

If we look back at Origen's work, we can see how different everything is here from what was originally represented by Jewish Christianity – which was still alive at this time. There is no doubt about it: here we have a great new 'constellation of beliefs, values and techniques' with a **Hellenistic** formulation which is quite different from that of Jewish apocalypticism. It is what we would now call a 'modern' paradigm for this period of Hellenism: 'Exemplifying as an individual the unfettered access of Christian faith to the universal culture to which he belonged,' says Kannengiesser once again, 'Origen experienced, with the unique capacities of his genius, what was to become a paradigm for the whole church of future generations: **the acceptance of 'modernity' in Christian theology.**[17]

The characteristics of this new constellation are:
– the completion of the biblical canon;
– the church's tradition of faith;
– the monarchical episcopate;
– Middle- and Neo-platonic philosophical thought used in the interpretation of scripture.

All this also forms the hermeneutical framework for Origen's allegorical interpretation of scripture, which superelevates the wording of the Bible, and beyond question in many ways also reinterprets it. Moreover this spiritual-pneumatic interpretation of scripture established itself in the long run – in the face of the more sober Antiochene school, with its literal and historical interpretation – in the theology of both East and West. And instead of that model of the imminent apocalyptic expectation of Jesus Christ as the 'end of time' taken over from Judaism, there now first appears in full the Hellenistic, salvation-historical conception of Jesus Christ as the middle of time already prepared for in Luke's two-volume work, the Gospel and Acts: the **incarnation of God** in Christ is seen as the **hinge of world history**, understood as the drama of God and the world. We cannot fail to examine it critically here.

Certainly the new Hellenistic paradigm was historically unavoidable, because it was **necessary** if early Christianity did not want to *a priori* to renounce the inculturation of Christianity in the now quite different world of Hellenism (the kind of opportunity which is often missed nowadays). Without a comprehensive new spiritual and ecclesial self-understanding on the part of early Christianity as embodied in Origen, the coming cultural and political shift would not have been possible either. And how could theologians who thought and felt as Greeks, how could already Justin and Irenaeus, Clement and then Origen, have thought through the Christian message, how could this self-awareness have been realized, other than in Greek - i.e. in Middle- or Neo-platonic – categories and conceptions? This process of transformation is not decadence, but bears witness to the extremely lively dynamic of Christianity. A category like 'lapse from the gospel' certainly does not do justice to the completion of the paradigm shift!

However, the decisive question – which was already put by Harnack – remains whether with such a completion of the Hellenistic paradigm shift the **spirit of Hellenism did not penetrate too far into the Christian centre** and whether justice failed to be done to those central elements of the original Christian message which have been an indispensable part of it from the beginning. So the decisive question is whether the shift of focus in Christian theology does not also represent a shift of meaning in the original Christian message, the gospel.

9. A problematic shifting of the centre

So looking without prejudice at the development of theology in the third century, we cannot denounce this first paradigm shift as a 'lapse from the gospel'. Conversely, though, we cannot glorify it as an organic 'development of the gospel'. What then? What in fact took place was a highly problematic shift of focus and meaning in Christian thought under the influence of a Hellenism with a Neoplatonic stamp. This shift was already taking place from the time of the early apologists and their metaphysical understanding of the Logos, but now it became abundantly clear. Even if one does not want to go so far as Harnack, who wanted to see the 'triumph of the Logos christology in the rule of faith **as a recognized part of the orthodox faith**' as being 'the transformation of faith into the compendium of **a Greek philosophical system**',[18] one cannot avoid putting critical questions to Origen:

– For Origen, what is the fundamental problem with which human beings see themselves faced? It is the **radical dualism** between spiritual and material cosmos, between God and human beings, which is known in neither the Old nor the New Testament.
– And what is the central event of revelation in this salvation history for Origen's systematic thought? The **overcoming of this** infinite **difference between God and human beings**, spirit and matter, Logos and flesh by the God-man Jesus Christ in a way which is alien to the New Testament.

For what is the price? Under the influence of Hellenism the centre of Christianity is no longer unequivocally the cross and resurrection of Jesus, as it is in Paul, the evangelist Mark, still also in Matthew and Luke (with their infancy narratives) and even still in John. Now, the centre is more the 'incarnation', or more precisely the speculative problem of the eternal pre-existence and incarnation of the divine Logos and thus the overcoming of the Platonic gulf between above and below, between the true, ideal, heavenly world and the untrue, material, earthly world. By whom? By the 'God-man' (*theanthropos*) Jesus Christ. His picture must now be increasingly divinized, removed from the senses and the body. For while a God-man, son of the Virgin Mary – who later is called not only 'mother of Christ' but also 'mother of God' (*theotokos*) – may still eat and drink, he feels no needs and has no sexual urge. Measured by the original message, this is a grotesque caricature. Or, more precisely, it is a paradigm shift in Christianity with far-reaching consequences.

What are the precise characteristics of this paradigm shift which reached its first climax with Origen? The historians of dogma have stressed in a variety of ways what dogmatic theologians generally have hardly taken seriously. Here are three perspectives:

– Instead of thinking in an **apocalyptic-temporal** scheme of salvation with a forward direction (Jesus' earthly life – suffering, death and resurrection – coming again) people now think primarily from above downwards in a cosmic-spatial scheme of pre-existence – descent – ascent of the Son of God and Redeemer.

– Instead of being explained **in concrete biblical language** (logia of Jesus, narratives, hymns, baptismal confessions), the relationship of Jesus to God is now explained in the **essential, ontological concepts** of contemporary Greek metaphysics. Greek terms like *hypostasis, ousia, physis, prosopon,* or Latin terms like *substantia, essentia, persona,* dominate the discussion.

– Instead of further reflection on the **dynamic revealing activity** of God through his Son in the Spirit **in the history** of this world, the focal point of reflection shifts to a more static **contemplation of God in himself in his eternity** in his innermost 'immanent' nature, and thus to the problems of the pre-existence of three divine forms, hypostases, persons. The decisive theological problem is no longer, as in the New Testament, what is the relationship of this Jesus, the Messiah, to God? It is, increasingly, what is the relationship between Father, Son and Spirit already before all time?

To take just one example of the shift of perspective: the difference between the old (probably even pre-Pauline) confession of faith from the introduction to Romans and the famous christological formula of Ignatius of Antioch, about two generations later. Both talk of Christ as **Son of God**, but in clearly different ways.

The **Pauline** confession, like the famous passage from Peter's speech in Acts,[19] briefly gives a sketch of the story of Jesus by beginning from below with the man Jesus from the tribe of David, who from the resurrection is appointed Son of God: 'The gospel concerning his Son, who was descended from David according to the flesh and designated Son of God in power according to the Spirit of holiness by his resurrection from the dead, Jesus Christ our Lord.'[20]

By contrast, **Ignatius** already says quite naturally that Jesus Christ 'was from eternity with the Father and appeared at the end of the times'.[21] Indeed he already unhesitatingly identifies God and Jesus and speaks of Jesus as 'God come in the flesh', which then leads to paradoxical formulae like this: 'There is one physician, both fleshly and spiritual, begotten and unbegotten, come in flesh, God, in death, true life, both of Mary and of God, first passible and then impassible, Jesus Christ, our Lord'.[22]

We cannot overlook the fact that in the subsequent period the **exaltation christology** (the exaltation of the human Messiah to be Son of God, the two-stage christology) with an originally Jewish Christian stamp, beginning from below and centred on the death and resurrection, was in fact increasingly **suppressed by an incarnation christology beginning from above** (Logos christology), which ontologically intensified the lines of the Gospel of John or individual statements about pre-existence and creation in the hymns of Philippians, Colossians and Hebrews: the pre-existence and incarnation of the Son of God, his emptying and humbling, as a presupposition for his later elevation to God.

We can also say that in Old Testament terms, for the 'ascending' christology, to be Son of God means an election and acceptance in the place of son (exaltation, baptism and birth). It is now supplemented or even replaced by a 'descending' christology. For this approach, to be Son of God means less a dignity and position of power in the sense of the Hebrew Bible than an **essential begetting** of a higher nature – to be described increasingly more precisely in Hellenistic terms and concepts – his heavenly descent and origin. Terms like essence, nature, substance, hypostasis, person, union become more and more significant. Now people wanted to use them to describe the relationship between Father and Son (and eventually also Spirit). But how? A long dispute over that now began.

10. The battle over orthodoxy

Indeed, what originally stood at the periphery of faith and confession now came to the centre and as a result was exposed to controversy. Christianity was now increasingly driven by a variety of speculative philosophical systems into a **crisis of orthodoxy** which was to have devastating consequences. For it was by no means the case that Origen exclusively dominated the theological scene at that time.

However, in particular in the second half of the third century after Origen the sources are extraordinarily sparse, and it is quite a dark period for historians. This is not only because we often have only very fragmentary evidence and do not know how far communities (larger or smaller) also stand behind particular names, but because:

1. Many independent theologians (like Paul of Samosata) were condemned as heretics although they were quite orthodox in their way, as their rehabilitation by historians in our century attests;

2. Most of the books of the 'heretics' (including some of Origen's after his condemnation) were destroyed, so that we are dependent on the often tendentious and selective quotations of their opponents;

3. The Hellenistic terms used at that time were ambiguous and often employed in contradictory ways: for example 'hypo-stasis' (in any case identical with the Latin *sub-stantia* only in its etymological significance) could be used both for God alone (thus only one divine hypostasis), for God, the Father, and the Son (two hypostases), or even also for the Holy Spirit (three divine hypostases).

Indeed who can count the names of those who were entangled in the course of the battles over the 'right faith', 'orthodoxy' – that unbiblical word which now become increasingly frequent in church terminology? The sorry conclusion is that as theology became increasingly scientific and intellectual – Origen and the consequences – it now increasingly ran into problems of orthodoxy, disputes over heresy, demarcations – and all this in the name of Jesus!

Only if we have understood this paradigm shift in christology can we understand:

– Why the messianic faith of Christians and Jews has drifted so far apart, as also the messianic faith of Gentile Christians and Jewish Christians;

– Why belief in Christ even within the Hellenistic Gentile Christian churches of the East led to splits in the church which have lasted to the present day; and

– Finally, why in the first millennium a deep gulf also opened up between the Eastern church and the Western church, which then led to a definitive schism in the second millennium. What emerges from this situation?

11. Christian self-criticism in the light of the future

To sum up: already with the early Greek fathers, the main interest of theology shifted from the concrete salvation history of the people of Israel and the rabbi of Nazareth to the great soteriological system. And in Origen it shifted from Good Friday (and Easter) – which were never kept silent about – to Christmas (Epiphany), indeed to the pre-existence of the Son of God, his divine life before all time. According to Origen, simple believers (the pistics) could hold to the earthly, crucified Jesus, but the advanced pneumatics (Gnostics) were now to rise to the transcendent Logos and divine teacher, whose relationship to God was now described in philosophical categories of Hellenistic ontology as the relationship between two or three hypostases.

But Harnack rightly asked about the original gospel. Today this question must be sharpened up against the background of a **markedly extended horizon of comparative religion**: today, more than ever, Christian theology has a responsibility to show ecumenical solidarity with other religions too. Questions arise.

– First of all with respect to **Christianity itself**: Are not the original message of Jesus and the New Testament proclamation of Jesus the Christ of God who was crucified and raised and is present in the Spirit distorted if in Christian theology, literature and piety the main interest has shifted from the cross and resurrection to the conception, birth and 'appearance' (Epiphany), indeed the pre-existence, of the Son of God and his divine life before all time? So has not the original gospel, the Pauline 'word of the cross', become *a priori* a triumphalist metaphysical doctrine, a 'theology of glory'?

– Then in respect of **Judaism:** Is it appropriate for Christian theologians, excessively heightening the Hebrew Bible's divine inspiration, to see the Old Testament as a book of deep Christian mysteries which they attempt to unveil with the help of the allegorical, symbolic method, so that they even think that they can discover a Trinity of Father, Son and Spirit in what becomes their 'Old Testament'?

– Finally, in respect of **Islam:** Is it in keeping with the Hebrew Bible, the Old Testament, when the salvation history narrated in the biblical books is forced more and more into an increasingly complicated dogmatic system which already split the church in the century after Origen and entangled it in increasingly complicated disputes, so that Islam could have such decisive success with its simple message – so close to Jewish Christianity - of the one God, the prophet and Messiah Jesus, and the 'seal' of the prophets, Muhammad?

Origen was firmly convinced that throughout his theology – in exegesis, apologetics and systematic theology – he had done no less than decipher his beloved Holy Scripture. But he was not aware how far he himself remained imprisoned in a quite definite philosophical world-view. That is why we have to speak at such length about these theological questions: to the present day in Eastern Orthodoxy people have maintained the all too natural conviction that the orthodox teaching of the church fathers is simply identical with the message of the New Testament, indeed that the Eastern churches and they alone stand in unbroken continuity with the early church – as though there had been no shift from the Jewish-Christian to the Hellenistic paradigm!

If we now look more closely at the development of Hellenistic christology and the formation of speculation on the Trinity, which makes a decisive beginning with Origen and which we shall soon be able to pursue further with Augustine, in connection with present-day preaching and present-day faith the need arises to consider more closely whether we can simply take over and repeat the christological formulations and notions of the time; whether, in this Hellenistic constellation, the biblical message was simply being interpreted for the abiding centre of the Christian faith, as traditionalist theologians assert, or whether the message of the New Testament was not being swamped by Hellenistic conceptuality and notions.

What is this **abiding centre**? What the Christian community believed from the beginning, what unites Paul and John, Matthew, Mark and Luke and all the rest of the New Testament witnesses:

– The man **Jesus** of Nazareth, the crucified one, has been raised to new life by God; appointed Messiah and Son, he rules as the exalted Lord;

– **God**, the one God of Abraham, Isaac and Jacob, is also the God who called Jesus his Father and our Father.

– The power of the **Spirit** who became powerful in and through Jesus is the Spirit of Godself, who not only permeates all creation but also gives power, comfort and joy to all who believe in Jesus as the Christ.

As a Christian one can hold firm to these indispensable basic elements; as a Christian one can speak of Father, Son and Spirit, without having to follow Origen in taking over the Middle Platonic/Neoplatonic doctrine of hypostases. That Origen attempted this in his time is his greatness. But we would be poor things if in our time we did not make the same attempt in our own way. Origen would have had the greatest understanding of this.

Augustine
The Father of All Western Latin Theology

Chronology (according to P. Brown)

354	Born in Tagaste.
371-3	Goes to Carthage for the first time. Death of his father Patricius; beginning of cohabitation with a woman; birth of his son Adeodatus.
383	Travels to Rome with wife and child.
384	Appointed teacher of rhetoric in Milan (autumn).
385	His mother Monica comes to Milan (late spring); separates from the woman.
386	Conversion to Christianity (end August); goes to Cassiciacum (September).
387	Returns to Milan (beginning of March); baptism; Ostia vision; death of Monica.
388	Moves from Ostia to Rome.
388-90	Returns to Carthage, then goes to Tagaste.
391	Moves to Hippo to found a monastery; ordained priest.
392	Debate in Hippo with the Manichaean Fortunatus.
394	First Synod of Carthage; reads about Romans in Carthage.
395	Successor to Bishop Valerius.
397-401	*Confessions*; debates with the Donatist bishop Fortunius.
399-419	The books *De Trinitate*.
410	Alaric enters Rome; Roman refugees come to Africa; Pelagius travels through Hippo; reversal of tolerance of Donatists.
411	Last great disputation with the Donatists; use of force.
413-25	The books *De civitate Dei*.
416	Provincial council of Miletus: condemnation of Pelagius and Celestius.
417	Innocent I condemns Pelagius and Celestius.
421	Eighteenth Synod of Carthage.
429	Vandals from Spain approach along the coast of Mauretania.
430	Devastation of Numidia by vandals; 28 August: death and burial of Augustine.

1. The father of a new paradigm

'Augustine is the only church father who even today remains an intellectual power. Irrespective of school and denomination he attracts pagans and Christians, philosophers and theologians alike by his writings and makes them come to terms with his intentions and his person. He also had an abiding indirect influence, more or less modified and broken, as a conscious or unconscious tradition in the Western churches, and through them in the general heritage of culture . . . Augustine was a genius – the only father of the church who can claim without question this pretentious title of modern personality-rating.'[1] Thus the Protestant historian Hans von Campenhausen in the Western tradition, for whom no praise is too high for Augustine.

But has Campenhausen – all too trapped in the Western perspective – deliberately or just unwittingly passed over Origen, that genius among the church fathers? At all events, it is true that the Christian West has dealt more graciously with Augustine's errors than the Christian East dealt with those of Origen. We need to be agreed on two things from the start:

– Augustine has **shaped Western theology and piety** more than any other theologian; in this way he became the father of the mediaeval paradigm.

– Augustine is **repudiated by the East** to a greater degree than perhaps any Western church father – a further indication of the shift in Christianity from the early church/Hellenistic paradigm to the Latin/mediaeval paradigm which in fact begins with him.

We shall be going on to talk about this in what follows: not about the wealth of Augustine's theological statements, which in any case are inexhaustible, but about his **paradigmatic significance** for the new Latin, Catholic paradigm, which is distinct from the Hellenistic, Greek paradigm. Eastern theology must not continue to ignore Augustine, but he may not be spared virtually all criticism, as he is in some Western accounts. A careful judgment should be passed on him as the **initiator of a new paradigm**. For any paradigm shift means not only progress, but also gain and loss. And in fact a new paradigm came about in theology when this originally extremely worldly man, this acute dialectician, gifted psychologist, brilliant stylist and finally passionate Christian began to work his extremely varied experiences into a powerful theological synthesis – as Origen had done a good century earlier.

2. Origen and Augustine – differences and common features

Like Origen, Augustine was a man of tremendous talent, passionate commitment, a unity of doctrine and life:
he attempted to reconcile Christian belief and Neoplatonic thought, the biblical and the Neoplatonic understanding of God; he understood theology as a methodical reflection on Christian faith which may not allow any contradiction between faith and reason: theology as thoughtful discourse or an account of God.

Like Origen, Augustine worked through all possible philosophical approaches and material in a way which was both conservative and innovative:
he devoted himself to both Christian apologetic and biblical exegesis, the systematic penetration and the practical preaching of the Christian message;
he used the allegorical explanation of scripture, which at some points prefers a spiritual sense to the literal sense.

For Augustine, as for Origen, God as he has revealed himself in his Logos and his Son stands at the centre of theology;
the spiritual soul, which is in the possession of the body, is to find ascent to God through Christ;
religion is to be a matter of the heart instead of just a form of cult and community. One of Augustine's many famous sayings is: 'You have created us for yourself, and our heart is restless until it finds rest in you.'[2]

But the **differences** between Augustine and Origen are already evident here. We should reflect:
that Augustine was born almost one hundred years after Origen's death in what was now the Christian empire;
that while Origen from the start was an exegete and knew Greek philosophy, Augustine was a professor of rhetoric and an amateur philosopher;
that while Origen wrote in a taut, gripping style, ~~Origen~~ Augustine wrote with literary brilliance in a highly personal, existentially committed style;

that Origen remained a theologian who was critical of the hierarchy, while Augustine eventually became a Catholic bishop.

But Augustine could have been all this in the Greek East instead of in Rome, Carthage, Milan or Hippo. Still, these more external observations lead us to an inner difference: Origen was **Greek** through and through (with an outstanding knowledge of Hebrew), while from the start and with all his heart Augustine was **Latin**:

– Augustine was a Roman citizen and son of a city official in the Roman province of Numidia, present-day Algeria.

– His language, of which he had sovereign control, was Latin; he had no desire to learn Greek, and he was the only significant Latin philosopher who in practice did not know Greek.

– The heroes of his youth were not the African Hannibal or the Greek Pericles but Romans like Regulus and the Scipios.

– He studied the Latin classics, above all Virgil, and then as an orator of course Cicero, the orator and philosopher; he learnt Greek material, whether pagan or Christian, only from translations or imitations.

– He did not feel in solidarity with Carthage from the start, far less with Athens or Byzantium, but with Rome, for him still the capital of the world and now the centre of the church.

– Augustine hardly sought any contact with the great Greek church fathers of the East, the schools of Cappadocia, Antioch and Alexandria. In short, 'Augustine's education is grounded in Western language, if not wholly in Latin.'[3]

There is one more thing: whereas in a still pagan and hostile environment Origen went his way from youth onwards as a convinced Christian ready for martyrdom, as a young man in an environment which was already widely Christianized Augustine at first rejected Christianity. Only after many wanderings did he find the way from worldliness to being a Christian. So the fact that Augustine could initiate a new theological paradigm was due first to his Latin origin, education and culture. At the same time, however, we must see that any new paradigm, including a new Latin paradigm, arises out of a **crisis** which leads to a new constellation. And Augustine himself, although living in the 'golden age of the church fathers', had to surmount a threefold crisis: first the crisis of his life, then the crisis of the church, and finally the crisis of the empire.

3. A life in crisis

Aurelius Augustinus had grown up in Roman North Africa. The emperor Constantine had already been dead almost two decades when he was born in the little town of Tagaste in the high country of Numidia in 354, the son of a pagan father, Patricius, and a pious Christian mother, Monica. She introduced her child to the beginnings of Christian faith and had him given the rites of the catechumenate. Augustine was not baptized, but he did receive an intensive education, made possible by his father, who unfortunately was to die early.

Rhetoric, technically highly developed in the North African capital, Carthage – a good basis for becoming a lawyer or state official – was the ambitious aim of Augustine's studies and his goal: success, status, wealth and a good marriage. As a student among young careerists, as early as seventeen he lived with a woman. He does not mention her name in his later autobiographical *Confessions*, but she was to be his fate, since after a year, before he became a professor of rhetoric, she bore him a child (whom he called 'Adeodatus', given by God). In intellectual circles of the time a strictly monogamous sexual relationship without legitimate Roman marriage, evidently with the use of some form of birth control, was not unusual. Augustine's relationship to this woman lasted for thirteen years – until he abruptly broke off the relationship.

This is not the place to describe in detail the **spiritual Odyssey** of this man with his different 'conversions'; through his writings and letters, his *Confessions* and the contemporary biography by Possidius, Augustine is in any case the best-known man of antiquity. It might just be mentioned that his course lay from political rhetoric, at first under Cicero's influence (*Hortensius*), to a serious quest for **wisdom**; then from Cicero's philosophy, which was not religious enough for him, as a 'hearer' to that dualistic **Manichaeism** which explains evil (and sexuality) with the aid of an evil principle (eternally equal to the good God), whose 'elect' live a life of continence; then from Manichaeism, which after nine years proved to be a not very philosophical, fantastic mythology, to the **scepticism** of the 'Academics'... How were things to continue?

Augustine was almost thirty years old when in 383 he set out 'overseas' and after a short period of teaching in Rome took the post of a professor of advocacy in **Milan**. Milan was the imperial residence, later also that of Theodosius, the emperor of the East, who had shortly beforehand declared Christianity the state religion and banned all pagan cults. Augustine's mother, who had followed him, now forced him to make an appropriate marriage; it was against the law for him to marry his lowly-born concubine. Monica found a young heiress, only twelve, but from the best Milan family, who seemed to offer her son the prospect of an outstanding career. Thereupon Augustine's life-companion and mother of his son made a 'vow of continence' and travelled back to Africa, there presumably to put herself under the protection of the Christian community as a widow. But Augustine, offended, first of all consoled himself with a substitute lover, though this did not give him spiritual fulfilment. An arranged marriage, a conventional future as a married man and government official – was that now to be his life? His self-doubt reached a climax.

However, in Milan Augustine now met a brilliant advocate of the Christian cause, Bishop **Ambrose**. Ambrose's sermons, which were both rhetorically and theologically brilliant, and his allegorical interpretation of scripture inspired by Origen (at that time Origen had not yet fallen out of church favour in the East), removed Augustine's intellectual hesitations about Christianity. Now he saw a way of transcending the naive anthopomorphic notions of God and the offensive and contradictory features of the Bible. Another, acceptable form of Christianity showed him how Christian faith and ancient culture could be combined.

4. The move to Christianity

Through Ambrose and his intensive preoccupation with Neoplatonism, Augustine overcame scepticism, found access to the true world of the spiritual, and immediately experienced its intense joy. The connection between the Greek Logos and the Logos of the Johannine prologue dawned on him. Then it took only a thorough study of the letters of the apostle Paul, and in August 386 an account of the conversion of Antony and the monastic settlements in the desert, to spark off a new, dramatic and now **final conversion**: from worldly life and hedonistic habits to being a Christian in the spirit of renunciation and asceticism. As Augustine describes his conversion experience ten years later in his *Confessions*,[4] in deep turmoil, he understood the words of a child in a garden, 'Take and read,' as a personal address from God. On the spur of the moment he opened the letters of Paul and read: 'Not in riots and drunken parties, not in eroticism and indecencies, not in strife and rivalry, but put on the Lord Jesus Christ and make no provision for the flesh in its lusts.'[5]

Now Augustine, supported by his friends, resolved on conversion, which under the influence of Neoplatonism, and following the example of the monastic father Antony, he understood as a **radical break**: a decision against sexual pleasure and for perpetual continence, against a worldly career and for a life of seclusion with friends; against riches and for poverty; against sensual delights of all kinds and for asceticism. On Easter Eve 387 Augustine and his gifted son, who was to die early, were baptized by Bishop Ambrose; but from then on Augustine does not say a single word in his *Confessions* about the mother of his child.

Augustine did not become a monk as a result. But he did live a *vita communis*, first in Milan and then a year later – after a memorable farewell conversation his mother had died in Ostia on her journey home – in his native African city of Tagaste, where he sold his father's property. That means that from then on Augustine lived without private possessions, in the company of like-minded friends, a life in common study of the Bible and philosophy, in conversation and prayer, in fact a 'synthesis between the *bios philosophikos* of the Greeks, Cicero's *otium liberale* and the life of the Christian hermit'.[6]

However, after only three years, in which he wrote his works against scepticism and against the Manichaeans, there followed a further turn in the life of the ascetic layman. On a visit to the port of Hippo Regius (present-day Bône/Annaba in Algeria), the most important city after Carthage, this man of faith, who had meanwhile become famous, was recognized in church and literally dragged before old Bishop Valerius, a Greek by birth, in the choir of the church. The bishop was asked to make Augustine presbyter and Latin preacher in place of another candidate, and was prepared to do this. Augustine, at first putting up a vigorous resistance, agreed, and put his personal interests aside. So he was ordained priest and, five years later, in 395, now at the age of forty-one, he became co-bishop, and then successor to the Bishop of Hippo, who died shortly afterwards. This was a move which was to have great consequences for the politics of the church and theology.

Augustine was to remain bishop for thirty-five years, unlike the other bishops, who were mostly married, living until his death a strictly regulated 'common life' with his priests, deacons and other clerics, separated from the people by vows of celibacy and poverty and by the wearing of black robes (some of these companions later became bishops); the Middle Ages with its cathedral communities could see its model in the Augustinian community of priests. And as bishop, Augustine was now to become the chief figure in the two crises which not only shook the church of North Africa but also compelled Augustine himself to make new changes. These were finally to have an effect on the whole Latin church of the West. Here in Africa the form of the church of Europe was decided.

5. The dispute over the true church: Donatus and the consequences

As bishop, Augustine had a tremendous programme to get through: services and sermons, instruction of converts and baptismal candidates, administration and works of charity, judgments and petitions to authorities, sessions, synods, an enormous correspondence (extending as far as Gaul and Dalmatia) and endless journeys on horseback. The mediaeval fusion of state and church competence was heralded in the legal competence accorded by the emperor to bishops in civil trials. It was a life of action rather than one of contemplation, as it had been previously. But it was also a life of interpreting scripture, as is shown by Augustine's extensive commentaries, say, on Genesis and the Psalms, on the Sermon on the Mount and the Gospel of John.

Nevertheless, this man who kept several stenographers and writers busy found time over the years to write the majority – and most profound – of his theological works, now in middle age above all the *Confessions* of his spiritual development to conversion and baptism. This is a unique confessional work, written in the form of a prayer, as much psychological analysis as theological commentary, by one who had still not found rest; he wrote it for himself and a new spiritual and clerical elite, for both apologetic and a therapeutical purposes. After the *Confessions* came the *De Trinitate* and the *De Civitate Dei*, all in all an amazing theological conspectus, which keeps referring back to the Bible (well over 40,000 scriptural quotations have been counted in Augustine's work). Augustine was capable of patiently and consistently thinking through and working out in detail a great idea which had occurred to him.

However, this theology was deeply stamped by two crises in the church and theology which proved to be of significance for the whole of Western theology and the church. The first of these was the **Donatist crisis,** which was to have consequences for Augustine's emphatically **institutional and hierarchical understanding of the church and then that of the whole West.** The background is this. In the fourth century the Catholic church had become an already quite secularized church of the masses. But in North Africa in particular, some circles remembered very clearly the time of martyrdom and the strict church discipline, and the more pneumatic understanding of the church and the sacraments in Tertullian and Cyprian. According to these North Africans, baptisms and ordinations which had been performed by unworthy bishops and presbyters who had been 'lapsed' in persecution (there seems to have been such a case earlier in Carthage as well) lacked the Holy Spirit and were therefore invalid; so they had to be repeated. There had already been a schism with the rigorists for around a century, even before the change under Constantine; the mainstream church was accused of laxity. Indeed, after the Constantinian change the majority of North African bishops were rigorists, and were now called **Donatists** after their leader Bishop Donatus (who died in 355).

All the negotiations, synod resolutions and persecutions over several decades were of little help: the Donatists regarded themselves as those who, compared with the great church, were a church unstained by anything unworthy, a pure and holy church whose bishops and priests alone possessed the Holy Spirit, so that they alone could dispense the sacraments validly. And when Constantine's son and successor Constans attempted to suppress Donatism by force, the opposition within the church fused with the social discontent and anti-Roman resentment of the Punic-Berber country population of North Africa, who were being increasingly impoverished by the large-scale agriculture of the Roman landlords. However, this social revolution was largely over when Augustine became bishop of the Catholics in Hippo, eighty-five years after the outbreak of the schism.

But the tensions within the church had not died away. And **the persecuted church** was now to become a **persecuting church**. How did this come about? After the Catholic church had been declared a state religion under Theodosius, and orthodoxy had been established, Theodosius's successor in the West, the emperor Honorius, decreed that the Donatists were to be brought back into the Catholic church by force. Only the Catholic church, whose authority Augustine had so admired since his conversion, would continue to be recognized by the state. Augustine would not have believed in the gospel, he had declared, had not the authority of the Catholic church moved him to it.[7] The subordination of the individual to the church as an institution, as the form of salvation, the means of grace – this was to become a characteristic of Latin Christianity.

The test case came soon, since from the start in Hippo Regius, where the majority were Donatists, Augustine had fought intensely for the **unity of the church**. As a Christian he was tormented by the broken unity of the African church, and as a Neoplatonist more than most he found the idea of unity a sign of the true and the good. No, for him the one true church could in no way be represented by a particular church which had split itself off, but only by the universal church – in communion with Jerusalem, Rome and the great Eastern communities: the great *Ecclesia catholica*, ever expanding and absorbing the world, endowed with sacraments and led by orthodox bishops, that church which Augustine called the 'mother' of all believers. Here, as Augustine stresses so strongly, the 'Catholic' becomes of the utmost significance for the paradigm of the Middle Ages.

But Augustine also knew that this one, holy, catholic church will never be perfect on this earth. Some belong to the church only in the body (*corpore*) and not in the heart (*corde*). The real church is a **pilgrim church** and will have to leave the separation of chaff and wheat to the final judge. To this degree the true church is the church of the saints, predestined, redeemed: a church contained in the visible church but hidden from human view. As for the **sacraments** of the church, a distinction must be made between validity on the one hand and legality and efficacy on the other. The decisive thing is not what is done by the bishop or priest (who is perhaps unworthy), but what is done by God in Christ. The sacraments are objectively valid (though they may not always be legitimate and effective), quite apart from the subjective worthiness of the one who dispenses them, provided that they are performed in order according to the church's understanding. *Ex opere operato*, people were to say in the Middle Ages: a sacrament is valid simply in the dispensation.

6. *The justification of violence in religious matters*

This great dispute without doubt led to fundamental clarifications, and in it Augustine largely gave to the whole of Western theology **categories, solutions and neat formulae for a differentiated ecclesiology and doctrine of the sacraments**: that the church can be understood as being at the same time visible and invisible, two entities which do not simply coincide; the understanding of the unity, catholicity, holiness and apostolicity of the church which follows from this; how word and sacrament go together; the word as audible sacrament and the sacrament as visible word; how in the theology of the sacraments a distinction can be made between the chief dispenser (Christ) and the instrumental dispenser (bishop, presbyter), and how the question of validity can be decided in that light.

And what about the **Donatists**? All the arguments, dialogues, sermons and more than twenty propaganda writings of Augustine, all the prohibitions of mixed marriages and gifts were of no avail. The situation came to a head: there were violent actions on both sides. In 411, on the orders of the imperial government, there was a last great disputation in Carthage, in which 286 Catholics and 279 Donatists took part. Augustine's superior arguments prevailed; at all events they served as a justification for the decision of the imperial commissioner (which had been settled from the start) now to implement the state orders through the police. This could not be done without violence and bloodshed.

Augustine and other bishops like Ambrose and Gregory of Nazianzus saw nothing un-Christian about this. They were convinced from the start that the state had the right to proceed against the heretics. But Augustine was to put this position more and more sharply over the years: in no way did he want hypocrites to populate the church. For him, initially compulsory state measures were a deterrent, and at first he protested against the imposition of the death penalty. But in the end, impressed by the success of crude police actions, he even justified the use of force against heretics and schismatics theologically. Indeed he did so with Jesus's saying from the parable of the great supper: '*Coge intrare*', in the emphatic Latin translation, 'Force (instead of compel) them to come in', those who are outside in the alleyways and hedgerows.[8]

And the success? Certainly Donatism had been broken. It had lost its bishops, church buildings and the support of the upper classes. The majority bowed to force. In this respect the Catholics had 'won'. But the price of this 'victory' was to be all too high in the long run. Historians today think that the forcible conversion of the Donatists ushered in the downfall of the African church which had once been so proud: that the former Donatists whose descendants were still causing trouble for Pope Gregory the Great at the end of the sixth century had no interest in defending the Catholic faith. So the African churches, even those of Carthage and Hippo, were overwhelmed by Islam in the seventh century without resistance and vanished without a trace into history.

Nevertheless, the mainstream church and the state (which of course was always interested in unity) did not succeed in completely eliminating all the schismatic and heretical subsidiary churches which kept reappearing. However, with his fatal arguments in the Donatist crisis, Augustine, the bishop and man of the spirit, who could talk so convincingly about the love of God and the love of human beings, was to be produced down the ages as the key witness: the key witness for the **theological justification for forcible conversions, the Inquisition and the holy war**, against deviants of all kinds; this was to become a characteristic of the mediaeval paradigm and was something for which the Greek church fathers had never argued. Peter Brown, who has written the most informed and most sensitive biography of Augustine, remarks: 'Augustine, in replying to his persistent critics, wrote the only full justification, in the history of the Early church, of the right of the state to suppress non-Catholics.'[9] Certainly Augustine could not exterminate the all too numerous non-Catholics in Hippo (as the Inquisition later exterminated the small sects), nor did he want to; he simply wanted to correct and convert. So – again according to Peter Brown – 'Augustine may be the first theorist of the Inquisition; but he was in no position to be a Grand Inquisitor.'[10]

7. The dispute over grace: Pelagius and the consequences

That Augustine, an indefatigable preacher and interpreter of scripture, had changed deeply on becoming a bishop – as so many were to do after him; that now more than before he tended towards institutional thinking, towards intolerance and pessimism, became even clearer in the second great crisis which his church had to undergo and in which he was again the main figure. This second great crisis is called the **Pelagian crisis**. It **sharpened and narrowed Augustine's theology of sin and grace**, but found decisive spokesmen not only in the Middle Ages but also in the Protestant Reformation and in Catholic Jansenism.

Pelagius, a highly respected ascetical lay monk and educated moralist from England, utterly opposed to Arianism, was active in Rome between 400 and 411, above all among lay people. He passionately attacked Manichaeism and the immoral paganism which was still widespread, and also the lax nominal Christianity of well-to-do Roman society. But in order to combat the evil, Pelagius, who had been inspired by Origen and his intellectualism

82

and optimism, and who wrote a commentary on Paul, attached great weight to **the human will and freedom**. He emphasized personal responsibility and practical action.

Certainly Pelagius also affirmed the necessity of the grace of God for all men and women, but he understood grace in a more external way, at all events not, like Augustine, as a force working within human beings, almost a material force. For Pelagius, grace was the forgiveness of sins, which for him, too, was the unmerited gift of God. Grace was also moral admonition and the example of Christ. And indeed, for Pelagius, too, the justification of men and women took place in baptism on the basis of faith without works and merits. But once a person had become a Christian – this was his concern – he or she had to make their way to salvation by their own actions – in accordance with the commandments of the Old Testament and the example of Christ.

So it was consistent that in contrast to Augustine, Pelagius should reject the notion of an 'original sin' which since Adam had been handed on to all human beings, a view which had already been put forward in a commentary on Paul falsely attributed to Ambrose (the author is now known as 'Ambrosiaster'). According to Pelagius, all human beings are born innocent; they fall by their own guilt. And with their own free will human beings can also repent and lead a new life. Pelagius was willing to recognize only a sinful bent in human beings, in voluntary imitation of the sin of Adam. When presented with Augustine's saying, 'Give what you command and then command what you will',[11] he rejected it as all too easy a way out. And his pragmatic Christianity found more admiration than criticism among the Romans, who were not interested in high dogmas but in law and morality. In some respects Pelagius was still advocating the old ideals of the past, of classical Stoic ethics. Augustine stood for ideas which were to belong to the future.

When Pelagius fled the West Goths, leaving Rome for North Africa, he did not come into contact with Augustine, and soon travelled on to Jerusalem. However, he had left behind his pupil in Carthage, the like-minded Celestius. And because Celestius now began openly to deny that infant baptism was also given for the forgiveness of sins, in 411 he was excommunicated at a synod of Carthage. Thereupon Augustine sent a personal messenger to

Jerome in Palestine also to obtain the condemnation of Pelagius in the East. However, Pelagius, who did not want a dispute, was able to justify himself: grace was necessary for good works, but there must also be a free act of the will for which human beings are really responsible. A synod of Eastern bishops, for whom the freedom of the will was no problem and the dispute over grace was more a product of Western scrupulosity, acquitted Pelagius in 415. This again caused indignation in Africa and prompted new activities on the part of Augustine who himself understood something else by 'grace', namely something inward; indeed, for Augustine, to assert an 'innocence of the newborn' was tantamount to a falsification of the relationship between God and human beings and a declaration that redemption was superfluous. So he could only feel that Pelagius's response was dishonest or deceitful.

In 416 Augustine therefore called a great synod of Numidian bishops in Milevis which, together with the Synod of Carthage, denounced Pelagius and Celestius to Pope Innocent I. The Pope then promptly excommunicated the two of them. And although Augustine was originally not a theologian fixated on the papacy (a papalist) but more a man of episcopal authority as Cyprian had been before him (an episcopalist), his comment on the action is said to have been '*Roma locuta, causa finita*', 'Rome has spoken, the matter is settled' (the statement in this form does not appear in his writings).[12] But of course this *causa*, too, was by no means settled by the pronouncement of Rome. Pelagius was rehabilitated at two Roman synods, but a Carthaginian synod condemned him again. And it was again the intervention of Augustine and his friends, this time at the imperial court, which led to Pope Zosimus reluctantly – because of an imperial edict – condemning the two main advocates of this theology, Pelagius and Celestius.

But even then the 'cause' was not at an end. For to the end of his life Augustine had to grapple with a spirited defender of Pelagius's cause, **Julian**, the bishop of Eclanum. For Julian, of an aristocratic family and a generation younger than Augustine, the son of a bishop who married the daughter of a bishop but lived a long life of continence, was a brilliant dialectician who could cope with Augustine and could advance good arguments in Pelagius's favour. Furthermore, Julian turned the tables and accused Augustine of Manichaeism, because he condemned the act of sex, which was good in itself, and regarded sin as entanglement in the evil principle of dark matter, from which human beings could free themselves only through abstinence from marriage and the pleasures of the flesh. Furthermore, Julian, who because of his support for Pelagius had been banished from southern Italy in 419, could speak Greek well and in contrast to the 'African' (*Poenus*), as he constantly called Augustine, referred to the much more liberal **Greek tradition** on marriage, which regarded sex as indispensable for the majority of Christians and had no moral problems with sexual intercourse between married partners, or with the statement in scripture that God wants all human beings to be saved. Against this, even in his very last work, which he was unable to complete, Augustine put forward his rigorist position as Catholic doctrine: 'That is the Catholic view: a view which can demonstrate a just God in so many and great punishments and torments of small children.'[13]

But is that really the Catholic view? A more important difference between the Latin West and the Greek East opened up here. Augustine rejected any semblance of Manichaeism. But above all, Augustine felt that Pelagius's teaching touched a sore spot in his own personal experience and struck at the heart of his faith. Had not he, who more than anyone else in antiquity had the capacity for analytical self-reflection, through all the wearisome years before his conversion to Catholic Christianity, experienced and described in his *Confessions* how little human beings can do of themselves? How weak their wills are? How much the fleshly desires (*concupiscentia carnis*) culminating in sexual lust keep human beings from doing the will of God? How much human beings from the start constantly need grace – not just afterwards, to support their wills, but already for the willing itself, which in itself can be evil and perverted. Hence the Augustinian counterpoint:

8. The theology of original sin and predestination

Many pagans in antiquity were also convinced that a great sin lay behind all the misery in the world. But Augustine heightened this view by historicizing, psychologizing and above all sexualizing the Fall. According to Augustine, from the start human beings are deeply corrupted by Adam's sin: 'In him all have sinned' (Romans 5.12). *In quo*: that is what Augustine found in the Latin translation of the Bible in his time, and referred this 'in him' to Adam. But the Greek text simply has '*eph'ho*' = 'because' (or in that) all sinned! So Augustine read from this statement in Romans not only a primal sin of Adam but even an **original sin** which every human being incurs right from birth, has as it were inherited – a reason why all human beings are poisoned in body and soul, are doomed to death.

But even worse, because of his personal experience of the power of sex and his Manichaean past, Augustine – in contrast to Paul, who does not write a word about it – connects this transmission of **'original sin' with the sexual act** and the 'fleshly' = selfish desires, concupiscence, which arise here. Indeed Augustine puts sexuality generally right at the centre of human nature. And what theologian in fact understood more about this than Augustine? Who could describe what goes on inside people better than he? All this influenced his biblical exegesis. For in contrast to most Greek and Syrian authors, Augustine understands the moment of sin after the first fall psychologically as a clearly felt sexual shame – punishment for sin! The inherited corruption of human nature since Adam's fall thus manifests itself particularly in the constant disruption caused by the sexual drive, which escapes the control of the will especially at the beginning and at the climax of the act, but also in sleep and in dreams.[14] Granted, it is not sexuality itself which is evil (as the Manichaeans believed), but the loss of control (thus Augustine). Even the newborn child is no innocent, but is rather a child born in sin who, if it is not to be damned eternally, needs liberation from original sin. And this act of liberation is baptism, so at all events this must be administered already to the newborn child. According to Augustine, not only the young man but also the older, married man has to strive for 'chastity' against sexual desires and take action against the sexual fantasies which constantly break in. Let us be clear about this: never before had an author in antiquity put sexuality so much under the spotlight of cool psychological analysis.

But this attempt at a solution raised a further question: if it is

God who brings about all good things in human beings (who are so corrupt in themselves), then the **problem of grace and freedom** arises. Where is human freedom, if everything takes place through God's grace, and the good will itself must be given by God's grace? Augustine was convinced that God's grace is not motivated through human freedom: on the contrary, the human will is first moved to freedom by God's grace. Grace is not acquired; grace is given. It is God's grace alone which brings about all things in human beings and which is the sole ground of human redemption. This freely given gift is constantly necessary for human beings until their end, but it requires their constant co-operation.

But in that case why are there so many people who are not saved? The more Augustine went into this controversy, the more his position hardened, as is clearest from his doctrine of **double predestination**, predestination to blessedness or to damnation.[15] To fill the gap brought about by the fall of the angels with other rational beings – here Augustine is manifestly taking up more a Manichaean than an Origenistic position – God has predestined a relatively small number of people, fixed in advance, to blessedness, and by contrast a great 'mass of damnation'.

– God's **mercy** is manifested in the **redemption** of human beings, which bestows eternal **bliss** without any legal claim (though envisaging human merits).

– However, God's **righteousness** is shown in the **rejection** of the majority of human beings. God does not will evil but does allow it (because of human free will), and thus lets human beings go on their way to eternal **damnation**. What a difference from Origen! This is a terrifying doctrine, which Calvin was to think through to the end. It raises a number of questions.

9. Critical questions to Augustine

There is no doubt that it is greatly to the credit of Augustine that he energetically directed Western theology, with its tendency toward righteousness by works, to **the Pauline message of justification**, which had lost all topicality with the disappearance of Jewish Christianity into Hellenistic Christianity, and thus indicated the **significance of grace**. Whereas Eastern theology

continued to have a strongly Johannine stamp and largely neglected the Pauline problem of justification with its antitheses in
favour of talk of the divinization of human beings, on the basis
of his experiences and his deeper study of Paul Augustine made
grace virtually the central theme of Western theology, and also
found numerous neat Latin formulations in this sphere. Against
the moralism widespread in the old Latin church which built
all too much on human achievement, he demonstrated how
everything is grounded in God's grace: 'What do you have that
you did not receive?' So according to Augustine Christianity
should present itself not as a religion of works and the law but as
a religion of grace.

This great achievement of Augustine's has often been praised,
and need not be emphasized further. Indeed, it is impossible here
to come anywhere near assessing this epoch-making work and all
the inspired and profound, brilliant and moving things he wrote
about the human longing for happiness and the human situation
in the world, under the rule of sin and the rule of grace, all
his deep thoughts on time and eternity, spirituality and piety,
surrender to God and the human soul. Within the framework of
our paradigm analysis, our prime concern must be to work out
the difference which gradually arose between Christian spirituality with a Hellenistic stamp and spirituality with a Latin stamp,
and the change from the early church/Hellenistic paradigm to the
Latin mediaeval paradigm. So what must occupy us here is
not the whole breadth and depth of the theological content
of Augustine's work but the paradigmatic shifts of this great
theologian, which can be traced into the Middle Ages and their
crisis, the Reformation, and on into modern times. And now there
can be no doubt that the same Augustine who put forward the
primacy of the will and love over against the Greek primacy of
the intellect and wrote such a generous statement as '*dilige, et
quod vis fac*', 'Love, and do what you will';[17] who could write so
generously about the grace of God, is also responsible for highly
problematical developments in the Latin church, at ~~three~~ decisive
points: four

1. The **suppression of sexuality** in Western theology and the
Western church: more than other Latin theologians (e.g. Jerome),

88

Augustine stressed the equality of man and woman at least on a spiritual level (in respect of rational intelligence), because both are in the image of God. But at the same time he maintained the physical subordination of woman which was general at the time – according to Genesis 2 woman is made from man and for man.[18] In all this Augustine's theory of sexuality and sin remains problematical: it was so important to him that at the age of seventy he even wrote a letter to the patriarch Atticus of Constantinople, the successor to John Chrysostom (this letter has only recently been discovered), summarizing his position like this:

'An urge (what he means is the evil 'urge of the flesh') which burns quite indiscriminately for objects allowed and disallowed; and which is bridled by the urge for marriage (*concupiscentia nuptiarum*), that must depend upon it, but that restrains it from what is not allowed... Against this drive, which is in tension with the *law of the mind*, all chastity must fight: that of the married couple, so that the urge of the flesh may be rightly used, and that of men and virgins, so that, even better and with a struggle of greater glory, it should not be used at all. This urge, had it existed in Paradise, would, in a wondrous pitch of peace, never have run beyond the bidding of the will... It would never have forced itself upon the mind with thoughts of inappropriate and impermissible delights. It would not have had to be held upon the leash by married moderation, or fought to a draw by ascetic labour. Rather, when once called for, it would have followed the will of the person with all the ease of a single-hearted act of obedience.'[19]

From Augustine's perspective it was clear that ideally sexual intercourse should take place only for the procreation of children. Sexual pleasure purely for its own sake is sinful and is to be suppressed; it was inconceivable for him that sexual pleasure could even enrich and deepen the relationship between husband and wife. What a tremendous burden this particular Augustinian legacy of Augustine's, of the vilification of the sexual libido, was for the men and women of the Middle Ages, the Reformation and far beyond! And still in our own day a Pope has in all seriousness proclaimed the view that even in marriage a man can look on his wife 'unchastely', if he does so purely for pleasure...

2. The **reification of grace** in Western theology and piety.

Whereas in the East no idea of a 'created grace' corresponding to the Latin Western doctrine of grace developed, and interest was wholly focussed on the hoped-for divinization of human beings and their 'immortality' and 'transitoriness', Tertullian already understood grace not so much biblically, as God's disposition and decree of sins, but – following Stoic ideas – as a *vis* in human beings, a power more powerful than nature (*natura*: the contrast between nature and grace appears for the first time in Tertullian).

So for Augustine too, the 'grace of forgiveness' is merely the preparation for the 'grace of inspiration', which is poured into human beings as a healing and transforming dynamic substance of grace: *gratia infusa*, something like a supernatural fuel that drives the will (which of itself is impotent). By grace here Augustine no longer means the living God who is gracious to us, but a 'created grace' which is distinct from God himself, made independent and usually attached to the sacrament. There is nothing about this in the New Testament, but the Latin theology and church of the Middle Ages – a church of grace and the sacraments – was to concentrate on it, in complete contrast to Greek theology.

3. The anxiety about **predestination** in Western piety. Whereas the Greek church fathers maintained the human capacity for decision before and after the Fall and did not recognize any unconditional divine predestination to salvation or damnation, indeed partly even tended to the reconciliation of all things, like Origen and the Origenists, as he grew old Augustine, in an over-reaction to Pelagianism, took over a mythological Manichaean notion and in addition neutralized the universal significance of Christ; in a completely un-Pauline way he individualistically narrowed the statements in Romans about Israel and the church.[20] What kind of a God is it who has *a priori* destined countless human beings, including countless unbaptized babies, to eternal damnation (though perhaps in a milder form) for the sake of his 'righteousness'?

Augustine's contemporary John Chrysostom had explicitly emphasized that small children are innocent, since in his community some people believed that they could be killed by witchcraft and that their souls were possessed by demons. But Augustine also made quite a substantial contribution to fear of demons in the Western church. His doctrine of predestination, although already repudiated by Vincent of Lérins as an innovation (against the principle of the Catholic 'what has been believed everywhere, always, by all') and thus in no way fully received by the mediaeval church, instilled in many people, including Martin Luther, an anxiety about the salvation of their souls which does not match the message of Jesus and contradicts God's universal will to save. Even the French patrologist Henri Marrou, who generally interprets Augustine in such a generous way, cannot avoid stating: 'If serious errors have often distorted his real thinking, as the history of his influence shows, Augustine bears a great deal of the responsibility.'[21]

4. The **new conception of the doctrine of the Trinity.** Whereas Augustine did little to stimulate the Christian life of 'lay people' in the world or a cosmic piety, his theology does contain a good deal of speculation about God. For Augustine set completely new accents not only in matters of sexual morality or the theology of grace and the sacraments, but also in the doctrine of God, above all in rethinking the Christian tradition about the Trinity, where he goes far beyond what we heard previously from Origen about oneness and threeness in God. Summed up in all too brief statements, we may say:

– The Greeks thought in terms of the **one God and Father**; the Father is '**the** God', the one and only principle of the Godhead, which he also gives to the Son ('God from God and light from light') and finally also the Holy Spirit. They are like three stars one after the other: each gives the light to the next, but we only see one.

– Augustine now begins with the **one divine nature or substance,** the one divine essence, glory, majesty common to all three persons. The starting point and foundation of his doctrine of the Trinity is this one divine nature which for him is the principle of the unity of Father, Son and Spirit, within which these three differ only as eternal relationships (these are the foundation of life within God): the Father knows himself in the Son and the Son in the Father, and proceeds from this as the personified love of the Spirit. So Augustine asserts a twofold principle for the Spirit: the famous later Latin addition to the Nicene Creed, 'the Spirit, proceeding from the Father **and the Son** (*filioque*)', which to this day is rejected by the Greeks as nonsense.

So the **originally simple triadic confessional statements** of the New Testament about Father, Son and Spirit developed into an **increasingly demanding intellectual trinitarian speculation** on '3 = 1'. It was almost like a higher trinitarian mathematics, but despite all attempts at conceptual clarity, lasting solutions were hardly reached. We might ask whether this Graeco-Latin speculation, which, far removed from its biblical basis, boldly attempted to spy out the mystery of God in vertiginous heights, did not perhaps like Icarus, the son of Daedalus, the ancestor of Athenian craft, come too near to the sun with wings made of feathers and wax.

In the light of the New Testament, no more is required than that the relationship between Father, Son and Spirit should be interpreted in a critical and differentiated way for the present. The 'heart' of Christian faith is not a theological theory but belief that God the Father works in a revealing, redeeming and liberating way in us through his Son Jesus Christ in his Spirit. Any theological theory must not complicate this basic statement; rather, it must be seen simply as an instrument for clarifying it against differing cultural horizons.

Generally speaking, Augustine, unlike Origen, did not work out any comprehensive system, but put forward a unitary conception. And he had not yet completed his work on the Trinity, when as a bishop he was confronted with an event which now clearly indicated a crisis for the empire and a change in world history. How did his story go on?

10. The great threat to the empire

News of unprecedented terror ran through the empire. On 28 August 410, Rome, which had believed itself to be 'eternal' – even Christians called it *Roma aeterna* – had been stormed by King Alaric, leader of the Western Gothic army fighting for a homeland, and plundered for days. In North Africa refugees had told of horrific atrocities: numerous burnings, women raped, even senators murdered, the rich hunted, whole families exterminated, houses plundered, valuables of all kinds carted off by the barbarians, the old government and administrative centre of the Western world destroyed... Uncertainty and defeatism were abroad: if Rome, the **ancient capital**, could **fall**, what was still safe? How could things reach such a pitch? There were very different responses to the catastrophe:

1. The response of **pagan old Rome,** those educated pagan aristocrats (along with the peasants = *pagani*, the last pagans) who fled to Carthage was clear: it was the **vengeance of the gods of Rome**. The Christians were responsible for the fall of the Roman state. They had evacuated the political and religious idea of the Roman empire, rejected the emperor cult, and thus undermined the authority of the state, the law and the army. They had driven out the gods and replaced them with the cult of the Christian God, putting the state under the protection of Peter, Paul and so many martyrs. But these had evidently offered no protection against murder, plundering, rape, kidnap and extermination.

2. The response of **Christian new Rome**: this catastrophe was **God's punishment**. According to the Byzantines the old Rome had had the Messiah and Son of God crucified by its governor in Jerusalem, had for centuries subjected his disciples to a bloody persecution, and even when it had become Christian, had still tolerated paganism within its walls to the end. So the second, new, Rome, the Christian Byzantium, had long since replaced the old Rome. Its end was now well-deserved retribution for a mistaken policy and false belief.

3. **Augustine's response**. As an African and a Latin, he ignored the existence and myth of the Second Rome and so never paid due attention to the Christian empire as a whole. He gave his extremely sophisticated answer in his last giant work, on the 'City of God' (*De civitate Dei*; we should not forget that here the term 'city' is virtually equivalent to the modern 'state', a term not in existence at that time). For when his open letters and sermons had had too little effect even in Carthage, Augustine's friend Marcellus, tribune and notary in Carthage, had invited him to produce a more substantial work because of so much pagan criticism and so much helplessness and defeatism among Christians. Augustine took up this challenge and now carefully planned a major new work which

he published in several stages: the twenty-two books *De civitate Dei*, on which he spent a large part of his last two decades (413-426/7), during which he also composed most of his anti-Pelagian writings.

The first ten books, produced in haste, are devoted to **apologetic and polemic**. The pagans ought really to have seen that the old gods of Rome had always been incapable of keeping famine, epidemics and wars from Rome – one had only to think of the Punic wars or the Roman civil wars. The behaviour of the Christian Germans might be called moderate compared with the harsh conduct of the pagan Romans. Indeed, one can see the whole history of Rome from the beginning as a long chain of violent actions and accidents which begins with the fratricide of Remus by Romulus and in no way corresponds to the ideal of the state as Cicero describes it in *De re publica*, since it has no righteousness. The goal of the state is the preservation of peace in an order which rests on righteousness. There is no question that what Augustine offers here is a bold and unprecedented demythologizing of the history of Rome supported by numerous quotations from Roman authors.

But there is more: at the same time he produces a **demythologizing of the old gods** which sums up all previous apologetic. Not only are Christians not guilty of Rome's downfall, but the gods are not responsible for Rome's rise either. The virtues of the ancient Romans, ambivalent though they have been, were responsible for that. The gods are not only impotent; they do not exist at all; their competence is arbitrarily divided and self-contradictory. In other words, through Varro's distinction between a poetic religion (*religio fabulosa*), a political religion (*religio civilis*) and a natural religion (*religio naturalis*), Augustine carries out such a comprehensive critical destruction of all Graeco-Roman belief in gods that it made any further apologia superfluous in the future.

But Augustine also turns to the Christians, who in their propaganda to pagans had all too often inappropriately brought in the protection of the Christian God. The God in whom Christians believe nowhere promised to safeguard possessions and happiness on this earth in order to protect human beings from any external misfortune. Anyone who believes that does not really believe in God, nor does he understand the meaning of his life. That is recognized only by someone who is humble of heart before God: on their journey through life such persons may not always be able to ward off suffering, but they can endure it. First the end will bring freedom from all suffering and eternal peace. To this degree suffering can purge and thus contribute towards seeking God, not only for earthly advantages, but also for God's own sake. No, there was no argument that Augustine did not take up in the course of his work, in order to offer a large-scale **theodicy**, a justification of God in the face of all the indissoluble riddles of this life. And all this with the aim of strengthening unconditional trust, faith in God.

11. *What is the meaning of history?*

Augustine's concern is the destiny of human beings, indeed the destiny of humankind. And so in the last twelve books his apologia issues in a large-scale **interpretation of history**: the battle between the *civitas terrena*, the earthly state, the world state, world citizenship, and on the other hand the *civitas Dei*, the city of God, the state of God, the citizenship of God. The great controversy between world state and God's state is the mysterious foundation and meaning of history, which is at the same time a history of salvation and disaster. Augustine describes its origin and beginning, then its progress through seven ages, and finally its outcome and goal.

The origin of the two civil communities lies in primal times, when the apostasy of proud angels led to a second empire alongside God's state – the devil's state. Consequently there was a need to make good the gap torn open by the fall of the angels, from those predestined from the human race, until the full number of the citizens of God was attained again. However, through the primal sin of Adam, which thus includes the city of God and the city of this world in itself, the angelic sin of pride has repeated itself, so that now among human beings an earthly world state has developed as an opposite to God's state. Its first representatives were on the one hand Abel, the just, and on the other Cain, the builder of cities and fratricidal murderer; then Israel and the Gentile world; then Jerusalem the city of God, and Babylon the city of this world; and finally in the end time Rome, the new Babylon, and the Catholic church. So the city of God and the city of this world are different right from the beginning:

– Their Lord and Governor is different: on the one hand God, and on the other the gods and demons.

– Their citizens are different: the elect worshippers of the one true God – the repudiated worshippers of gods and the selfish.

– Their basic attitude is different: the love of God rooted in humility, going as far as despising the self – the self-love grounded in pride going as far as despising God.

So now both world history and the history of individuals runs in six periods, formed after the pattern of the week of creation, which in world history becomes a world week. Since its creation the world has gone through six great world ages. Thus for Augustine the transitoriness of cultures, the reality of breaks in eras and 'paradigm shifts', was already manifest from the Bible. With Jesus Christ, the Lord of the city of God has appeared corporeally in the world – the God-man as the climax of world history! Since then humankind has been living in the sixth day of the world week, in the end-time, at the end of which will come the Last Judgment. This is heralded in the downfall of the last world state, the Roman empire, which unmasked itself as the devil's state in the persecution of Christians, but now has the merit of having secured a peace from which God's state has also profited. But Augustine himself remains mistrustful of the Christian empire, as pagan forces are still at work in it. Augustine says hardly anything about the future of the Roman empire (whether Rome in the West or Rome in the East). By contrast, he is utterly certain that the kingdom of God in this earthly age has an empirical form: the **Catholic church**. It is the concrete embodiment, the manifestation, of the kingdom of God on earth. However, it is not simply identical with the city of God, since the city of this world is still at work in it. For Augustine, God alone knows the elect.

Of course Augustine is not a historian in the modern sense, but a theological interpreter of history; he is not primarily interested in the development of humankind, but in God's plan. And yet, unlike Homer and Virgil, he is concerned not with a mythology of history but with real history and its deepest ground. With the help of the Bible and ancient historians, Augustine wants to achieve two things: first, to present numerous historical details with all possible parallels and analogies, allegories and typologies; and secondly, precisely in this way to offer a **meaningful overall view of world history** as the great clash between faith and unbelief, humility and arrogance, love and striving for power, salvation and damnation – from the beginning of time until today. So it is Augustine who created the first monumental **theology of history** in Christianity – which had an influence deep into the whole of mediaeval Western theology and the theology of the Reformation, up to the threshold of the modern secularization of history. Before Augustine, in antiquity, there was neither a philosophy of history nor a theology of history. Augustine thus took seriously the fact that in the Jewish-Christian understanding – so completely different from the circular Hellenistic, Indian understanding – history is a movement towards an end, guided and directed by God: the eternal city of God, the kingdom of peace, the kingdom of God.

In this way the *magnum opus et arduum*, the 'great and difficult work', was completed.[22] But hardly two years had passed before Augustine, who in the meantime, because of the difficulties of his old age, had chosen a coadjutor with the right to succession, saw that the Arian Vandals, who in a single generation had come from Hungary and Silesia right through Europe to Spain and Gibraltar, were now marching along the Mauretanian coast of North Africa. In 430 Numidia too was devastated by the Vandals, and three months later now Hippo also was already under siege from them. Augustine, now seventy-five and a victim of fever, saw that his end had come. He had David's penitential psalms pinned to the wall and spent his time in prayer. The one who all his life had enjoyed having friends around him and never liked to be alone, wanted to die alone. Before the Vandals broke through the ring of defence, on 28 August 430 – precisely twenty years to the day after the conquest of Rome by the Goths – he died, the undisputed spiritual and theological leader of North Africa. Now Roman rule of the world had also collapsed here, but Augustine's theology was to make world history on another continent, that of Europe.

Down to our own days, this theologian and stylist, incomparable despite his limitations, reminds us not only of the meaning of history but also of the meaning of our life, when in the closing sentence of his *City of God* he conjures up that seventh world age, that indescribable and undefinable eighth day, on which God completes his creative work, the church achieves the goal of its pilgrimage, and the world recognizes its Lord: 'There we shall be still and see; we shall see and we shall love; we shall love and we shall praise. Behold what will be, in the end, without end! For what is our end but to reach that kingdom which has no end? (*Ibi vacabimus et videbimus, videbimus et amabimus, amabimus et laudabimus. Ecce quod erit in fine sine fine. Nam quis alius noster est finis nisi pervenire ad regnum, cuius nullus est finis?*).'[23]

Thomas Aquinas
University Science and Papal Court Theology

Chronology (according to J.A. Weisheipl)

1224/5	Born in Roccasecca.
1230/31-39	Benedictine Oblate in Monte Cassino.
1239-44	Student at the University of Naples; death of his father.
1244	Enters the Dominican order in Naples; abducted on the journey to Paris and taken to a family castle.
1245	Returns to the order.
1245-48	Paris: novitiate and study.
1248-52	Cologne: studies with Albert the Great; ordained priest.
1252-56	Returns to Paris: *sententiarius*.
1252	Becomes Magister of theology.
1256-59	Teaches as Magister of theology.
1259-64	The first great *Summa*: *Summa contra gentiles*.
1260-61	Stay in Naples.
1261-65	Teacher in Orvieto.
1266	Beginning of the second great *Summa*: *Summa theologiae*.
1267	Stay in Viterbo.
1269-72	Magister in Paris for the second time.
1270	10 December: condemnation of Averroism (Thirteen Propositions).
1272	Teaches as Magister of theology in Naples.
1273	6 December: Breaks off the *Summa theologiae*.
1274	February: invitation to the Council of Lyons. 7 March: dies on the journey in Fossanova.
1277	Condemnation of 219 propositions in Paris. 18 March: condemnation of propositions in Oxford.
1323	18 July: Beatification of Thomas by Pope John XXII in Avignon.

Without the theology of Aurelius Augustine there would have been no theology of Thomas Aquinas. The Catholic fundamental theologian Heinrich Fries has rightly pointed to the great historical influence of Augustine's theology, which reaches deep into mediaeval theology and beyond: 'Augustine's theology influenced the whole of Western Christianity after him. He is the greatest theologian of the Christian West. One can say that the content and method of philosophy and theology up to the scholasticism of the thirteenth century was influenced by him. The *Sentences* of Peter Lombard, for centuries the textbook and handbook of theology, are primarily taken from Augustine's work. The programme of scholasticism, which is defined by Anselm of Canterbury's *Credo ut intelligam*, goes back to Augustine. And even when the work of Aristotle was received with Albert the Great and Thomas Aquinas, and theology methodologically took on a new form as a science, in the separation of knowledge and faith, philosophy and theology, in the distinction between nature and grace, Augustine's significance remained, as the work of Thomas Aquinas shows, as normative for mediaeval theology as that of Aristotle.'[1]

Aristotle – alongside Augustine, he is the second great figure without which the theology of Thomas Aquinas is inconceivable. His philosophy – which was rediscovered in the Christian Middle Ages – had a decisive influence in shaping Thomas's philosophy. In the thirteenth century in particular, Thomas's century, when the monasteries were replaced as centres of education by the universities with their sciences, this pagan philosopher was to have an epoch-making effect. We shall be seeing this in more detail later.

Thomas was born in 1225 (or at the end of 1224), the youngest son of the knight Landulf of Aquino, in the family castle of Roccasecca, precisely midway between Rome and Naples. At the early age of five he was taken to the powerful abbey of Monte Cassino as a *puer oblatus*. An 'offered' child – for what? For the service of God and thus for religious and intellectual schooling. However, because of the war between the pope and the emperor Frederick II – the powerful clan of Aquinos were among those on the imperial side – Thomas had to move his son to **Naples,** to the Studium Generale founded by Frederick, there to qualify in the propaedeutic studies in the arts faculty, which consisted of the seven *artes liberales*: grammar, rhetoric, dialectic (known as the trivium), and arithmetic, geometry, music and astronomy (known as the quadrivium).

What motivated Thomas to this study? He wanted to follow a **spiritual calling,** in other words not just to study Aristotle, though in Naples he got to know his natural philosophy and in all probability also his metaphysics at a time when these were still forbidden territory to Paris students. Thus prepared, at the age of nineteen Thomas made a decision which was to have great consequences for his life. In 1244 he entered the Dominican order. In so doing he opted for a life in accordance with the gospel. He had to fight for his choice – like Francis of Assisi – against the massive resistance of his powerful family: if he had to be a monk, they would rather have seen him as the abbot of the rich monastery of Monte Cassino. His brothers even abducted him on his journey to Paris and put him in a family castle. For about a year Thomas resisted not only a staged attempt at seduction by a courtesan but also the constant pressure of his relations.

He won. But he did not want to spend his life in personal sanctification, in a remote feudal monastery, where one was condemned to immobility by the vow of *stabilitas loci* and bound by the patriarchal authority of an abbot. Nor did he want to live a well-endowed, comfortable life as a canon, according to specific rules, in the shadow of a cathedral. Although born into a land-owning aristocracy, he had been attracted by the simple **'apostolic life' of the Mendicants,** a collective name for all the begging orders (from the Latin *mendicare*, beg), especially the Franciscans and the Dominicans. They formed a highly democratized international community of like-minded people, and it was evident that Thomas was seeking precisely that: another form of life in another world.

What kind of a world was this **other world**? Let us be clear that this was a time of transition: from a feudal type of **allegiance,** in which duty and an oath of allegiance bound people personally to their lord and landowner, to a common life, a **commonwealth,** in which the citizens of the towns had their own rights and freedoms within the framework of their guilds and corporations. In this situation the new anti-feudal orders which followed the mendicant movement offered quite different possibilities even to a young nobleman like Thomas; one could move in the midst of the great cities, the economic and scientific centres which were now forming, and involve oneself spiritually there. This was particularly true of the centres of the European spirit which came into being between the seventh and the middle of the thirteenth century from the city schools (not the conservative, monastic feudal schools, remote from the cities): the **universities**. Here private schools of scholars had joined together, and pupils from various regions flocked to hear famous teachers: for the first time there was a free community of teachers and taught, in which those being taught were sometimes even allowed to choose their rector.

Moreover very soon such universities sprang up in many European cities: in Bologna, Paris, Oxford, Cambridge, Padua, Naples and Salamanca, the constitution of whose faculty became the model for the universities which were soon also founded in the German empire: Prague, Krakow, Vienna, Heidelberg, Cologne and Leipzig. They had a strong legal position. For on the basis of imperial and papal privileges, as independent corporations the universities enjoyed autonomous statutes, the right to bestow academic awards, exemption from taxation, their own jurisdiction, safe conduct, freedom of teaching – all this, provided that they were not in conflict with church dogmas. For Thomas, now Paris, Cologne, Paris again, the Roman Curia, Paris a third time and finally Naples again were to be the stages of his life and teaching.

Thomas had resolved on a mendicant order which is also called the Order of Preachers, *Ordo fratrum praedicatorum*. Founded by the Spaniard **Dominic** (1170-1221) with papal approval, this order used 'sermons' in the style of the heretics (Albigensians, Catharists) both to attack these heretics and to deal with the wretched state of preaching in the church generally. Moreover, from the beginning the disciples of Dominic had a concern for solid university study, which was also Thomas's goal. He was attracted by a simple life of poverty, though without just making poverty absolute. For, as Thomas was to put it later, 'Perfection does not consist essentially in poverty, but in the discipleship of

Christ.'[2] That left scope for various forms of discipleship of Christ, of which the monastic-ascetic form was just one.

Of prime importance to the Order of Preachers was a concern for **Holy Scripture**, for revised editions of the Bible, a Bible concordance and Bible commentaries. Thomas Aquinas was also to combine his teaching activity with biblical exegesis and to write a whole series of commentaries on the Old and New Testaments.[3] All his life, he too saw himself primarily as a *doctor in divina pagina*, a teacher of Holy Scripture, which moreover he was constantly expounding in sermons. This makes it clear that the spiritual basis of his existence was not the study of Aristotle but the **discipleship of Christ**. This made Thomas capable of steeping himself fully in the philosophical thought of antiquity precisely for the sake of Christian faith: in a concern for a reconciliation of Christian faith not only with Neoplatonic thought, like his great predecessors Origen and Augustine, but also with the thought of Aristotle, which was very much less 'pious'. For this, Thomas was later censured by Luther and then by some Lutherans, who hardly knew Thomas on the basis of his original series of lectures. Were they right? Let us look more closely.

2. Aristotle – the danger

Brilliantly gifted as he was, Thomas was almost automatically drawn into the **second Renaissance** of the high Middle Ages which followed the early mediaeval Carolingian renaissance. By that we understand that movement of renewal inspired by the spirit of antiquity which in the twelfth century comprised not only literature (Ovid, Virgil), but also above all Roman law and politics. Now, in the second third of the thirteenth century, in Paris, the 'city of the philosophers' and the centre of European cultural life, it also reached a climax through the renewal of the *artes liberales*, philosophy and theology.

This became possible above all through the **reception of the whole of Aristotle**. Previously, Aristotle had been known to mediaeval scholars only as a logician and then mostly indirectly, but now his original thought developed tremendous power. Translations first from the Arabic and then also from the Greek, and knowledge through the intermediary of Arab Jewish philosophy – the most important transit points were Spain and Sicily – quickly made him known despite church bans on reading him, and Aristotle was soon **the** philosopher. Why? Because the discovery of his truly encyclopaedic thought amounted to a tremendous **extension of knowledge** for European scholars, particularly in the sphere of the natural sciences, medicine, anthropology and metaphysics. This in turn resulted in a further quest for knowledge, another spiritual atmosphere: a new university of interests, a new independence in thought, a new concern with natural science.

When Thomas, aged twenty, arrived at the study centre of his order in Paris – Notre Dame had just been completed – he had the inestimable good fortune to meet a uniquely learned teacher, around twenty-five years older, who rightly bore the title *Doctor universalis*. Three years later, Thomas was able to accompany this teacher for four years to **Cologne**, where he was ordained priest (he was nicknamed the 'dumb ox'). Thomas was so close to his teacher all his life that when Thomas was posthumously condemned by the church this elderly man rushed to Paris to defend his pupil. Who was he? The Swabian **Albert the Great**, from Lauingen near Ulm (1200-1280). Albert was the man who over twenty years had laboured to produce an encyclopaedia of Aristotelian thought. He had courageously sought to disseminate and evaluate the Aristotelian, Arabic and Jewish writings which had newly been discovered in the twelfth century. Since some of them were still banned at the time, Albert did not develop them further, but paraphrased them. He was courageous. But how so?

What we take for granted today was not at all the case at that time. For many people thought that a pagan philosopher like **Aristotle** was extraordinarily **dangerous** and disturbing. And with good reason. Did not Aristotle advocate the eternity of the world instead of a creation and thus the temporality of the world? The blind compulsion of history instead of a divine providence? The mortality of the soul tied to its body instead of its immortality? Generally speaking, did not this philosopher embody such a concentration on empirical and visible reality that heaven, God and his revelation seemed to be being neglected? As late as 1263 Pope Urban IV had once again banned the study of the writings of Aristotle – but in vain. For Aristotle, passed on through

Arabic scholars in Spain (Averroes!), also found his way into the intellectual centres of France and Germany.

I need not spend long explaining how both Aristotelianism and Arabism must have been a tremendous intellectual **challenge to the young Thomas** when at twenty-seven he returned to **Paris** in 1252 from Cologne, to prepare himself to teach theology as an assistant (*Baccalaureus*) at the Dominican study centre. What was his starting point? Already in Cologne he had to give an introduction to the Bible; now, in Paris, as *sententiarius* he had to expound the theological textbook of the Middle Ages: the *Four Books of Sentences* of Peter Lombard. This Paris professor and later bishop (he died in 1160) had made a collection of texts from the church fathers and above all Augustine, and systematically divided the material, using John of Damascus as a model, into the doctrine of God, the doctrine of creation, christology and the doctrine of redemption, the doctrine of the sacraments and eschatology – a structure and a sequence which have been maintained in theological curricula down to the present day. After four years, Thomas and the Franciscan Bonaventura were made **Magister of theology** in the University of Paris, in 1256. He was now *ordinarius* professor, and his task consisted in *legere* (lecturing), *disputare* (disputation) and *praedicare* (preaching).

This extraordinarily young Magister now faced the gigantic task of combining the new knowledge from ancient philosophy with scripture and traditional theology. But Thomas did not resort to antiquity for its own sake, so to speak out of philological and archaeological interest, but for the sake of people in the present, **with a theological and pastoral intent.** For as Étienne Gilson and Josef Pieper have shown, in so far as Thomas was a philosopher, he was a **Christian philosopher.** He was interested not in what Aristotle and other thinkers of antiquity had to say to the Athens and Rome of their day, but in what they had to say to the Paris of his day – presuming that they would have accepted Christian faith. To this extent we may not apply today's historical-critical criteria to Thomas's interpretation of Aristotle. The philosopher Thomas was a passionately **Christian theologian** and remained so. Certainly he wanted to understand Aristotle authentically, and therefore took the trouble to read translations and commentaries all his life. But at the same time, fusing the chronological horizons, he wanted to understand Aristotle better in Christian faith than Aristotle understood himself 1500 years earlier.

So Aquinas did not intend a revival of Aristotle but his transformation. However – *pace* Gilson and Pieper – he held firm to one thing: scientific and philosophical thought, empirical thought from below, was best learnt from the works of Aristotle himself. For this reason, Thomas took enormous trouble, in addition to his great theological works, to write extensive commentaries on Aristotle's most important works. Here, in the Aristotle commentaries, very much more than in the so-called 'philosophical' arguments of his theological works, we can grasp his philosophical thought. In particular his clear distinction between Aristotelian philosophical and Augustinian theological thought made it possible for him to give a new basis to theology.

3. Theology – now a rational university science

For Thomas it was clear, even if he did not say so, that traditional **Augustinianism**, which hitherto had governed everything, was in **a crisis**. In this new time one could no longer solely refer in questions of faith to the previous authorities – Bible, church fathers, councils and popes – which were often contradictory. Rather, one had to make much more use than before of reason and conceptual analysis to achieve clarity. At all events, Thomas did this both resolutely and boldly, with not a little objectivity and logical acuteness, but also often uncritically, and reinterpreting the statements of the authorities unhistorically – in the *expositio reverentialis*, respectful exposition, customary at the time.

However, we should be clear that Thomas's theology – unlike the more contemplative monastic theology of the church fathers and still that of Augustine – is quite essentially a **rational university theology**, composed by professors in the *schola*, the school, and intended primarily not for the people and pastoral care, but for students and colleagues in theology. All the works of Thomas Aquinas – whether the *Summas* or the questions for disputation, the commentaries on Aristotle, Pseudo-Dionysius, Peter Lombard and Boethius or those on a variety of Old and New Testament books, or finally the various opuscula – are utterly stamped with the 'scholastic' approach to learning. They are all exclusively composed in Latin (Thomas did not learn either German in Cologne or French in Paris); all are very clear, terse and compact, but impersonal and monotone compared with Augustine, because their procedure is constantly analytic, with numerous divisions and subdivisions, with sharp definitions of concepts and formal distinctions, with objections and answers, with all the means of grammar, dialectic and disputation.

But there is no doubt that for all his tremendous use of highly-developed and often over-developed scholastic technique, Thomas Aquinas never lost sight of the great task of his life. Right at the beginning of his first great personal work, the *Summa contra gentiles*, he formulated as his lifelong task: 'I am aware that I owe it to God as the first task of my life to let him speak in all my discourses and senses.'[4] So for Thomas, the university professor, as for Augustine, the bishop, 'theo-logy' was responsible talk of God.

With this basic theological and pastoral intention, Thomas created a new philosophical and theological synthesis for the new time: brilliant, constructed with methodological rigour and didactic skill, of an unprecedented unity. And it was presented in two *Summas*, one philosophical and theological, against the 'Gentiles' (*Summa contra gentiles*), and one theological and philosophical, for Christian faith (*Summa theologiae*). Why, one might ask, this division, which neither Origen nor Augustine would have allowed?

4. The discovery of the power of reason

The influence of Aristotle is particularly evident from the fact that Thomas gave, had to give, knowledge gained by human reason quite a different value from what was usual in the theological tradition. For there was no disputing the fact that reason has its independence, its own right, its own sphere, over against faith. The new desire for knowledge, for science, had to be taken seriously. Earlier theologians had had things easier here: they proved as it were the justification for reason alongside faith. But as he shows in the introductions to his two *Summas*, Thomas felt compelled to prove the justification for faith alongside reason (*rationem fidei*). This was a completely new challenge, which forced him to think through the relationship between faith and reason in a new, fundamental way. How?

For Thomas, there is no question that philosophy exists in its own right alongside theology. Not by permission of the church, but because of the nature of the order of creation. The creator God himself has endowed human beings with understanding and reason. Science is a 'daughter of God' because God is the 'Lord of the sciences' (*Deus scientiarum dominus*). If one takes this seriously, the result is a liberating **shift for all theology**:
– a shift towards the creaturely and empirical,
– a shift towards rational analysis,
– a shift towards scientific research.

To be more precise: more than any other theologian of his time, Thomas understood that in view of the new significance of reason, in view of Aristotle and Averroes, it was no longer appropriate to seek to combine the whole of reality without distinction into one great philosophical and theological union of reason and faith. Augustine's thought, which did not know any independent philosophical system, was no further use here, important though it remained in other spheres. No, in this new time, no thought was publicly defensible in which philosophical truth was not *a priori* one with revealed truth, in which philosophical arguments could not be used for the interpretation of the Bible and, conversely, biblical quotations could not be used as a basis for philosophical thought. So what was required? Another, purer **method** which created an utterly **rational basis** for theology.

So we understand Thomas only if we have understood his basic hermeneutical methodological decision. It consists in a fundamental **distinction** between the modes of knowledge, levels of knowledge and thus the sciences:
– There are two different human **modes of knowledge** (directions of knowledge): it is important to analyse precisely what natural reason is capable of and what comes from faith through grace.
– There are two different human **modes of knowledge** (perspectives of knowledge): it is important to distinguish precisely what human beings know as it were 'from below', within the limits of their horizon of experience, from what they know

'from above', from God's own perspective through inspired Holy Scripture: in other words, what belongs on the lower level of natural truths and what belongs on the upper level, that of revealed, supernatural truth.

– So there are two different **sciences**: a precise distinction must be made between what philosophy can know in principle and what theology can know. What are we to learn from Aristotle, 'the philosopher' (hence the commentaries on Aristotle), and what are we to know from the Bible (hence the Bible commentaries)?

So according to Thomas, **human reason** is given a wide sphere in which it can be independently active in knowledge. For even the existence and properties of God, God's work as creator and God's providence, the existence of an immortal soul and many ethical insights, are natural truths which human beings can know, indeed demonstrate by reason alone, without revelation. And **faith**? Faith in the strict sense is necessary for the acceptance of certain higher truths of revelation. These include the mysteries of the Trinity or the incarnation of God in Jesus of Nazareth, and also the primal state and the last state, the fall and redemption of human beings and the world. These truths transcend human reason; they cannot be proved rationally but are beyond reason, though they should not be confused with irrational 'truths', which can be refuted rationally.

5. *Two* Summas – *a formal principle*

Because of this twofold possibility of knowing God, and the twofold mode of knowing the truth about God, while **philosophy** (including the philosophical doctrine of God) and **theology** are not to be separated, since they speak of the same God, they are to be distinguished, since they speak differently of God. Here philosophy proceeds rationally 'from below', from the creation and creatures, while theology proceeds in faith 'from above', from God. Nevertheless, reason and faith, philosophy and theology, should support each other since, being both rooted in the one truth of God, they are compatible. In this theology, *intelligo ut credam*, 'I know in order to believe', rather than Augustine's *credo ut intelligam* ('I believe in order to know'), stands in the foreground.

The very first part of the *Summa theologiae* – beginning with twelve long chapters on the one God, his life, knowledge and will,[5] and going on to sixteen equally long chapters on the threefold God[6]! – makes it clear that the starting point is to be two spheres, two levels of knowledge, metaphorically **two storeys**, which are clearly distinguished but not simply separated: one of higher certainty, the other fundamental and rationally clearly superior, both of which are in the last resort not contradictory but in fundamental accord. The First Vatican Council in 1870, 600 years later, was to define the relationship between faith and reason in a similar Neoscholastic, Neothomistic way.

Thus beyond question Thomas Aquinas **created for theology the mature, classical form of the mediaeval Roman Catholic paradigm**. His restructuring of all theology includes an evaluation:
– reason as compared with faith,
– the literal sense of scripture as compared with the allegorical-spiritual sense,
– nature as compared with grace,
– the natural law as compared with a specifically Christian morality,
– philosophy as compared with theology; in short,
– the human as compared with the distinctively Christian.

Moreover, it was quite coherent and in no way inconsistent for Thomas to work out **two different *Summas***, two overall accounts for two different purposes, although in both he deals with the same God, the same world and the same human beings, and in both also uses **the same cyclical formative principle, understood primarily in spatial terms** which come from Neoplatonism: the scheme of departing and returning. In their first halves, both of Thomas's schemes deal with the *exitus*, the issuing of all things from God (God as origin), and in the second with the *reditus*, the return of all things to God (God as goal) – however, they do so without the cosmic determinism of the Neoplatonists. All things are to be understood from God, their supreme ground of being and their ultimate goal. So why two *Summas*, despite the same basic pattern? Because the two *Summas* serve different purposes and could operate at different levels.

1. The *Summa* against the Gentiles. It was written for Christians who found themselves arguing with Muslim (and also Jewish and heretical) opponents, whether with Muslims in Spain, Sicily and North Africa, or Jews and heretics in Christian Europe. In the thirteenth century, Islam, which was advanced culturally, was not only a political and military but also an intellectual and spiritual challenge. Therefore an alternative had to be provided to the Graeco-Arab world view. This was the aim of the *Summa contra Gentiles*: an overall view of Christian convictions with an apologetic, missionary and scientific purpose. But precisely because it is aimed at convincing non-Christians, except in the fourth apologetic part it largely operates at the level of **natural reason**. Scriptural statements are at best used in isolation to confirm it. In the introduction Thomas says that one cannot discuss about God, creation and the moral life (the three themes of the first three parts) on the basis of the Old or New Testaments, 'so it is necessary to resort to the natural reason, to which all are compelled to assent'.[7]

2. The *Summa theologiae*. This is intended for theologians, indeed for 'beginners' in theology (a typical professorial overestimation of the capacities of students). The theological *Summa* is a handbook with a clear pedagogical and scientific aim within the church, which is meant to provide a systematic survey of the whole of 'sacred doctrine'. Here, despite all the rational arguments, in principle the biblical message and thus **Christian faith** is constantly presupposed, though here too, often, as already in the doctrine of God and also in the ethical section, the procedure is on two levels. But Thomas succeeds impressively in interpreting personal language about God, the Father who speaks and can be spoken of, with concepts from Greek philosophy: God as the supreme being (*summum esse*), being itself (*ipsum esse*), the greatest truth (*maximum verum*), the truth itself (*ipsa veritas*), the supreme good (*summum bonum*).

6. *A new theology – at first regarded as heresy*

With his two *Summas*, Thomas set a high standard for theology, and moreover with him this literary genre of theology breaks off.

But his *Summa theologiae* in particular, his *magnum opus*, has shown him to be a master among theologians for all time. However, this was a late insight. For how could someone like him, who at that time changed the hermeneutical and methodological premises so radically compared with the tradition and at the same time presented a variety of novel theories, like the doctrine of transubstantiation for the eucharist (which unfortunately was defined at the Council of Trent), remain an uncontroversial theologian? Had he not delivered over the gospel to the conceptuality of Aristotelian philosophy?

Moreover Thomas was regarded by the traditionalist (Augustinian) theologians of his time as the advocate of a 'new theology' (Aristotelian and Averroistic). No wonder that he was increasingly contested as a modernist and branded a **heretic**: in 1270, theses of Siger of Brabant and probably also Thomas Aquinas were condemned by the Bishop of Paris (an early chancellor of the university); at any rate Thomas was so sharply attacked in a formal academic session by a young Franciscan colleague, the brilliant John Pecham (who was later to become Archbishop of Canterbury), that the Bishops of Paris appointed a commission of theologians to investigate the radical Aristotelianism which had evidently broken out here. In 1272 – after only three and a half years, his most fruitful – Thomas was given a new post in Italy by the general of his own order. But the agitation in Paris continued. Finally in 1277, on precisely the third anniversary of his death, a whole series of theses of Thomas Aquinas were formally **condemned** by the Bishop of Paris, within whose jurisdiction Thomas was, and also by the Bishop of Oxford (a Dominican!).[8] This condemnation meant that (outside the Dominican order) the neo-Augustinianism advocated by Bonaventure had conquered at least for the next fifty years; it would later issue in Scotism (the teaching of the Franciscan Duns Scotus), which was at first to play a more significant role than Thomism at the Counter-Reformation Council of Trent.[9]

So it is understandable that – although forty-nine years after his death he was beatified by a pope in Avignon and therefore eighteen months later was acquitted of his condemnation and excommunication by the Bishop of Paris – Thomas Aquinas was far from being a classical Catholic. It is understandable that after

113

his death a period of apologia for Thomas and the *Defensiones* had to follow. It was only at the end of the fifteenth century that the first commentaries on the *Summa theologiae* appeared. The whole *Summa* was first commented on by the classic interpreter of Thomas, Cardinal Cajetan de Vico, who was to preside over a hearing of Martin Luther at the Reichstag in Augsburg in 1518.

It was 1567 before Thomas was formally elevated to the status of teacher of the church – by the Dominican pope Pius V, an early Grand Inquisitor. But it then took another three hundred years, until the first Vatican Council and afterwards, for popes to promote Neo-Thomism (rather than Thomas!) with all the power at their disposal: encyclicals on Thomas, naming Thomas the authentic teacher of the church and patron of Catholic schools, a new critical edition of Thomas, the commitment of Catholic theology to twenty-four normative basic philosophical theses, and indeed finally the legal regulation in the *Codex Iuris Canonici* of 1917/18 that philosophy and theology were to be treated in Catholic education institutions 'according to the method, teaching and principles of the *Doctor Angelicus* (the angelic teacher)'.[10] Up to 1924 one can count no less than 218 commentaries on the first part of the *Summa theologiae* and 90 on the whole *Summa*. It is true that Thomas Aquinas played virtually no role at the Second Vatican Council, which was concerned with *aggiornamento* and the problems and hopes of Christianity which had recently appeared; since then, moreover, there has not been a Thomistic school. But in the new 1983 *Codex Iuris Canonici* he is again 'especially' commended, and in the traditionalist Roman World Catechism which was published in 1993, of all the post-biblical church writers – apart from Augustine (88 times) and John Paul II (137 times) – he is quoted by far the most frequently.

Today even opponents no longer dispute that Thomas Aquinas created a grandiose new theological synthesis for his time. But the question must be asked: did Thomas also create a really new paradigm for theology? The answer is 'No'. Why that is the case should become clear in the following sections.

7. A problematical dependence on Augustine

Why could not Thomas – unlike Augustine – create a new paradigm, make possible a new overall constellation? Why did he not become – as Luther did later – the initiator of a paradigm shift in theology and church history, although he did not lack either a new milieu (the university), nor knowledge, perceptiveness and courage? The answer is that while with his philosophical theological system Thomas Aquinas quite substantially **modified Augustine's Latin paradigm,** he did not replace it. Indeed, despite its encyclopaedic (but ultimately fragmentary) greatness – his theology has its indisputable **limitations** and **defects.**

However much Thomas may have corrected Augustine in some details, modified him and sometimes even ignored him, at the level of the truths of faith he remained essentially **bound to the prevalent Augustinian theology.** Certainly as a philosopher Thomas was no Augustinist, but as a theologian he was - loyal to the distinction in his system. Thomas largely retained the second 'storey', the theological superstructure, the sphere of the 'supernatural' and the mysteries of salvation, in the Neoplatonic Augustinian tradition. Certainly he constantly pointed out that the theology of Augustine and the church fathers used Platonic conceptuality. But neither in the doctrine of the Trinity nor in christology, in soteriology nor in the doctrine of the church and the sacraments, did he fundamentally investigate behind the patristic positions. He reflected these with his Aristotelian conceptuality, in order to bring them up to date, refine them and confirm them; but only rarely, and then sometimes more tacitly, as in the doctrine of predestination, did he fundamentally correct them.

But in so doing Thomas also shares the fundamental **weaknesses** of Augustine's theology. For Thomas does not see through either the one-sidednesses and defects of Augustine's 'psychological' **doctrine of the Trinity** (starting from the one divine nature) or the narrowing of the **doctrine of redemption** (which was accentuated by Anselm of Canterbury's doctrine of satisfaction). He does not criticize Augustine's notion of an **original sin** which has been handed down since Adam to all human beings through the sexual act. Against the Greeks he defends the doctrine of a **purgatory,** which was similarly developed by Augustine. And he takes the reification of the understanding of grace (a concentration on 'created grace') considerably further, though at the same time, within the framework of his doctrine of grace,[11] he happily develops a *quaestio* of his own on the 'justification of the sinner'.[12] But he neglects 'grace' as God's disposition, benevolence, graciousness[13] – as his teacher Albert the Great already did. Instead, with the help of Aristotelian physiology and psychology, he analyses the different kinds of that *gratia creata* (which cannot be found in the New Testament), that 'created grace' or 'gift of grace' (to be understood as something like a supernatural fluid or fuel) and its effects on the substance of the soul, the intellect, the will, before, during and after the act of knowing and willing. Thus typical scholastic distinctions of grace come into being: active and cooperative, prevenient and subsequent, habitual and actual grace. These were all very impersonal, over-complex distinctions which would already be obsolete in Luther's time. And there is a further factor: his dependence on the ancient world-view.

8. An ancient world-view: a test case – the place of women

Most of the Neo-Thomists would not see that although at that time Thomas boldly confronted an immense wealth of new and specifically scientific knowledge which came to him from Aristotelian and Arab philosophy, his new philosophical-theological system remained deeply rooted in the **world-view of Greek antiquity**. This is not an accusation, but a statement.[14] For there can be no authentic understanding of Thomas's theology without an understanding of his metaphysics, and no understanding of his metaphysics without an understanding of his physics, chemistry and biology. Anyone who reads the two *Summa*s attentively will make a discovery which is at first perplexing: that Thomas draws his models of theological explanation not so much from metaphysics as from Aristotelian science, e.g. gravitation, light, heat, chemical process and properties, biological procreation and growth, the physiology of the senses and emotions. Even the most important metaphysical concepts like being as such, act and potency, relation, *actus purus*, rest on insights from science and natural philosophy.

It is therefore undeniable that Thomas has taken over almost unchanged the world-view of Greek antiquity – including the notion of a begetting of human beings in the interplay between human beings and the sun. He unhesitatingly affirms it all: that all mixed bodies consist of four elements; that the seven planets are moved and guided by seven pure spirits (angels); that there are three heavens. For him the world is a perfect order, immutable from beginning to end, a cosmos in which being is more powerful as it ascends, a strictly hierarchical, geocentric and anthropocentric cosmos.

Indeed, with the aid of the Platonic concept of an unchangeable, static order (*ordo*), Thomas constructs an all-embracing interpretation of the world from Christian faith, which at the same time represents a thoroughgoing interpretation of faith in terms of the geocentric view of the world. That means that the Bible is understood cosmologically and the cosmos biblically. Christian faith guarantees the world-view, and conversely the world-view guarantees Christian faith. It is a perfect harmony of theology and cosmology, the order of salvation and the world order. Not only is knowledge of God possible from the order of creation, but astrology too is largely acceptable; so too is an angelic hierarchy corresponding to the heavenly spheres, and even (we are reminded of Origen) the number of the elect (to replace the fallen angels).

But even more, Thomas justifies from the Bible and reason the composition and origin of human beings with body and soul; the primal state of paradise and original sin; then the descent of Christ from heaven to earth and the underworld and his subsequent ascent; then grace and the seven sacraments, the hierarchical order of church and state, an ethic of order and obedience: and lastly precise notions about the end of the world and the bodies of those who are resurrected. There is no doubt that down to the last detail this mediaeval theology is dependent on the world-view of Greek antiquity; indeed it is an amalgam of the Middle Ages and antiquity. And we can now already guess what must happen to the content of this theology once its physical, chemical, biological, medicinal and cosmological presuppositions collapse – following the Copernican revolution and the victory of mathematics and experimentation, to which Aristotle and, of course also Thomas, completely fail to do justice. A test case is the position of women.

By way of excuse, it has been said that for all his universality, Thomas Aquinas did not understand three things: art, children and women. Because of his monastic way of life, of course he had been surrounded almost only by males. But did he not say quite basic and historically influential things about women and their nature? Defenders of Thomas point out that he only dealt with women here and there throughout his work, as it were incidentally. But at two crucial points even in the *Summa theologiae* there are quite basic statements about women: within the doctrine of creation a whole *quaestio* with four articles on the 'bringing forth (*productio*) of the woman (from Adam)',[15] and within the framework of the doctrine of grace an important article on the right of women to speak in church.[16]

Now it must be said straight away that for Thomas Aquinas there was no doubt:

– that **woman**, like man, is **created in the image of God**;
– that woman therefore in principle has the same dignity and the same eternal destiny for her soul as man;
– that woman was created by God not only for procreation but also for a shared life.

No, Thomas Aquinas may not be depicted as a dark mediaeval misogynist. But is that a reason for playing down his other statements? In matters relating to the theology of the feminine did not Thomas **accentuate** and refine many of **Augustine's remarks** and as a result not tone down but intensify the contempt for women? In all seriousness he asserts that:

– man is the starting point (*principium*) and goal (*finis*) of woman;
– woman was not created from head of the man (so that she should not rule over him), nor from his feet (so that she should not be despised), but from his rib, so that man and woman should remain together inseparably all their lives;
– by 'nature' woman is subjected to man, since in man the rational power of discernment is present more abundantly and so the woman falls short of the man in power and dignity;
– in relation to the whole of creation, while woman is among its good things, individually woman is '**something deficient and**

unsuccessful' (*aliquid deficiens et occasionatum*) compared with the man.[17]

There is no disputing the fact that for Thomas Aquinas, on closer inspection a woman is a man who by chance is defective and unsuccessful, a *mas occasionatus*. This finding from the doctrine of creation explains why **women** had absolutely no say at all in the **mediaeval church**. Granted, in the light of the Old Testament they could not in principle be denied the gift of prophecy. But the ordination of women as priests? While Thomas was not able to discuss this in more detail in the *Summa*, since he broke off working on it in his younger days he had come to a negative decision on this question in the commentary on the *Sentences*.[18] Not only the illegitimacy but even the invalidity of such an ordination is asserted here, and moreover this view was promptly taken up in the posthumous supplements to the *Summa* (*Supplementum*) as Thomas's valid position.[19]

The same holds for **women's preaching**. In view of the heretical movements, lay preaching at that time was in any case a provocative topic. And what about a preaching and teaching office even for women, a 'grace of the discourse of wisdom and knowledge', exercised publicly? No, Thomas excludes this with special arguments:[20]

– Above all because it is the condition of the female sex to be subject to the male: teaching as a public office in the church is a matter for those set over others (*praelati*) and not subordinates, which now essentially include the women precisely because of their sex (and not accidentally like the simple priest, who is at any rate a man);

– The senses of males are not to be stimulated to lust by women preaching (lust = *concupiscentia* or *libido* was a widespread theme after Augustine);

– Women were generally not so distinguished in matters of wisdom that one could appropriately entrust a public office of teaching to them.

But anyone who on the basis of all these negative statements should immediately want to pass a definitive verdict (in the negative) on Thomas should remember three things. First, Thomas is anything but original in many of his sayings; rather, in many cases he simply expresses what people (men) thought at that time.

Secondly, in many of his statements Thomas is simply basing himself on the Bible, on the Old Testament (for example women inherit only when there are no male descendants; no men in women's clothes) or the New Testament (for example, woman created for the sake of man, women to keep silent in church). And in his knowledge of women Thomas simply followed the greatest scientific and philosophical authority of his time, **Aristotle**. It was Aristotle who in his treatise 'On the Procreation of Living Beings' provided the biological basis for a fatal 'sexual metaphysics' and 'theology of sex' by attributing all the activity in the act of procreation to the male sperm (the female ovum was discovered only in 1827!). None of this excuses him (Galen, the most famous doctor of Roman antiquity, had assumed an active biological share of the woman in the origin of the foetus), but it does explain some things. But yet another weakness is intrinsic to Thomas's theology.

9. Despite everything, a court theology: the papacy safeguarded

One can easily overlook these weaknesses if one first (rightly) emphasizes the innovative power of Thomas's theology and even refers to his history of conflict with the magisterium of the church. But they cannot be concealed, sobering though that may be for Thomas's admirers. For in his understanding of the church and above all the papacy, Thomas Aquinas differs both from Origen, who as a theologian remained critical of the hierarchy, and Augustine, who even as a bishop was anything but fixated on the pope (a papalist), but more an episcopalist like Cyprian. In the end – and this must be said quite clearly – Thomas became the great **apologist of the centralist papacy** in the spirit of Greogry VII and Innocent III and remains so today. He put his theology at the service of dogmatic papolatry. He became a court theologian like others. This is understandable, since for nine years, from 1259 to 1268, he taught colleagues in the order in the Roman Curia (in Anagni?, at all events in Orvieto and Viterbo) and in Rome (S.Sabina), and had a close friendship with Popes Urban IV and Clement IV. That is also understandable, for though he was personally quite unpretentious (the Pope vainly offered him the archbishopric of Naples), he belonged to an order which was directly under papal authority. So he was *de facto* a court theologian.

Certainly Thomas was the one who claimed a **magistral** teaching office for theologians, which in contrast to the **pastoral** teaching office of the bishop was not to proceed authoritatively but by argumentation, and to rest on the academic competence of the Magister. But at the same time he was able to incorporate the new political and juristic development towards an absolutist papalism in the second half of the thirteenth century into the dogmatic system of theology. To what extent? One might compare him with Augustine. Whereas Augustine still does not think in terms of any primacy of jurisdiction for Peter, this primacy is at the centre of Thomas's view of the church. If for Augustine Christ himself and belief in him is the foundation of the church, for Thomas this foundation is the person and office of Peter. Whereas for Augustine the ecumenical council is the supreme authority, for Thomas this supreme authority is the Pope. In contradiction to the paradigm of the early church and still to Augustine, this is a Gregorian **view of the church, completely derived from the papacy**: a papalist ecclesiology in the framework of a theological systematics which at all points provides ideological backing for the new absolutist church system and both the ecclesiastical and secular claims of the papacy. Against the view of the Greek church (and the early church), he demonstrates the thesis that the Pope 'has the fullness of power in the church',[21] 'that it is for the Pope to define what faith is', indeed 'that it is necessary for salvation to be subordinate to the Roman Pope'.[22] All this is an ideological preparation for Pope Boniface's bull *Unam sanctam*, the classical document of the mediaeval papacy.

We cannot avoid the conclusion that if we leave aside the philosophical substructure and see Thomas's system from the perspective of his theology, and above all his ecclesiology, Thomas Aquinas has a new theology only to a limited degree. What we find in him is a systematic and speculative shaping of the Roman Catholic paradigm which had been initiated above all by Augustine and Pope Leo in the fifth century, achieved with Aristotelian categories and arguments, but above all a **cementing**

of this paradigm in dogma. So on the whole this is more a reinforcement, accentuation and completion of the traditional paradigm than an overcoming of it. The speculative scholastic system had first to reach crisis point – in late mediaeval nominalism (Ockhamism) it had become increasingly remote from the Bible and had neglected the basic truths of faith and its existential character simply by virtue of its rational conclusions – for a new starting point to be created for a paradigm shift: the paradigm shift in the direction of the Reformation.

Otto Hermann Pesch, the specialist on Thomas, is therefore right in seeing as 'the objective basic error of Neo-Thomism' that it started from '**directly** regarding Thomas as relevant without examining his work and in advance of all detailed questions'; Thomas can be rightly understood today only 'through a fundamental experience of his alien character'.[23] So with a departure from the Thomistic claims to absoluteness, it has rightly become established that 'Thomas's theology is to be seen as a model, not so much in its material content as in the public nature and courage of the questions it asks'.[24]

10. Dialogue with Islam and Judaism?

Indeed, who would dispute that with no little courage and great openness Thomas Aquinas also accepted the challenge of non-Christian thinkers, whether these were 'pagan' philosophers of antiquity like Aristotle, or Muslim and Jewish philosophers of his time like Averroes and Moses Maimonides. So there is no doubt that Thomas Aquinas was involved in **living discussion of the challenge of Judaism and Islam.** Nor did he content himself with the ignorance that was customary in the early Middle Ages and ugly polemic against Islam and the Qur'an. Indeed his *Summa contra gentiles* cannot be understood unless we sense the pressure that must have burdened some Christian intellectuals of the time: is not Islam both spiritually and culturally far in advance of Christianity? Does it not have the better philosophy? How can the option for Christianity rather than Islam and Judaism be justified?

Granted, 'Thomas did not travel to Morocco nor to the land of the Mongols, and he did not utter a single remark about the Crusades' – thus, once again, M-D.Chenu, who continues: 'But he always had the works of the great Muslim philosophers on his desk, and he measured the dimensions of a Christianity which, having hitherto been included within the geographical and cultural frontiers of the Roman empire, now suddenly became aware that it embraced only a part of humankind and discovered the immeasurably secular condition of the cosmos.'[35] That is admirably put, but it is correct only if once again at precisely this point we also take note of the limitations of Thomas Aquinas.

The limitations do not so much lie in the fact that Thomas 'did not travel to Morocco nor to the land of the Mongols'; Spain and Sicily would have been far enough. Rather, the problem is that Thomas did not know any Muslims personally, and did not engage in personal dialogue with any of them. But it is more suspicious that Thomas 'did not utter a single word about the Crusades', though Dominicans were also active in Palestine and though it had already proved that the Crusades were not having the hoped-for effect upon the Muslims. And it is most suspicious that Thomas knew Islam at best from the 'works of the great Muslim philosophers', who in any case were more philosophers than Muslims, but not from the Qur'an itself, which was now already available in more than one Latin translation as a result of the initiative of Petrus Venerabilis (died 1156), the last significant abbot of Cluny. Thomas evidently did not study this translation – at the cost of having only a very **rudimentary knowledge of Islam**. He had no access to the self-understanding of Muslims, who regard the Qur'an as the definitive revelation of God. His main informants may have been Christian missionaries, who evidently had had difficulties arguing against Islam. Whereas the Franciscans only attempted to influence the Muslims by simple preaching and practical example, at a very early stage the Dominicans also engaged in intellectual argument with them.

Precisely because of this method, we can no longer regard the *Summa contra gentiles* today as a model of Christian apologetic against Islam. Granted, in contrast to most of the early apologists of Latin or Byzantine origin Thomas argued in a way which was pleasantly neither polemical nor argumentative, and attempted to adapt to the horizon of his conversation partner's understanding as far as possible. But all this was not an *apologia ad extra* but at best an *apologia ad intra*, i.e. for those already converted. At that time only isolated individuals thought of an authentic inter-religious dialogue, indeed in twelfth-century Paris the dialogue with the Jews which was still going on had now been interrupted as a result of the Crusades, the expulsion of the Jews, pogroms and all their atrocities.

11. *The mysterious breaking off of the* Summa

In retrospect we can say that Thomas Aquinas would have been the last person to strive for any form of 'canonization' or even 'absolutization' of his theology. Within certain limits he was well aware of the contextuality of statements of faith and thus of their relativity. More than anyone else he embodied **a contemporary theology**, a theology in living exchange with the great spiritual trends of its time, a theology which can only make its distinctive statement in this way. If we take the 'spirit' and 'nature' of the theological work of this great thinker seriously in this way, even today theology has to stand on the spiritual fronts which move a time – equipped with the whole range of critical methods without which scholarly work since then is quite unthinkable: historical criticism, hermeneutics, comparative and interdisciplinary studies. A theology which masters this academic 'technique' is truly theology in the spirit of Thomas Aquinas. But a Thomism which repeats theses in a sterile way does not provide any stepping stones on to which the spirit can leap.

Even now it remains a biographical enigma why **Thomas broke off work on the *Summa theologiae*** in the middle of the third part, in his discussion of the sacrament of penance. It is attested beyond all doubt that on 6 December 1273, Thomas Aquinas, who according to his contemporaries studied, taught, wrote and prayed all the time and hardly wasted a moment, declared to his faithful companion Reginald of Piperno after morning mass that he could no longer go on. Why? 'I can do no more, for all that I have written seems to me like straw!'[26] *Omne foenum* – all straw? What had happened? Even now people puzzle over this self-assessment and over what had happened at that service: did this man with a notoriously massive body have a stroke? Did this man who was not yet fifty but had already written more than forty extensive works have a breakdown of health? Or an ecstatic experience? Or both together? A visionary experience of heavenly glory or insight into the transitoriness of his two-storey theological system? All straw?

The only certain thing is that from that hour on Thomas did not write or dictate any more (like Origen and Augustine he often even had several secretaries and himself wrote almost illegibly on small pieces of paper). At any rate, he had four months still to live, but did not produce another single line. Still, he accepted Pope Gregory X's invitation and made his way to the Council of Lyons, which among other things was to be concerned with negotiations for union with the Greeks. He wanted to take a copy of his work *Against the Errors of the Greeks* with him. However, exhausted after a few hours' journey he asked if he could stop and stay with his niece Francesca, Countess of Ceccano, at Maenza castle. When his state deteriorated there, Thomas asked to be taken to the nearby Cistercian abbey of Fossanova. Here, on 7 March 1273, he passed peacefully away. It was noted at the time with disapproval that no Superior of the Dominican order from Naples or Rome was present at the burial. After some extremely macabre manoeuvres over his body in Fossanova, he was finally laid to rest almost a century later (1369), in Toulouse, where the founder of his order had brought the first Dominican house into being.

Thomas Aquinas's gigantic work represents a tremendous piece of thought, an abiding obligation for all theology for all time. At the same time, though, for all his intellectualism Thomas also constantly remained aware of the **limits of his own understanding of God**. Indeed for him any definition transferred from human beings or the world to God at the same time called for a negation: the negation of any human-worldly limitations and imperfection. For Thomas, too, God's real being remained hidden, inaccessible to human reason. To this degree he can agree with Pseudo-Dionysius, whom he also regarded as a pupil of Paul: 'Therefore this is the last (*ultimum*) of human knowledge of God; that he (the human being) knows that he does not know God (*quod sciat* *se Deum nescire*), and that in so far as he knows, what God is transcends all that we understand of him (*illud quod Deus est, omne ipsum quod de eo intelligimus, excedere*).'[27]

Martin Luther
Return to the Gospel as the Classical Instance
of a Paradigm Shift

Chronology (according to R.Schwarz)

1483	10 November: Luther born in Eisleben.
1505	Enters the monastery in Erfurt.
1510	Travel and pilgrimage to Rome.
1512	Gains his doctorate in theology.
1513	First lectures on the psalms to the University of Wittenberg.
1515/16	Produces his work *Ein Theologia Deutsch*.
1517	95 theses on indulgences: 'Sermon on Indulgences and Grace'
1518	Interrogation before Cardinal Cajetan in Augsburg.
1519	Charles V elected emperor: Leipzig disputation.
1520	'To the Christian Nobility of the German Nation' (June). 15 June: Leo X's bull *Exsurge Domine*; threat of excommunication, call for repentance and burning of all his writings. 17 June: Luther appeals to a general council: *De captivitate Babylonica ecclesiae praeludium* (late summer). 'The Freedom of a Christian' (autumn). *Adversus execrabilem Antichristi bullam* (November). 10 December: burning of the papal bull and of the papal church law in Wittenberg.
1521	January: bull *Decet Romanum Pontificem*. 18 April: appearance before the Reichstag in Worms. 26 May: Emperor Charles V places Luther and his followers under the imperial ban (Edict of Worms).
1521/22	Wartburg: translation of the Bible, unrest in Wittenberg; Luther's return.
1524/5	Parts company with the enthusiasts.
1525	Peasants' War; marriage; break with Erasmus.
1526-30	Territorial extension of the Reformation.
1528	Dispute with the Swiss theologians.
1529	Reichstag at Speyer; protest of the 'Protestants'. Religious dialogue in Marburg with Zwingli and Bucer.
1530	Reichstag at Augsburg (*Confessio Augustana*); failure over reconciliation; foundation of the Schmalkald League of Protestant German princes.
1531-39	The Reformation safeguarded politically by the empire.
1521	Jean Calvin establishes his church republic in Geneva.
1546/47	Schmalkald wars.
1546	18 February: Luther dies in Eisleben.

1. Why there was a Lutheran Reformation

Hardly a single one of Luther's reform concerns was new. But the time had not been ripe for them. Now the moment had come, and it needed only religious genius to bring these concerns together, put them into words and embody them personally. Martin Luther was the man of the moment.

What had been the **preparation** for the new paradigm shift in world history immediately before the Reformation? Briefly:[1]
– the collapse of papal rule of the world, the split in the church between East and West, then the twofold, later threefold, papacy in Avignon, Rome and Pisa along with the rise of the nation states of France, England and Spain;
– the lack of success by the reform councils (Constance, Basel, Florence, Lateran) in 'reforming the church, head and members';
– the replacement of the natural economy by a money economy, the invention of printing and the widespread desire for education and Bibles;
– the absolutist centralism of the Curia, its immorality, its uncontrollable financial policy and its stubborn resistance to reform, and finally the trade in indulgences for rebuilding St Peter's, which was regarded in Germany as the pinnacle of curial exploitation.

However, even north of the Alps, as a result of the Roman system, some of the abuses were quite blatant:
– the retrograde state of church institutions: the ban on levying interest, the church's freedom from taxation and its own jurisdiction, the clerical monopoly of schools, the furthering of beggary, too many church festivals;
– the way in which church and theology were overgrown with canon law;
– the growing self-awareness of university sciences (Paris!) as a critical authority over against the church;
– the tremendous secularization even of the rich prince bishops and monasteries; the abuses caused by the pressure towards celibacy; the proletariat, which comprised far too many uneducated and poor people:
– the radical critics of the church: Wycliffe, Hus, Marsilius, Ockham and the Humanists;

– finally a terrifying superstition among the people, a religious nervousness which often took enthusiastic-apocalyptic forms, an externalized liturgy and legalized popular piety, a hatred of work-shy monks and clerics, a malaise among the educated people in the cities and despair among the exploited peasants in Germany... All in all this was an abysmal crisis for mediaeval theology, church and society, coupled with an inability to cope with it.

So everything was ready for an epoch-making paradigm shift, but there was need of someone to present the new candidate for a paradigm credibly. And this was done by a single monk, in the epoch-making prophetic figure of Martin Luther, who was born on 10 November 1483 in Eisleben in Thuringia. Although as a young monk and doctor of theology Luther certainly did not understand himself primarily as a prophet but as a teacher of the church, intuitively and inspirationally he was able to meet the tremendous religious longing of the late Middle Ages. He purged the strong positive forces in mysticism, and also in nominalism and popular piety, confidently centred all the frustrated reform movements in his brilliant personality, which was stamped with a a deep faith, and expressed his concerns with unprecedented eloquence. Without Martin Luther there would have been no Reformation in Germany!

2. The basic question: how is one justified before God?

But when did things get this far? As a result of acute fear of death during a violent thunderstorm and constant anxiety about not being able to stand in the final judgment before Christ, at the age of twenty-two, in 1505, Luther had entered a monastery against the will of his father (who was a miner and smelter by trade). But when did the Augustinian monk who loyally obeyed the rules and was concerned for righteousness by works become the ardent Reformer of 'faith alone'? Historians argue over the precise point in time of the 'breakthrough to the Reformation'.

Be this as it may, there is no disputing the fact that Martin Luther, who had a very similar scholastic training in philosophy and theology to Thomas Aquinas, was in deep crisis over his life. Being a monk had not solved any of his problems, but had accentuated many of them. For the works of monastic piety like choral prayer, mass, fasting, penitence, penance to which Luther submitted himself with great earnestness as an Augustine eremite could not settle for him the questions of his personal salvation and damnation. In a sudden intuitive experience of the gracious righteousness of God (if we follow the 'great testimony' of 1545), but presumably in a somewhat longer process (if we look at his earlier works more closely), in his crisis of conscience a new understanding of the justification of the sinner had dawned on Luther. Whenever precisely the 'breakthrough to the Reformation' took place (more recent scholarship is predominantly for a 'late dating' to the first half of 1518[2]), the '**shift to the Reformation**' happens here.

So the starting point of Luther's reforming concern was not any abuses in the church, not even the question of the church, but the **question of salvation**: how do human beings stand before God? How does God deal with human beings? How can human beings be certain of their salvation by God? How can sinful human beings put right their relationship with the just God? When are they **justified** by God? Luther found the answer above all in Paul's Letter to the Romans: human beings cannot stand justified by God, be justified by God, through their own efforts – despite all piety. It is God himself, as a gracious God, who pronounces the sinner righteous, without any merits, in his free grace. This is a grace which human beings may confidently grasp only in faith. For Luther, of the three theological virtues faith is the most important: in faith, unrighteous sinful human beings receive God's righteousness.

That was the decisive theological factor. But there was a second one: starting from a new understanding of the event of justification Luther hit upon a new understanding of the **church**. This was a radical criticism of a secularized and legalized church which had deviated from the teaching and praxis of the gospel, and of its sacraments, ministries and traditions. But in this criticism had not Luther broken completely with the Catholic tradition? With his understanding of justification was he not *a priori* un-Catholic? To answer this question, for all the discontinuity one must also see the great continuity between Luther and the theology which preceded him.

3. The Catholic Luther

An **interrupted train of tradition** binds Luther to the church and theology of the preceding period precisely in his understanding of justification. We must look briefly at four lines of historical continuity, all of which are important for Luther's understanding of Reformation and which in part overlap: the Catholic piety which Luther encountered in the monastery; in connection with that, mediaeval mysticism; then Augustine's theology; and finally late mediaeval nominalism in the form of Ockhamism.

Catholic piety? Granted, the traditional Catholic piety caused a crisis for Luther in the monastery. And so all his life, for him the monastic way of perfection remained the way of legalistic works and wanting to be something before God, which did not bring him peace of mind and inner security, but anxiety and desperation. Nevertheless, Luther salvaged the best of Catholic piety through his crisis. For the doctrine of justification it is particularly significant that it was Luther's superior in the monastery, Johannes von Staupitz, a man with a concern for reform, who diverted him from his heart-searchings over his own predestination and pointed him to the Bible, to God's will for salvation and the picture of the crucified Jesus, before whom all anxiety about whether or not one is elected disappears.

Mediaeval mysticism? Granted, the pantheizing features of mysticism and its tendency to blur the line between the divine and the human were quite remote from Luther. Nevertheless, it is known that Luther had knowledge of the mysticism of Dionysius the Areopagite and Bernard of Clairvaux. Moreover, he discovered the mystical work *Die Theologia deutsch*, studied it with enthusiasm and brought out an edition in 1515/16 (completed in 1518). Furthermore he called the mystic Tauler one of the greatest theologians and continued to commend him. There is no doubt that Luther's sense for being humble, small, nothing before God, to whom alone honour belongs; his insight that piety by works leads to vanity and self-satisfaction and away from God; and finally his faith in the suffering Christ, particularly as he took this from the words of the Psalter – all these ideas which were decisive for his understanding of justification are traditional material of mediaeval mysticism.

Augustine's theology? Granted, it was not least the doctrine of predestination and the understanding of the perfect love of God as developed by the old anti-Pelagian Augustine which were responsible for Luther's crisis. And all his life Luther understood grace differently from Augustine, in a more personal way. Nevertheless, insight into the deep corruption of sin as human selfishness and a distortion of the self remained decisive for Luther's understanding of justification, as did insight into the omnipotence of the grace of God, which he learned above all from Augustine. So Luther remained tied to one of the basic components of mediaeval theology, the theology of Augustine, whose *Confessions* and great treatises *On the Trinity* and *The City of God* he had studied at a very early stage, Augustine, who was not only dominant in pre-Aristotelian early scholasticism and in the high scholasticism of Alexander of Hales and Bonaventure, but who also could not be overlooked in Thomas Aquinas and his school (though there he had clearly been forced into the background) and finally also in the late Middle Ages. The continuity was much stronger than Luther himself realized, not only in the doctrine of the Trinity and christology, but also in the theology of grace. It dawned on Luther that Romans 1.17, the passage about the 'righteousness of God', which was decisive for his breakthrough to the Reformation, does not speak of the inexorable judgment of God's righteousness, before which no sinner can stand, but of his righteousness as a gift. The passage was understood in this way not just by Augustine, as Luther thought, but, as Catholic scholars have demonstrated,[3] by the majority of mediaeval theologians.

Ockhamism? Granted, in his doctrine of justification Luther reacted most vigorously against the Pelagianism of the late-Franciscan Ockhamist school which is found both in Ockham himself and in his great pupil Gabriel Biel, and also in Bartholomew Arnoldi of Usingen, Biel's pupil and Luther's teacher. Nevertheless, there is also a way from Ockham and Biel to Luther's doctrine of justification. The Thomistic school was certainly not right in slating late mediaeval theology in general and Ockhamism (nominalism) in particular as a disintegration of mediaeval theology. But on the other hand Protestant Reformation scholarship has been equally wrong in treating late mediaeval theology only as the dark background against which Luther's doctrine of justification could shine out particularly brightly. Attention must not be limited, as it usually is in the Protestant sphere, to Luther's dependence on Paul and Augustine; his positive connection with Ockham and Biel must also be considered: for example in respect of particular aspects of his concept of God (the absolute sovereignty of God), his view of grace as favour, the acceptance of human beings by free divine choice which has no ground in humankind.

What follows from this fourfold connection with the tradition? That it is *a priori* **impossible** for Catholics **sweepingly to condemn** Luther. The mediaeval Catholic tradition has far too much in common with Luther's great theological concentration. However, it is important not to lose sight of what is particularly characteristic of Luther. What is this? We can demonstrate it from the famous dispute over indulgences.

4. *The spark of Reformation*

The dispute over indulgences was neither the internal cause nor the fortuitous external cause for the Reformation, but the catalyst, the factor which sparked it off. Should, can, may the Pope grant indulgences? May he grant to the living and even to the dead (in purgatory) partial or total remission of the temporal punishments for sin which God may have imposed before entry into eternal life? At that time this was not only a highly theological but also a highly political question. Luther had taken it up in view of an unprecedented campaign for indulgences which had been staged in Germany on the orders of Pope Leo X, with all available means of propaganda, for the rebuilding of St Peter's in Rome.[4] The Commissioner General for these so-called Peter's indulgences was the Archbishop of Mainz, Albrecht of Brandenburg.

Penance – what is it? Luther gave a theologically radical answer to this question. For Christians, penance is not limited to the sacrament of penance; it should embrace the whole of life. And the decisive thing is that forgiveness of guilt is God's concern alone; at best the Pope can confirm by a subsequent declaration that a sin has already been remitted by God. At all events, the authority of the Pope is limited to this life and ends with death.

To think that the salvation of souls could be bought by expensive indulgence certificates created to pay for an ostentatious papal church: what a perversion of the great notion of the free gift of God to the sinner!

But at the same time this attack meant that at a stroke Luther had not only robbed the whole business of indulgences of its theological legitimation but at the same time shattered the authority of those who had set up this trade in their own favour: the Pope and the bishops. Luther summed up his position in **ninety-five theses**, sent them to Archbishop Albrecht of Mainz under whose jurisdiction he was, and at the same time made them known to the academic public. It may be a legend that, as is so often depicted in pictures, he personally affixed these theses to the door of the Schlosskirche in Wittenberg on 31 October (or 1 November) 1517 (it goes back to a remark made by Melanchthon, Luther's most capable and loyal companion; however, Melanchthon was still teaching at the University of Tübingen at the time and made this remark only after Luther's death).[5]

Be this as it may, at all events we can say that to begin with Luther was in no way 'boldly steering towards a break with the church'; in fact he 'became a Reformer unintentionally', as the Catholic church historian Erwin Iserloh writes. Iserloh concludes from this: 'However, that puts even greater responsibility on the bishops concerned.'[6] Another thing is certain: Luther's theses were rapidly disseminated everywhere, with Luther making his own contribution. He commented on them through Latin 'Resolutions'[7] and popularized their main ideas in a 'Sermon on Indulgences and Grace',[8] deliberately speaking increasingly direct to the people in German, their mother tongue. The deep and widespread discontent with the indulgences and the curial fiscalism now exploded in a storm of indignation.

Counter-action soon followed. A **heresy investigation** into Martin Luther had already opened in Rome, his accusers being the Archbishop of Mainz and the Dominican order. In spring 1518 Luther was summoned before the **Reichstag at Augsburg** and interrogated for three days by the papal cardinal legate. The legate was Cajetan, the leading Thomist of his time, who shortly beforehand had written the first commentary on the whole *Summa theologiae* of Thomas Aquinas. However, the hearing did not lead to any agreement, so Cajetan ultimately gave the stubborn Augustinian monk the choice: recant – or be imprisoned and burnt. His prince, Frederick of Saxony, was asked to hand Luther over, but Luther had secretly left Augsburg.

Two completely different perspectives, indeed two different 'worlds', two different worlds of thought and language, **two different paradigms**, met in Luther, the Reformer, and in Cajetan, the Thomist and papal legate. The result was only to be expected: total confrontation, a hopeless debate, understanding impossible to reach. Essentially the church authorities, who were unwilling for reform, had only one thing to set against Luther's call for reform: a demand for capitulation and submission to the papal and episcopal magisterium. And now with Luther the whole nation faced the hitherto unprecedented alternative: **recant and 'return' to the old** (to the mediaeval paradigm), **or convert to the new** (to the Reformation-gospel paradigm). An unprecedented polarization began which soon divided the whole church into friends and enemies of Luther. 'Reformation' was for some the great hope for a renewal of the church – for others the great apostasy from Pope and church.

Luther, who appealed to the gospel, reason and his conscience, and so would not and could not recant, had fled from Augsburg and appealed against the Pope to a general council. But instead of investigating the reform ideas, the church authorities attempted to deal with Luther theologically, in order finally to quench the flame of dispute. In the summer of 1519 there was a **disputation in Leipzig** lasting for three weeks. Luther's main Catholic opponent was now Johann Eck, who adopted skilful tactics. Instead of taking up Luther's criticism of the church, he concentrated the whole problem on the question of papal primacy and infallibility. Luther did not in fact want to continue to recognize the primacy as a divine institution necessary for salvation, but saw it as an institution of human law. So a trap had been laid, and it snapped to when the question of **the infallibility of councils** was raised, above all that of the Council of Constance, which had condemned and burnt Hus. There was nothing left for Luther than to concede the possibility that even councils could err, since in the case of Hus the council had even condemned some statements which were in accord with the gospel. But with that

Luther had left the ground of the Roman system. And without Rome having had to go into his demands for reform, Luther was now finally branded a heretic, publicly unmasked as a Hussite in disguise. For his part, Luther, who at first had not rejected the authority of Pope, episcopate and councils, but relativized them historically, was now completely convinced: his opponents were incapable and unwilling even to consider a reform of the church in the spirit of scripture.

The **heresy investigation** was moving to a fatal conclusion. After an unusually long postponement by the Roman Curia because of the election of the emperor (in which the prince of Saxony had an important vote), on 15 June 1520 – a year after Leipzig – Luther was confronted with the papal bull *Exsurge Domine*.[9] This papal document not only designated forty-one of Luther's statements, selected without any understanding, as 'heretical', but threatened Luther with excommunication and the burning of all his writings if he did not recant within sixty days. Instead of relevant theological argumentation, Luther now felt the whole power of papal jurisdiction (the Roman body set over him consisted almost entirely of canon lawyers). Luther reacted by appealing once again on 17 November to a general council[10] (as the Sorbonne had done shortly beforehand, despite two papal prohibitions of such an appeal). Furthermore, he wrote the work *Adversus execrabilem Antichristi bullam* ('Against the accursed bull of the Antichrist')[11] against the Pope, whom, because of his usurpation of all scriptural exegesis and rejection of any reform, he increasingly saw as the Antichrist.

Now the crisis came to a dramatic head; when Luther got hold of a printed copy of the bull and learned of the burning of his books in Louvain and Cologne ordered by the nuncio Aleander, he responded on 10 December 1520 in Wittenberg with a spectacular act: accompanied by colleagues and students, he burned not only the papal bull but also the books of papal church law (the Decretals): a clear sign that he no longer recognized Roman jurisdiction and the legal system built up on it, since they condemned his teaching – which was in keeping with the gospel. This amounted to raising a banner for the whole nation, and three weeks later, at the beginning of January 1521, Rome sent the bull containing Luther's excommunication ban (*Decet Romanum*

Pontificem). At first little note was taken of it in Germany, but the die in the 'Luther case' was now finally cast. The Reichstag at Worms in the same year, 1521, to which Luther was invited by the young emperor Charles on the prompting of his cautious prince Frederick the Wise, was not to change matters.

5. The programme for Reformation

1520, the year of the breakthrough in church politics, was also a year of theological breakthrough for Martin Luther. The great programmatic writings for the Reformation were composed. And while Luther was hardly a man with a deliberately planned theological system, he was a man who could confidently make theological proposals to suit the situation and carry them through effectively:

– The **first writing** of this year was the long sermon 'On Good Works' (beginning of 1520), addressed to the churches, written more in an edifying than a programmatic way.[12] It is theologically fundamental, in that here Luther dealt with 'his' basic question, which is the question of Christian existence: the **relationship between faith and works,** the innermost motive of **faith** and the practical consequences which follow from it. Using the Ten Commandments, he demonstrated that faith which gives God alone the glory is the foundation of Christian existence; only from faith can and should good works follow.

– **The second writing,** addressed to the emperor, princes and other nobility, took up the *gravamina* (objections) of the German nation and is also a passionate call for the **reform of the church,** similarly written in the vernacular: *To the Christian Nobility of the German Nation Concerning the Reform of the Christian Estate* (June 1520).[13] Here Luther launches the sharpest attack so far on the papal system, which is preventing a reform of the church with its three pretensions ('walls of the Romanists'): 1. spiritual authority stands above worldly authority; 2. the Pope alone is the true interpreter of scripture; 3. the Pope alone can summon a council. At the same time, a programme for reform, as comprehensive as it is detailed, is developed in twenty-eight points. The first twelve demands relate to the reform of the papacy: a renunciation to claims to rule over world and church; independence of the emperor and the German church; the abolition of the many forms of curial exploitation. Then it deals with the reform of church life and secular life generally: the monasteries, priestly celibacy, indulgences, masses for souls, feasts of the saints, pilgrimages, mendicant orders, universities, schools, care of the poor, abolition of luxury. Here already we have the programmatic statements on the priesthood of all believers and ministry in the church, which, according to Luther, rests on a commissioning for public exercise of the priestly authority which is common to all Christians.

– The **third writing** in the late summer of 1520 is addressed to scholars and theologians and is therefore written in Latin in a formal academic way: *The Babylonian Captivity of the Church*.[14] This work, probably the only work of strict systematic theology that Luther the exegete wrote, is devoted to the sacraments – highly explosive, because it was about the foundation of Roman church law. According to Luther the **sacraments** themselves are constituted by a promise and a sign of Jesus Christ himself. If here we take the traditional criterion 'institution by Jesus Christ himself' really seriously, then only two sacraments, baptism and the Lord's Supper remain – three at most, if one adds penance: the other four sacraments (confirmation, ordination to the priesthood, marriage, final unction) are therefore pious church customs, but not instituted by Christ. Luther again makes many practical proposals for reform of the sacraments and customs – from communion with the cup for laity to the remarriage of innocent parties in divorces.

– The **fourth writing**, *On the Freedom of a Christian*,[15] published in the autumn, develops the thoughts of the first work and offers a summary of Luther's understanding of justification on the basis of I Cor.9.19 in two statements: 'A Christian is a perfectly free lord of all, subject to no one' (in faith, according to the inner man), and 'a Christian is a perfectly dutiful servant of all, subject to all'[16] (thus in works, according to the outer man). It is faith which makes someone a free person who may serve others in their works.

In these four writings we have the foundation stone of the Reformation. And now we can also answer the questions relating to Martin Luther's ultimate concern, what moves him in all his writings, what motivates most deeply his protest, his theology, and indeed his politics.

6. *The basic impulse of the Reformation*

Despite his enormous political explosive force, Luther remained a man of deep faith, a theologian who out of existential need struggled over the grace of God in the face of human fallenness. It would be quite superficial to think that he was concerned only with the fight against indescribable church abuses, especially the indulgences, and the liberation of the papacy. No, Luther's personal impetus towards Reformation and his tremendous historical explosive effect came from the same thing: **a return of the church to the gospel of Jesus Christ** as it was experienced in a living way in **Holy Scripture** and especially in **Paul**. In concrete, this means (and here the decisive difference from the mediaeval paradigm clearly emerges):

– Against all the traditions, laws and authorities which have grown up in the course of the centuries Luther sets the **primacy of scripture,** 'scripture alone' (*sola scriptura*).
– Against all the thousands of saints and tens of thousands of official mediators between God and human beings, Luther sets the **primacy of Christ**: 'Christ alone' (*solus Christus*).
– Against all pious religious human achievements and efforts ('works') to achieve the salvation of the soul, Luther sets the **primacy of grace and faith**, 'grace alone' (*sola gratia*), of the gracious God as he has shown himself in the cross and resurrection of Jesus Christ and unconditional human faith in this God, unconditional trust in him (*sola fide*).

But at the same time, much as Luther originally came to know the private pangs of conscience of a tormented monk and aimed at the conversion of the individual, his theology of justification went far beyond the creation of privatistic peace for the soul. Rather, the theology of justification forms the basis for a **public appeal to the church for reform** in the spirit of the gospel, a reform which is aimed not so much at the reformulation of a doctrine as at the renewal of church life in all areas. For it was the religious practice of the church which was forcing itself between God and human beings; it was the Pope who had in fact in his authority put himself in the place of Christ. In these circumstances a **radical criticism** of the papacy was unavoidable. However, Luther was not concerned with the Pope as a person, but with the institutional practices and structures encouraged and legally cemented by Rome, which manifestly contradicted the gospel.

For its part, the Roman church thought that it could quickly either force this heretical young monk in the far north to recant, or (as in the cases of Hus, Savonarola and hundreds of 'heretics' and 'witches') bring him to the stake with the state's help. So from a historical perspective there can be no doubt that Rome **bears the main responsibility** for the way in which the dispute over the right way to salvation and practical reflection on the gospel very quickly turned into a fundamental dispute over authority in the church and the infallibility of Pope and councils. For in Rome – and also in the German episcopate – people at that time could not and would not publicly hear this call to repentance and conversion, to reflection and reform. Think of what would have to have changed there! There was too much at stake for Rome, taken completely by surprise by the 'new' message (and politically involved in dealings in Italy, with the Turks and the church state): not only the tremendous financial needs of the Curia in rebuilding St Peter's, which was to be paid for by indulgences and levies, but above all the principle 'in the end Rome is always right', and thus the whole mediaeval Roman Catholic paradigm.

That is also how things looked to the Spanish Habsburg, brought up a strict Catholic, who at the age of twenty-one became the emperor Charles V. He was the one who at his first **Reichstag** held on German soil, **at Worms,** sat in judgment over Luther at the memorable session of 18 April 1521. This was a session at which Luther, as a professor of theology – facing the emperor and the imperial staff – showed unique theological courage when despite the tremendous pressure he did not deviate from his conviction of faith, appealing to scripture, reason and his conscience.[17]

Charles V made unmistakeably clear what was at stake for Luther here: the following day he had his personal, very impressive confession on the tradition of Catholic faith read out in German.

And at the same time he declared that while granting Luther free conduct he would without delay initiate proceedings against him as a notorious heretic. Moreover in the **Edict of Worms** on 26 May Charles V put Luther and his followers under the imperial ban. All Luther's writings were to be burned and an episcopal censorship of books was to be introduced for all religious works appearing in Germany.

As Luther was in extreme personal danger, his prince had him hidden away on the Wartburg. As 'Knight George', in his ten months there he completed his translation of the New Testament – on the basis of Erasmus's Greek and Latin edition – the masterpiece of High German. The Bible was to be the foundation of gospel piety and the new community life. And Luther's Reformation paradigm, totally constructed on the Bible, was now to be the real, great alternative to the mediaeval Roman Catholic paradigm.

7. The Reformation paradigm

The return to the gospel in protest against the false development and wrong attitudes in the traditional church and traditional theology was the starting point for the new **Reformation paradigm**, the **Protestant-evangelical paradigm of church and theology**. Luther's new understanding of the gospel and the completely new status of the doctrine of justification in fact gave the whole of theology a new orientation and the church a new structure; this was a **paradigm shift** *par excellence*.[18] In theology and the church too, from time to time such **processes of paradigm shift** take place not just in limited micro- or meso-spheres of individual questions and tractates but also in the macro-sphere: the shift from mediaeval to Reformation theology is like the shift from the geocentric to the heliocentric view:

– Fixed and familiar terms change – justification, grace, faith, law and gospel – or are abandoned as useless: Aristotelian terms like substance and accidents, matter and form, act and potency;
– Norms and criteria which determine the admissibility of certain problems and solutions shift: holy scripture, councils, papal decrees, reason, conscience;

– Whole theories like the hylomorphic doctrine of the sacraments and methods like the speculative deductive method of scholasticism are shattered.

Not least, the attractive language of the new paradigm was decisive for countless clergy and laity of the time. From the beginning many were quite fascinated by the internal **coherence**, the elemental **transparency** and pastoral **effectiveness** of Luther's answers, with the new simplicity and creative linguistic force of Lutheran theology. Moreover, the art of printing books and a flood of printed sermons and pamphlets, along with the German hymn, proved to be essential factors in the rapid popularization and extension of the alternative constellation.

Thus the model of interpretation changed, along with the whole complex of different concepts, methods, problem areas and attempted solutions as hitherto recognized by theology and the church. Like the astronomers after Copernicus and Galileo, so the theologians after Luther got used as it were to **another way of seeing**, of seeing in the context of another macro-model. That means that some things were now perceived which had not been seen earlier and possibly some things were overlooked which had been seen earlier. Martin Luther's new understanding of word and faith, God's righteousness and human justification, the one mediator Jesus Christ and the universal priesthood of all believers led to his revolutionary **new biblical-christocentric conception** of all theology. From his rediscovery of the Pauline message of justification there followed for Luther;

– a new understanding of **God**: not a God abstractly 'in himself', but a God who is quite concretely gracious 'for us';

– a new understanding of **human beings**: human beings in faith as 'at the same time righteous and sinful';

– a new understanding of the **church**: not as a bureaucratic apparatus of power and finance but renewed as the community of believers on the basis of the priesthood of all believers;

– a new understanding of the **sacraments**: not as rituals which worked in a quasi-mechanical way, but as promises of Christ and signs of faith.

Western Christianity had got itself into a hopeless situation: for traditional Roman Catholicism the Reformation represented apostasy from the true form of Christianity, but for those inclined towards the gospel it represented the restoration of its original form. The latter abandoned the mediaeval paradigm of Christianity with joy. Rome might be able to go on to excommunicate the Reformer Luther, but it could not stop the radical reshaping of church life in accordance with the gospel by the Reformation movement, which progressed and stirred up all Europe. The **new Reformation constellation of theology and the church** was soon solidly established. From 1525 the Reformation was carried through in countless German territories, and after the failure at reconciliation at the Augsburg Reichstag in 1530 (the *Confessio Augustana*) the Schmalkald League of Protestant German princes was formed, which perfected the combination of Lutheran Reformation and political power.

It was thus clear that to the great schism between East and West a no smaller schism had been added between (roughly speaking) North and South – an event of prime importance in world history, with incalculable consequences also for state and society, economics, science and art, which (with all their ambivalence) have extended even to North and South America.

Indeed it has taken a long time, almost 450 years, for Catholics and Protestants to find a way out of their polemical confrontations and approach one another. Today the question is: have the churches still not got clear of the old controversial questions raised by Luther? How can they finally come together again? By what criterion can they establish their unity?

8. *The criterion of theology*

We have already seen how the mediaeval understanding of justification was not simply out of keeping with the gospel, and how Luther's understanding was not simply un-Catholic. Only a differentiated and nuanced assessment does justice to both sides. And this differentiated and nuanced assesment will not harmonize, but at the same time see discontinuity in all the continuity: Luther's decisive new beginning.

The decisive **theological** argument, which is primarily to be put forward not by the church historian but by the systematic theologian, may not simply be carried on with the 'Catholic'

Luther – with a Luther who was still Catholic or remained Catholic.[19] It must be carried on with the **Reformation Luther,** who with Paul and Augustine attacked scholasticism generally and Aristotelianism in particular. It is Luther's distinctive Reformation doctrine which needs to be taken seriously, not just historically and psychologically, i.e. what it meant for the history of the church and theology and for Luther personally, but also theologically.

By what **criterion?** Unfortunately Catholic church historians have seldom reflected on this decisive question. Moreover, their judgments on Luther's theology are often less historical than dogmatic evaluations. As a criterion for their judgment they have often taken the Council of Trent, whose basic theological weaknesses they have overlooked (thus the conciliar historian Hubert Jedin), or the theology of high scholasticism, the Catholicity of which has not been critically investigated (e.g. by the Catholic Reformation historian Joseph Lortz), or Greek and Latin patristics, the distance of which from scripture has manifestly not been seen (thus French theologians).

Here it must be said that anyone who does not want to suspend theological judgment cannot avoid a purely **exegetical** study of Luther's theology and especially his understanding of justification. As we have seen, Luther's doctrine of justification, his understanding of the sacraments, his whole theology and his explosive effect on world history are grounded in one thing: in the return of the church and its theology to the gospel of Jesus Christ as originally attested in Holy Scripture. So can one really argue with the most distinctive features of Luther if in the last resort one avoids this battleground, on which schism and church union are ultimately decided, whether out of superficiality, convenience or incompetence?

No, neo-scholastic theology, Trent, high scholasticism and patristics are all only secondary criteria compared with this **primary, fundamental and permanently binding criterion:** scripture, the original Christian message to which both the Greek and Latin fathers and the mediaeval theologians, the fathers of Trent and the neo-scholastic theologians appealed, and before which of course Luther himself also has to answer. In other words, it is not decisive whether this or that saying of Luther in this form or that can already be found in a pope, in Thomas Aquinas, in Bernard of Clairvaux or Augustine, but whether or not it has behind it the original Christian message on which all subsequent tradition, including the Gospels, depends.

9. Where Luther can be said to be right

Does Luther have the New Testament behind him in his basic approach? I can venture an answer which is based on my previous works in the sphere of the doctrine of justification.[20] In his basic statements on the event of justification, with the 'through grace alone', 'through faith alone', the 'at the same time righteous and a sinner', **Luther has the New Testament behind him,** and especially Paul, who is decisively involved in the doctrine of justification. I shall demonstrate this simply through the key words:

– 'Justification' according to the New Testament is not in fact a process of supernatural origin which is understood physiologically and which takes place in the human subject, but is the verdict of God in which God does not impute their sin to the godless but declares them righteous in Christ and precisely in so doing makes them really righteous.

– 'Grace' according to the New Testament is not a quality or disposition of the soul, not a series of different quasi-physical supernatural entities which are successively poured into the substance and faculties of the soul, but is God's living favour and homage, his personal conduct as made manifest in Jesus Christ, which precisely in this way determines and changes people.

– 'Faith' according to the New Testament is not an intellectualist holding truths to be true but the trusting surrender of the whole person to God, who does not justify anyone through his or her grace on the basis of moral achievements but on the basis of faith alone, so that this faith can be shown in works of love. Human beings are justified and yet always at the same time (*simul*) sinners who constantly need forgiveness afresh, who are only on the way to perfection.

So Catholic theology today will be able to **take note** more openly than a few decades ago of the **evidence of scripture** and thus also Luther's doctrine: first, because Catholic exegesis has made considerable progress; secondly, because the time-conditioned nature of the Council of Trent and its formulations have been demonstrated to everyone by the Second Vatican Council; thirdly, because the anti-ecumenical Neo-scholastic theology which was so dominant between the councils clearly manifested at Vatican II its inability to solve today's new problems; fourthly, because the changed atmosphere since the Council has opened up incalculable and formerly undreamed-of possibilities for ecumenical understanding; fifthly, because while the discussion over justification carried on in recent years has shown great differences in the interpretation of the doctrine of justification, it has not brought out any **irreducible differences** between the Protestant and the Catholic doctrines of justification **which would split the church**. A number of officially agreed documents from both sides have confirmed that the doctrine of justification no longer divides the churches.[21]

Of course all this does not mean that there were not already differences between Paul's and Luther's doctrines of justification simply on the basis of their different starting points; Protestant scholars themselves often note them, in particular too individualistic an orientation on Luther's part. Nor does it mean that in some statements of his doctrine of justification Luther did not lapse into one-sidedness and exaggeration; some formulations with *solum* and works like *De servo arbitrio* and *On Good Works* were and remain open to misunderstanding and need supplementation and correction. But the basic approach was not wrong. This approach was right, as was its implementation – despite some defects and one-sidedness. The difficulties and problems lie in the further conclusions drawn, above all in questions of understanding the church, ministry and the sacraments; these, too, have largely been resolved in theory today but are awaiting practical realization.

So, welcome though it is that even Rome now recognizes that in abstract theological terms the doctrine of justification no longer splits the churches, this cannot disguise the fact that Rome has not drawn the consequences which followed for Luther for the structure of the church. Indeed the present clerical, unspiritual dictatorship of Rome again mocks the basic concern of the

Reformation, which is also a good Catholic concern (the Pope is not above scripture). Rome still has little understanding of what Luther wanted in the light of the gospel.

But – here a counterpoint is due – for all our assent to Luther's great basic insight in keeping with the gospel, who could overlook the fact that in its results the Lutheran Reformation remained divided, was two-faced.

10. The problematical results of the Lutheran Reformation

The Lutheran movement developed a great dynamic and was able to spread powerfully not only in Germany but beyond, in Lithuania, Sweden, Finland, Denmark and Norway. Parallel to the events in Germany, in Switzerland, which had already begun to detach itself from the empire since the middle of the fifteenth century, an independent, more radical form of Reformation had been established by Ulrich Zwingli and later Jean Calvin which, with its understanding of the church, was to make more of an impact than Lutheranism in both the old world and the new. But it was Luther himself at any rate who in the 1520s and 1530s succeeded in establishing the Reformation movement within Germany.

Indeed, Germany had **split into two confessional camps**. And in view of the threat to the empire from the Turks, who in 1526 had defeated the Hungarians at Mohács and in 1529 had advanced as far as Vienna, Luther had even asked which was more dangerous for Christianity, the power of the papacy or the power of Islam; he saw both as religions of works and the law. At the end of his life Luther saw the future of the Reformation churches in far less rosy terms than in the year of the great breakthrough. Indeed in the last years of his life, although he was indefatigably active to the end, Luther became increasingly subject, on top of apocalyptic anxieties about the end of the world and illnesses, to depression, melancholy, manic depressions and spiritual temptations. And the reasons for this growing pessimism about the world and human beings were real – not just psychological and medical. He was not spared great disappointments.

First, the original **Reformation enthusiasm** soon **ran out of**

steam. Congregational life often fell short of it; many who were not ready for the 'freedom of a Christian' also lost all church support with the collapse of the Roman system. And even in the Lutheran camp, many people asked whether men and women had really become so much better as a result of the Reformation. Nor can one overlook an impoverishment in the arts – other than music.

Secondly, the Reformation was coming up against **growing political resistance.** After the inconsequential Augsburg Reichstag of 1530 (the emperor had 'rejected' the conciliatory 'Augsburg Confession' which Melanchthon had the main part in drafting), in the 1530s the Reformation was able at first not only to consolidate itself in the former territories, but also to extend to further areas, from Württemberg to Brandenburg. But in the 1540s the emperor Charles V, overburdened in foreign politics and at home constantly intent on mediation, had been able to end the wars with Turkey and France. Since the Lutherans had refused to take part in the Council of Trent (because it was under papal leadership: Luther's work *Against the Papacy in Rome, Founded by the Devil*, 1545),[22] the emperor finally felt strong enough to enter into military conflict with the powerful Schmalkald League of Protestants. Moreover the Protestant powers were defeated in these first wars of religion (the Schmalkald wars, 1546/47), and the complete restoration of Roman Catholic conditions (with concessions only over the marriage of priests and the chalice for the laity) seemed only a matter of time. It was only a change of sides by the defeated Moritz of Saxony – he had made a secret alliance with France, forced the emperor to flee through a surprise attack in Innsbruck in 1552, and so also provoked the interruption of the Council of Trent – which saved Protestantism from disaster. The confessional division of Germany between the territories of the old faith and those of the 'Augsburg Confession' was finally sealed by the religious peace of Augsburg in 1555. Since then what prevailed was not religious freedom, but the principle *cuius regio, eius religio*, i.e religion went with the region. Anyone who did not belong to either of the 'religions' was excluded from the peace.

Moreover the Protestant camp itself was unable to **preserve**

unity. At a very early stage Protestantism in Germany split into a 'left wing' and a 'right wing' of the Reformation.

11. The split in the Reformation

Luther had roused the spirits, but there were some that he would only get rid of by force. These were the spirits of **enthusiasm,** which while certainly feeding on mediaeval roots, were remarkably encouraged by Luther's emergence. A great many individual interests and individual revolts began to spread under the cloak of Luther's name, and soon Luther found himself confronted with a second, 'left-wing' front. Indeed Luther's opponents on the left (enthusiastic turmoil, riots and an iconoclastic movement as early as 1522 in his own city of Wittenberg!) were soon at least as dangerous for his enterprise of Reformation as his right-wing opponents, the traditionalists orientated on Rome. If the 'papists' appealed to the Roman system, the 'enthusiasts' practised an often fanatical religious subjectivism and enthusiasm which appealed to the direct personal experience of revelation and the spirit ('inner voice', 'inner light'). Their first agitator and Luther's most important rival, the pastor Thomas Münzer, combined Reformation ideas with ideas of social revolution: the implementation of the Reformation by force, if need be with no heed to existing law, and the establishment of the thousand-year kingdom of Christ on earth!

But **Luther** – who politically was evidently trapped in a view 'from above' and has been vigorously criticized for that from Thomas Münzer through Friedrich Engels to Ernst Bloch – was not prepared **to draw such radical social conclusions** from his radical demand for the freedom of the Christian and to support with corresponding clarity the legitimate demands of the peasants (whose independence was manifestly threatened and increasingly exploited) against princes and the nobility. Despite all the reprehensible outbursts, were not the demands of the peasants also quite reasonable and justified? Or was it all just a misunderstanding, indeed a misuse, of the gospel? Luther, too, could not deny the economic and legal distress of the peasants.

But a plan for reform would by no means *a priori* have been an illusion. Why not? Because the democratic order of the Swiss confederacy, for the peasants of southern Germany the ideal for a new order, could have been a quite viable model. However, all this was alien to Luther, trapped in his Thuringian perspective and now with his conservative tendencies confirmed. Horrified by news of the atrocities in the peasant revolts, he fatally took the side of the authorities and justified the brutal suppression of the peasants.

12. The freedom of the church?

As well as the left-wing Reformation there was the right wing. And here we must note that the **ideal of the free Christian church**, which Luther had enthusiastically depicted for his contemporaries in his programmatic writings, was **not realized** in the German empire. Granted, countless churches were liberated by Luther from the domination of secularized bishops who were hostile to reform, and above all from 'captivity' by the Roman Curia, from its absolutist desire to rule and its financial exploitation. But what was the result?

In principle Luther had advocated the dotrine of state and church as the 'two realms'. But at the same time, in view of all the difficulties with Rome on the one hand and with enthusiasts and rebels on the other, he assigned to the local rulers (and not all of them were like Frederick 'the Wise') the duty of protecting the church and maintaining order in it. As the Catholic bishops in the Lutheran sphere had mostly left, the princes were to take on the role of 'emergency bishops'. But the '**emergency bishops**' very soon became 'summepiscopi' who attributed quasi-episcopal authority to themselves. And the people's Reformation now in various respects became a princes' Reformation.

In short, the Lutheran churches which had been freed from the 'Babylonian captivity' quickly found themselves in almost complete and often no less oppressive dependence on their own rulers, with all their lawyers and church administrative organs (consistories). The princes who even before the Reformation had worked against peasants and citizens for the internal unification of their territories (which had often been thrown together haphazardly) and a coherent league of subjects had become excessively powerful as a result of the secularization of church land and the withdrawal of the church. The **local ruler** finally became something like a **pope in his own territory**.

No, the Lutheran Reformation did not directly prepare the way (as is so often claimed in Protestant church historiography) for the modern world, freedom of religion and the French revolution (a further epoch-making paradigm shift would be necessary for this), but first of all for princely absolutism and despotism. So in general, in Lutheran Germany – with Calvin, things went otherwise – what was realized was not the free Christian church but **the rule of the church by princes,** which is questionable for Christians; this was finally to come to a well-deserved end in Germany only with the revolution after the First World War. But even in the time of National Socialism, the resistance of the Lutheran churches to a totalitarian regime of terror like that of Hitler was decisively weakened by the doctrine of two realms, by the subordination of the churches to state authority which had been customary since Luther, and the emphasis on the obedience of the citizen in worldly matters. It can only be mentioned in passing here that in the sermons before his death Martin Luther had spoken in such an ugly and un-Christian way against the Jews that the National Socialists did not find it difficult to cite him as a key witness for their hatred of Jews and their antisemitic agitation.[23] But these were not Luther's last words, nor should they be mine.

I would like to close with three great statements which are utterly characteristic of Luther.

First, the dialectical conclusion of his work 'The Freedom of a Christian': 'We conclude, therefore, that a Christian lives not in himself, but in Christ and in his neighbour. Otherwise he is not a Christian. He lives in Christ through faith, in his neighbour through love. By faith he is caught up beyond himself into God. By love he descends beneath himself into his neighbour. Yet he always remains in God and in his love... As you see, it is a spiritual and true freedom and makes our hearts free from all sins, laws and commands. It is more excellent than all other liberty which is external, as heaven is more excellent than earth. May Christ give us liberty both to understand and to preserve.'[24]

Then Luther's summary plea before the emperor and the Reichstag at Worms: 'Unless I am convinced by the testimony of the Scriptures or by clear reason (for I do not trust either in the Pope or in councils alone, since it is well known that they have often erred and contradicted themselves), I am bound by the Scriptures I have quoted and as my conscience is captive to the Word of God, I cannot and I will not retract anything, since it is neither safe nor right to go against the conscience. God help me. Amen.'[25]

And finally, the last thing that Luther wrote: 'Nobody can understand Virgil in his *Eclogues* and *Georgics* unless he has first been a shepherd or a farmer for five years. Nobody understands Cicero in his letters unless he has been engaged in public affairs of some consequence for twenty years. Let nobody suppose that he has tasted the Holy Scriptures sufficiently unless he has ruled over the churches with the prophets for a hundred years. Therefore there is something wonderful, first, about John the Baptist; second, about Christ; third, about the apostle. "Lay not your hand on this divine Aeneid, but bow before it, adore its every trace." We are beggars. That is true.'[26]

Friedrich Schleiermacher
Theology at the Dawn of Modernity

Chronology (according to M. Redeker)

1768   21 November: born in Breslau.
1783   Enters the Paedagogium of the Brethren community in Niesky, Oberlausitz.
1785   Enters the theological seminary of the Brethren community in Barby, Elbe.
1787   Studies at the University of Halle.
1790   First theological examination in Berlin; tutor in the house of Count Dohna in Schlobitten, East Prussia.
1794   Passes second theological examination and is ordained; auxiliary preacher in Landsberg.
1796   Pastor at the Charité in Berlin; enters the circle of friends of the Berlin Romantics (Henriette Herz, Friedrich Schlegel).
1799   *On Religion*. Unhappy relationship with Eleonore Grunow.
1800   *Monologues*.
1802   Court preacher in Stolp, Pomerania.
1804   Professor of theology and university preacher in Halle.
1805   *Christmas Eve*.
1806   University of Halle closed in the course of the Napoleonic wars.
1807   Moves to Berlin. At first freelance work.
1809   Preacher at the Trinity Church. Marries Henriette von Willich.
1810   Professor at the new University of Berlin and first dean of the new theological faculty.
1813   Political involvement as the editor of the *Preussischer Korrespondent*.
1814   Secretary of the Berlin Academy of Sciences; suspected of being a political reactionary; dismissed from the Department of Education.
1815   Rector of the University of Berlin.
1817   Plays leading role in the union of the Prussian state church.
1821-22 *Magnum opus, The Christian Faith described according to the Principles of the Protestant Church*
1824-25 Climax of church-political disputes with the Prussian king.
1833   Travels to Sweden, Norway and Denmark.
1834   12 February: death and burial in Berlin.

1. Beyond pietism and rationalism

'The first place in a history of the theology of the most recent times belongs and will always belong to Schleiermacher, and he has no rival.' So says Schleiermacher's most vigorous opponent, who was to drive him from his pinnacle, and continues: 'It has often been pointed out that Schleiermacher did not found any school. This assertion can be robbed of some of its force by mention of the names of his successors in Berlin, August Twesten, Karl Immanuel Nitzsch of Bremen, and Alexander Schweizer of Zürich. But it is correct in so far as Schleiermacher's significance lies beyond these beginnings of a school in his name. What he said of Frederick the Great in his Academy address entitled "What goes to make a great man" applies also to himself: "He did not found a school but an era".' So spoke the one who saw to it that Schleiermacher, 'the church father of the nineteenth century', did not also become the church father of the twentieth century: Karl Barth in his *Protestant Theology in the Nineteenth Century*.[1]

Friedrich Daniel Ernst Schleiermacher was the offspring of two Reformed clergy families (both his grandfather and father were theologians, and his mother was the daughter of the Berlin chief court preacher Stubenrauch). He was born in Breslau in 1768 and took the name by which he was called from Frederick the Great, under whom his father had served as a Prussian military chaplain for soldiers of the Reformed confession. He was a highly talented young man, and because of the possibilities open to him could go several ways, though of course hardly into Lutheran orthodoxy – which was still strong in some circles.[2]

For already his **grandfather** Daniel Schleiermacher had been a **Pietist**. As a Reformed preacher he had been active in a radically pietistic community of apocalyptists and finally after disturbances in this sect (which was accused of magic and witchcraft) had to move to Holland.

His **father**, Gottlieb Schleiermacher, was also a Pietist; he too was at first the member of a Pietist community, but was to be alienated from it for a long time: it was only at the age of fifty that finally he felt at least inwardly that he belonged to the Herrnhuter Community of Brethren.

Moreover the young Friedrich could also have become a pietist when at the age of fourteen he saw his mother (who was soon to die) and his father (who was soon to remarry) for the last time, and was handed over to the care of the Brethren community, first at boarding school in Niesky, near Görlitz. Then, at the age of seventeen, he **studied theology** at the strict theological seminary of **Barby** near Magdeburg. Here the religion was one of the heart, which centred less on feelings of repentance and penitence as it did in pietistic Halle than on joy at redemption.

However, the young Schleiermacher hunted in vain at that time for the supernatural feelings and familiar converse with Jesus that the pious milieu required. Instead of this he found himself drawn to forbidden books, like Kant's *Prolegomena to a Future Metaphysics* (1783). The result was what might have been expected, for Schleiermacher now began increasingly to see the world no longer with pietistic eyes but with the eyes of the rational Enlightenment. Moreover after two years of theological study the student, now nineteen, wrote to his father (2 January 1787): 'I cannot believe that he was the true eternal God who only called himself the Son of Man; I cannot believe that his death was a vicarious atonement, because he never explicitly said as much and because I cannot believe that it was necessary, for it was impossible that God should have wanted to punish for ever men and women whom he evidently did not create for perfection but for striving towards it, because they had not become perfect.'[3] This letter must have prompted bad memories for his father, and now it was only with some reluctance that he allowed Friedrich to study in **Halle**. For:

Friedrich's father, the pastor, had himself long been a **rationalist**, and indeed was a freemason stamped by the Enlightenment. Moreover in a letter to his son he explicitly confessed that 'for at least twelve years' he had 'preached as a real unbeliever'.[4]

Moreover they were also rationalists at the University of **Halle**, founded barely a century beforehand in the pietistic spirit of August Hermann Franke: it was now a **bastion of the Enlightenment**. The leading German Enlightenment philosopher Christian Wolff had worked here and established numerous schools. Moreover the theological faculty had become open to the spirit of the Enlightenment. Its leading figure was Johann Salomo Semler (died 1791), who in his treatise on the free investigation of the canon had founded the historical-critical exegesis of the Bible in Germany and thus introduced a shift from the old orthodox theology to enlightened 'neology', to 'new teaching'.

So it seemed most likely that Friedrich Schleiermacher would also become a rationalist. For at the age of nineteen he now – we are still talking of 1787 – moved to this University of Halle, there to spend the next two years studying theology. He lived in the home of his uncle on his mother's side, Samuel Ernst Timotheus Stubenrauch, an enlightened Reformed theologian who became almost a second father to him. Indeed in his four semesters in Halle (until 1789) Schleiermacher studied not so much theology – he even had a pronounced antipathy to dogmatics – as philosophy, under Wolff's pupil Johann August Eberhard.

Schleiermacher the student wanted to create for himself the philosophical foundations for his own view of the world. And to this end he steeped himself in the Greek classics, above all Plato, and wrote his first academic work on Aristotle's *Nicomachean Ethics*. To this end he steeped himself further in the main works of **Immanuel Kant**, which had been appearing in rapid succession since 1781; he also devoted most of his early, almost exclusively philosophical, works to Kant. No wonder that all this reinforced his scepticism towards traditional Lutheran orthodox dogmatics. Indeed, reading Kant would shape him for life; in his epistemology Schleiermacher remained a Kantian all his days. For him, too, pure reason has no competence outside the horizon of human experience.

And yet, specifically in matters of ethics and religion, Schleiermacher would **not follow Kant**. Kant's moral proofs for God and immortality seemed to him to have too little foundation, despite everything. How could God be the regulative principle of our knowledge if he is not at the same time the constitutive principle of our being? Schleiermacher remained convinced that in the world of thoroughgoing natural laws there is a last mystery which human beings have to respect. Here may be the deepest reason why Friedrich Schleiermacher, the passionate philosopher, in the last resort remained a theologian. Although he kept his love of philosophy to the end of his life, although he initiated modern Plato scholarship (in his obituary he was called a 'Christian Plato') with a translation of Plato's works (with introductions to all the Dialogues), and although, like Kant, Schelling, Hegel and Hölderlin, he became a tutor after his studies (for more than six years, first at the castle of Count Dohna in **East Prussia**, from where he also visited Kant in his old age), Schleiermacher did not become a professional philosopher – unlike the Tübingen theologians Schelling and Hegel. Moreover Schleiermacher ended his theological study with the two ordination examinations (getting good to excellent marks in everything but the dogmatics whch he hated) and finally became a preacher in the remote little town of **Landsberg**. Here he preached regularly in the spirit of the Christian Enlightenment, commending a reasonable faith, incessant moral striving and Jesus as the model of a right way of life; in addition he had already translated several volumes of English sermons. And a preacher he was to remain, indefatigable and loyal to his life's end.

However, in 1796 there was a decisive new move in Schleiermacher's life. He received a post in **Berlin**. At the age of twenty-eight he now became Reformed preacher at the great German hospital, the Charité, where he was to spend the next six years (until 1802). These were to be decisive, formative years, which were to give Schleiermacher the characterististics which distinguished him later. He had bidden farewell to both pietism and rationalism and yet had retained the legacy of both. As he once put it later, after all he had 'again become a Herrnhuter', but now 'of a higher order'.[5] Indeed during this Berlin period Friedrich Schleiermacher, this physically rather small, neat and slightly deformed man, but with great liveliness and agility, became the modern theologian, a man in whom piety and modernity were combined in an exemplary way.

2. A modern man

Schleiermacher's post as hospital chaplain in Berlin, where he had to preach to simple people, left him time to himself. He made use of this time. The man who hitherto had argued with modernity only in silence and solitude (conversations above all with philosophical books) now entered the social life of a modern city. He moved in the salons of educated Berlin society, where people talked about poetry and art, history, science and politics. It was an exciting time, still deeply marked by the French Revolution, though a counterpoint was already emerging. How much had changed in culture and society, in the sciences and in everyday life, as a result of the philosophical and literary Enlightenment and the political upheavals! Were not important corrections also due in the sphere of theology? Schleiermacher followed everything with a lively mind – without ecclesiastical blinkers and moralistic Christian prejudices.

A new period in church history did not begin with Schleiermacher, as was said in a communication to the students after his death, but it did come to theological maturity in him. Here the theological paradigm shift from the Reformation to **modernity** virtually takes on bodily form: Schleiermacher no longer lived like Martin Luther (and Melanchthon), still largely in a pre-Copernican mind-set, in a mediaeval world of angels and devils, demons and witches, borne along by a basically pessimistic and apocalyptic attittude, intolerant of other confessions and religions. It would never have occurred to him to have someone burned for having problems with a dogma of the early church, as Calvin did with the anti-trinitarian Servetus. Nor did he have difficulties with modern science, with Copernicus and Galileo, as did the Roman popes imprisoned in the mediaeval paradigm; in the nineteenth century the writings of the modern scientists remained on the Index of books forbidden to Catholics alongside the Reformers and modern philosophy (from Descartes to Kant). No, Schleiermacher, who even as a professor still went to lectures on science, remained convinced by Kant all his life that there is a thoroughgoing regularity in nature, which allows no 'supernatural' exceptions. A supernaturalism in theology? That was not Schleiermacher's affair.

So in Schleiermacher we meet a theologian who is a **modern man** through and through. That means:

He knows and affirms the modern **philosophy** with which he had grown up and which had reached its challenging heights with Kant, Fichte and Hegel; as a classical philologist he had also gained the respect of classical scholars by his masterly translation of Plato.

He affirmed historical **criticism** and himself applied it to the foundation documents of the biblical revelation; in the great dispute over the fragments of Reimarus he would have certainly been on Lessing's side against Goeze, the chief pastor of Hamburg; at any rate, later he inaugurated historical criticism of the Pastoral Epistles with a critical study of I Timothy, which he said could not come from the apostle Paul; later he attributed the writings of Luke to the community life of earliest Christianity and its oral tradition; he demonstrated the presence of a collection of sayings in the Gospel of Matthew; the writings of the New Testament were to be treated like any others; his hermeneutics (introduction to the understanding of texts) became a basic work for theological, philosophical and literary interpretations.

He affirmed and loved modern **literature, art and social life** above all. He himself played an active part here through his close links with the Berlin Romantic circles which were striving to get beyond the Enlightenment, above all with their leader, the twenty-five-year-old Friedrich Schlegel, who lived with him for almost two years, and Henriette Herz, the beautiful and witty thirty-two-year-old wife of Marcus Herz, the highly respected Jewish doctor who had been a pupil of Kant; he visited their salon almost every day, where the spirit of Goethe and Romanticism replaced that of the Enlightenment. So he was a theologian in the closest contact with writers, poets, philosophers, artists and political enthusiasts of every kind. That is how we are to imagine the young Friedrich Schleiermacher. Only now does his thought and writing achieve a broad horizon and finally succeed in combining the Romantic religion of feeling with scientific culture.

3. Belief in a new age

So it is not surprising that Schleiermacher also had works published in the key journal of early Romanticism, the *Athenaeum*, edited by the Schlegel brothers. In addition to other anonymous fragments, he wrote, for example, the 'Idea for a Rational Catechism for Noble Ladies.'[6] The first commandment? It runs: 'You shall have no lover but him; but you shall be able to be a friend without playing and flirting or adoring in the colours of love.' Or the seventh to tenth commandments? They run: 'You shall not enter into any marriage which would have to be broken. You shall not want to be loved where you do not love. You shall not bear false witness for men; you shall not beautify their barbarity with your words and works. Let yourself long for men's education, art, wisdom and honour.' He was truly a theologian who simply in his attitude to **women** and **their emancipation** is far removed from the mediaeval and the Reformation paradigm, from their paternalism and sexism, and who not least had a living experience through women of the ethos of a spiritualized, interiorized Christianity.

However, the fact must not be concealed that in Berlin Schleiermacher finally fell passionately in love with Eleonore Grunow, the deeply religious wife of a Berlin pastor. Her marriage was an unhappy one, but although she loved Schleiermacher in return, she would not leave her husband even when in 1802, well advised by the anxious church authorities, Schleiermacher went into 'exile' in the small Pomeranian town of **Stolp**, a community of about 250 Reformed Christians. There he hoped that he would be able to marry Eleonore inconspicuously – to no avail, as the next three years were to prove. In his unhappiness Schleiermacher kept his sanity by translating Plato and producing the outlines of a critique of moral theory to his day (that of Kant and Fichte). Five years later, at the age of forty-one, he was then to marry Henriette von Willich, the twenty-year-old widow of a pastor friend who had died early. She was certainly a good housewife, but a less good partner (as she later fell completely under the influence of a clairvoyante and a revivalist preacher). Schleiermacher later revoked his seventh rational commandment for noble ladies, which could be understood as an invitation to divorce, in a sermon on the Christian household.

That Schleiermacher was also anything but conventional in his thinking about **children** – he himself had three daughters and a highly-gifted son who to his abiding sorrow died at the early age of nine – is shown in the same context by his fifth commandment: 'Honour the idiosyncracies and whims of your children, that all may go well with them and they may live a mighty life on earth.' Moreover Schleiermacher was to become a **pioneer of modern education**. Through his planning and organization he later not only left his stamp on Prussian **schools** but was also a co-founder of Berlin **University** and a decisive figure in establishing the Berlin **Academy of Sciences**. He was truly a theologian who in an astonishing way quite naturally took a place at the centre of modern life and played an active part in shaping it.

What did Schleiermacher believe in this new time? The spiritual foundation of all his activities was a new extended **ideal of humanity**. And he once formulated his 'faith' like this:

'1. I believe in **infinite humanity** which was there before it took the guise of masculinity and femininity.

2. I believe that I am not alive to be obedient or to dissipate myself, but to be and to become; and I believe in the **power of the will and education**, again to approach the infinite, to redeem me from the fetters of miseducation and to make me independent of the limitations of gender.

3. I believe in **enthusiasm and virtue**, in the worth of art and the attraction of science, in friendship among men and love of the Fatherland, in past greatness and future nobility.'[7]

Belief in infinite humanity, in the power of the will and education, in enthusiasm and virtue: should we make all this grounds for censuring Schleiermacher, as Karl Barth did? Should he be criticized for feeling responsible for the intellectual and moral foundations of society? For being concerned for the elevation, development and ennobling of individual and social life? For not only being interested in culture but also being increasingly involved in it – as preacher, writer, teacher, researcher and organizer? Indeed, for virtually embodying this modern culture as a man with a thorough intellectual and moral education? Indeed, we might ask back: how else should Schleiermacher have done theology in the Berlin of his time? On the basis of other, pre-modern presuppositions, as they had been worked out by philosophy, history and science in his time? Should he have remained, like others, in the mediaeval or Reformation paradigm instead of resolutely doing theology in the new modern paradigm, in his quite decisive concern for culture and therefore for **education**? But here a fundamental question arose for many of his contemporaries.

4. Can one be modern and religious?

The young Schleiermacher primarily had contact with the **educated** among his contemporaries. And when on the occasion of his twenty-ninth birthday he was asked by those celebrating it to write a book by his thirtieth birthday (on the topic of how religion could be expressed in a new way today), he took up the challenge and in fact expressly addressed only the educated classes (he thought that one should **preach** to the uneducated). Of course Schleiermacher was well aware of how ambivalent the picture of religion was, particularly among these educated people, how it wavered between affirmation and rejection, assent and mockery, admiration and contempt. So while he addressed his book to the educated, he explicitly addressed it above all to the educated among the **despisers of religion**, who were at least to know what they either despised, or did not know properly because of their prejudices. Thus came into being his famous first work, *On Religion. Speeches to its Cultured Despisers*[8] which appeared in 1799, when Schleiermacher was in his thirty-first year.

There is no doubt that all was not well with religion and theology at this time. Moreover, in these years some of Schleiermacher's most famous contemporaries – Fichte, Schelling, Hegel and Hölderlin – had moved from theology into philosophy (or poetry). Certainly they had not given up 'religion' completely, and had incorporated it into their speculative metaphysical system – as philosophical thinkers who certainly cannot be said to have denied religion completely (above all not the 'piety of thought' claimed by Hegel); however, they themselves lived and thought on the basis of genuinely philosophical roots. Many of Schleiermacher's new friends showed only an incomprehension of religion.

It needed someone of the stature of Schleiermacher to adopt a counter-position here that was worth taking seriously. Moreover, generally speaking there was no one on the church theological scene who in these stormy times between revolution and restoration, Enlightenment and Romanticism, could ask the question 'What about religion?' as urgently, credibly and effectively in public as he could.

So this was Schleiermacher's concern on the threshold of a new century: a bold and original attempt to **recall to religion, after the**

Enlightenment, a generation which was weary of religion and to which religion was alien and 'to reweave religion, threatened with oblivion, into the incomparably rich fabric of the burgeoning intellectual life of modern times'.[9] Or were only poetry and literature, holy philosophy and the sciences and the humanities, to determine the hopeful century that was dawning? Had not the poets and seers, the artists and orators, already always been mediators of the eternal and the most high, 'virtuosi of religion'? Was a 'sense of the holy' to be the mark only of ordinary people, and not also of the educated? No, the topic of religion was a live one, because it was raised by the whole human disposition and was therefore undeniable. But everything depends on what one understands by 'religion'.

5. What is religion?

Religion is not science, nor does it seek 'like metaphysics to determine and explain the nature of the universe'. Nor is religion morality, nor action: having an influence on the universe by moral action, 'to advance and perfect the Universe by the power of freedom and the divine will of man'.[10] Not that religion has nothing to do with understanding and morality. What 'religion' is about is something independent, original, underivable, immediate.

The peculiar feature of religion is a mysterious **experience**; it is **being moved by the world of the eternal**. So religion is about the heavenly sparks which are struck when a holy soul is touched by the infinite, a religious experience to which the 'virtuosi of religion' give direct expression in their speeches and utterances and which is communicated by them also to ordinary people. To be more precise, religion seeks to experience the universe, the totality of what is and what happens, meditatively in **immediate seeing and feeling** (these categories come from Fichte): 'It is neither thinking nor acting, but intuition and feeling. It will regard the Universe as it is. It is reverent attention and submission, in childlike passivity, to be stirred and filled by the Universe's immediate influences.'[11]

One can also say that religion is a religion of the heart: in it human beings are encountered, grasped, filled and moved in their innermost depths and their totality – by the infinite which is active in all that is finite. No, religion is neither praxis nor speculation, neither art nor science, but a 'sense and taste for the infinite'.[12] This living relationship to the eternal, the infinite, represents the original state of each individual 'I', but this must be aroused. Religious experiences are countless, and patience is called for. So in the religious consciousness the two limits, individuality and the universe, make contact. From a historical perspective this means that religion is:

– no longer as in the Middle Ages or even the Reformation a departure, transition into something beyond the world, supernatural;

– nor as in Deism and in the Enlightenment a departure into something behind the world, metaphysical;

– rather, in a modern understanding, it is the intimating, the seeing, the feeling, the **indwelling of the infinite in the finite.** The infinite in the finite or God as the eternal absolute being that conditions all things – this, we can say, is the modern understanding of God and not (as Schleiermacher adds in the second edition at the end of the excursuses on the idea of God) 'the usual conception of God as one single being outside of the world and behind the world'.[13] Like Kant, Fichte, Schelling and Hegel, Schleiermacher with philosophical strictness rejects any anthropomorphizing of God. God in the modern understanding is the immanent-transcendent primal ground of all being, knowledge and will.

This feeling is not to be understood in a restricted psychological sense as Romantic enthusiastic emotion, but in a comprehensive, existential way: as human beings being encountered at the centre, as immediate religious self-awareness (Ebeling compares this function with that of the conscience in Luther). Schleiermacher will later himself make this notion more precise, will withdraw the term 'contemplation' of the universe, which is open to misunderstanding (with the senses or spiritually?), in favour of the term 'feeling' and, as we shall see, speak more precisely in his *The Christian Faith* of religion as the **feeling of absolute dependence.**

6. The significance of 'positive religion'

Now if religion is the feeling of 'absolute dependence', then is not a dog the best Christian?[14] – thus one of the most malicious *bon mots* about Schleiermacher's thought, made by Georg Friedrich Wilhelm Hegel, from 1818 his Berlin colleague in philosophy as successor to Fichte? No, witty and spiteful as this *bon mot* is (Schleiermacher ignored Hegel's polemic), it does not get to Schleiermacher's position. It is unjust, because it ignores not only the total, spiritual nature of 'feeling' but above all Schleiermacher's understanding of God with its emphasis on Christian freedom as compared with any religious servitude. So in 'feeling' before their God Christians are not as 'dependent' as dogs on their master.

No, on the contrary Schleiermacher is concerned with the inner **freedom** of the moral person – the source of eternal youth and joy – moreover freedom is also a key word in the *Monologues*, the second major work which Schleiermacher published after the *Speeches* (as a New Year's gift at the begining of 1800) and in which he attempted to describe his religious view of life and the world in the form of a 'lyrical extract from a permanent diary'.[15] And in complete contrast to Hegel, already in the *Speeches* Schleiermacher is decidely against the state church. For him, as a Reformed Christian, this is the source of all corruption. He called passionately for the separation of church and state following the French model, and in his fourth Speech on Religion virtually developed the programme for a radical reform of the church in which the parish communities would be replaced by personal communities (of the kind that he was later to have himself).

Anyone who thinks that in his *Speeches* Schleiermacher is simply practising 'natural theology' (something abhorred by many since Karl Barth) should note that he makes it emphatically clear over against the whole theology of the Enlightenment that for him there is **no such thing as 'natural religion'**. This would in fact be a rational matter with a moral orientation, so that everything going beyond such a religion of reason would have to be rejected as 'superstition'. No, for Schleiermacher such a natural religion or rational religion was an artificial product of philosophical reflection without that life and immediacy which characterize an authentic religion. So from the beginning, part of

Schleiermacher's concern is that religion can be understood rightly only if it is not simply considered 'in general' but in the individual, living, concrete, 'positive' religions (Judaism, Christianity, Islam, etc.).

So the *Speeches* end in a reflection on the 'positive' element in the religions. The basic notion is this. There is no 'Infinite' in itself, in pure abstraction. The infinite can always be grasped only in the finite: it empties and manifests itself in an infinite variety of forms. The view of the universe is always an individual one, and none of these countless views can be excluded in principle. So 'religion' must individualize itself in different religions. As a result, anyone who wants to understand 'religion' must understand the different religions. The individual religions may have lost their original lives and be identified with particular formulae, slogans and convictions; in the course of their long history they may have been distorted and deformed; nevertheless, they are authentic and pure individualizations of 'religion' if and to the extent that they make possible an experience of the infinite in the human subject, to the extent that they make a particular view of the infinite their central point, their central view, to which everything in this religion is related.

Thus in his *Speeches* Schleiermacher took great pains not only generally to disperse all the prejudices of his modern contemporaries about religion, but also to make them open to the **positive element in religions**, the positive element ('the given') in all religions. However, here we should note that in Schleiermacher the individual religions by no means all stand on the same level: Schleiermacher takes it for granted that what religion is has individualized itself most in Christianity. **Christianity** is thus **relatively the best of all religions** in human history. Christianity need not fear comparison with other religions.

Here we can only regret that Schleiermacher did not have more precise knowledge of the **non-Christian religions** (apart from Greek religion). Though with his stress on religious experience he had also brought out an important aspect of 'religion', in later years he never had so broad a knowledge of the history of religion as, say, his later Berlin colleague and rival Hegel. Hegel in his lectures on the philosophy of religion treated the religions of humankind in a quite concrete way: as the great historical forms of the absolute Spirit revealing itself in the human spirit – beginning with the nature religions (the deity as a natural force and substance) in Africa, China, India, Persia and Egypt through Judaism, Greek and Roman religion, the religions of spiritual individuality, to Christianity, which, as the highest form of religion, includes in itself all its previous forms.[16]

And yet there is no denying that no theologian was to give such a boost to the future history, phenomenology and psychology of religion; no theologian worked it out intellectually to such a degree as Schleiermacher. If there is so much talk of **experience** in religious studies and theology, this is essentially because of him. If religion is no longer understood as mere private religion but in communal terms, this again is largely due to Schleiermacher. If Christianity can be understood as the best and supreme individualization of religion and so can be included in the comparison of religions, this too finds its legitimation, at least in principle, in Schleiermacher.

7. The essence of Christianity

For Schleiermacher, the easiest way of finding access to the spirit of religions is to have one oneself. And this is certainly particularly important for the one who 'approaches the holiest in which the Universe in its highest unity and comprehensiveness is to be perceived':[17] Christianity. Nor can it be disputed, despite all criticism, that Schleiermacher made an essential contribution towards providing a constructive answer to the question of the **essence of Christianity,** which had been posed by the Enlightenment. His view is that the essence of every religion must be seen in a 'basic vision', its 'vision of the infinite'.[18]

So what is the central vision, the original being, the spirit of **Christianity,** which can be defined despite all the historical distortions, despite all disputes over words and despite all the bloody holy wars? Schleiermacher sees the relationship between the finite and the infinite in Christianity as differing from that in Judaism. It is not determined by the idea of retribution, but as a relationship of **corruption and redemption, hostility and mediation.** Christianity is polemic through and through, to the degree that it recognizes the universal corruption and proceeds against the irreligion outside and inside itself. However, Christianity has the aim of pressing through to an ever-greater holiness, purity and relationship to God: everything finite is to be related everywhere and at all times to the infinite.

So Christianity represents religion in a higher potency, even if as a universal religion it should not exclude any other religion and any new religion. It does not have its origin in Judaism, but underivably and inexplicably in the one **emissary** on whom first dawned the basic idea of universal corruption and redemption through higher mediation. What does Schleiermacher admire in Jesus Christ? Not simply the purity of his moral doctrine and the distinctiveness of his character, which combines power and gentleness; these are human features. The 'truly divine' in Christ is the 'glorious clearness to which the great idea he came to exhibit attained in his soul. This idea was, that all that is finite requires a higher mediation to be in accord with the Deity.'[19] What does this 'higher mediation' mean?

All that is finite needs the mediation of something higher for its redemption, and this 'cannot be purely finite. It must belong to both sides, participating in the Divine Essence in the same way and in the same sense in which it participates in human nature.'[20] Therefore he is not the only **mediator** but the **unique** mediator, of whom it is rightly said, 'No one knows the Father but the Son and the one to whom he wills to reveal it': 'This consciousness of the singularity of his religion, of the originality of his view, and of its power to communicate itself and to awake religion, was at once the consciousness of his office as mediator and of his divinity.'[21] It is beyond question that such a formulation of the significance of Jesus Christ even at that time made more than the orthodox frown.

8. A modern faith

From the beginning, Schleiermacher's **christology of consciousness** was sharply attacked: does not the revelation of God here become a mode of human knowing and feeling? Does not belief in Christ become an illuminating universal human possibility? Does Jesus Christ here still remain an objective historical entity which is distinct from pious feeling? Or is christology dissolved into psychology, a universal christological psychology instead of a concrete historical christology? And in all this is not the deity of Christ ultimately left out of account?

After the *Speeches* and *Monologues*, Schleiermacher clarified his christological position in a poetical-theological work, ***Christmas Eve***[22], composed as a 'conversation', which appeared in 1805. A year previously Schleiermacher had been rescued from his exile in Stolpe by a call to the University of Halle as *extraordinarius* Professor of Reformed Theology and University Preacher. In his 'conversation', which is set at a family Christmas celebration with music, songs and food, in imitation of Plato's 'Dialogues', various conversation-partners, all of whom he presents sympathetically with inner understanding, show how differently they understand the experience of Christmas and the person of Christ. Even now there is discussion as to which conversation-partner Schleiermacher identifies himself with, if he identifies himself with any of them. So we shall have to wait for Schleiermacher's 'Dogmatics' to get a clear answer to the question of his christology.

However, in the following years there was not much time to clarify his christology. In 1806 Napoleon inflicted a lightning defeat on the Prussians at Jena, also occupied Halle and closed the university. Schleiermacher, originally enthused by the French Revolution, changed under the pressure of events from being a Romantic cosmopolitan to being a **Christian Prussian patriot**; now he worked with the leaders of Prussian reform (above all with Freiherr vom Stein on a new constitution for the Prussian church), went off on secret missions, recruited volunteers, and in all this hoped for a fundamental change in political conditions under the leadership of Prussia – but in vain, as was soon to prove. However, the combination of Christianity and patriotism which he expressed even in sermons was not to benefit German Protestantism.

When Halle was attached to the kingdom of Westphalia which was founded by Napoleon, in 1807 Schleiermacher moved to **Berlin,** where he first gave private lectures on history and philosophy for a pittance, continued his lectures for educated people, went on working for the Patriotic Party, was active as a journalist, and took part in the discussions on the refounding of the University of Berlin (the model for German university reform in the nineteenth century): in his view, in its constitution it should be marked by autonomy, freedom of spirit and independence from the state.[23] Then in quick succession followed the **honorary appointments** which mark out the framework of his Berlin activity: in 1809 preacher at Trinity Church and marriage; 1810 professor at the university; 1811 a member of the Prussian Academy of Sciences. Several times in the next years he was dean of the theological faculty: at that time he wrote his *Brief Outline of Theological Study in the Form of Introductory Lectures* (1811).[24] From 1810 to 1814 he worked as a member of the Education Commission in the Ministry of the Interior on the reform of Prussian schools. But in the restoration he was suspected by the reactionaries as being a revolutionary, and in 1814 he was dismissed because he argued for a constitutional state.

Schleiermacher's lectures in Halle and Berlin had now been sufficient preparation for him to write his theological *magnum opus*, which was to become the **most significant Dogmatics of modern times**. However, he deliberately avoided the word 'dogmatics', and instead of this chose the title *The Christian Faith* – but now with the significant addition 'described consecutively in accordance with the Principles of the Protestant Church'.[25] It is a systematic theology with an artistic structure, which for its ingenious uniqueness and otherness can certainly be set alongside the *Summa* of Thomas Aquinas and Calvin's *Institutes*. It sought to be believing and pious, critical and rational, all at once – in its own way.

Schleiermacher's modern doctrine of faith thus differs both from mediaeval *Summas* and from any orthodox Reformation dogmatics which thinks of faith primarily as holding particular objective facts of revelation or truths of faith to be true.

By contrast, Schleiermacher's work:

– **has a strictly historical construction**: for it, dogmatic theology – and this is said against both biblicism and rationalism – is not the science of an (allegedly) timeless, unchanged Christian doctrine, but is 'the science which systematizes the doctrine prevalent in a Christian church at any one time' (§ 19);

– **has an ecumenical form**: the reference to a 'church' does not of course mean the authority of a magisterium but the confessional writings of the churches and their prime document, Holy Scripture. Here Schleiermacher did not think that the controversies between Lutheran and Reformed doctrine (unlike the opposition between Protestantism and Catholicism) split the church; Schleiermacher argued more than anyone else for the Lutheran-Reformed Union, introduced in Prussia at the Feast of the Reformation in 1817 with joint eucharistic celebrations; he understood his *Christian Faith* as a dogmatics of union;

– **is related to experience**: as was his wont, Schleiermacher begins from religious experience, the disposition or consciousness of Christians, the piety of the church community, in short from pious human consciousness (which, however, is collective and communal). The dogmatic statements in scripture and tradition certainly cannot be proved, but Schleiermacher can rightly claim to stand in the Christian tradition. For he explicitly does theology from the community of faith, from the church; not, though, to prove its faith but to make its innermost essence understandable in a critical and constructive way. So both the sayings of Anselm on the title page of his *The Christian Faith* are not just decoration from the tradition but express a consciousness of the tradition: 'I do not attempt to know in order to believe, but I believe in order to know. For anyone who does not believe will not experience, and anyone who does not experience will not know.'[26]

But what is the **essence of Christianity** according to Schleiermacher's *The Christian Faith*? The famous definition runs: 'Christianity is a monotheistic faith, belonging to the teleological type of religion, and is essentially distinguished from other such faiths by the fact that in it everything is related to the redemption accomplished by Jesus of Nazareth' (§11).

If we are to understand this definition of essence, which while simple is not all that easy to understand, we must remember four things:

– In the three stages of religious development presupposed by Schleiermacher, fetishism – polytheism – **monotheism** (universally advocated in the Enlightenment) – Christianity stands at the uppermost level, not only as an 'aesthetic' religion (a religion of nature or destiny), but as a religion which corresponds to human nature in a 'teleological' way – i.e. is determined by a goal and thus is an ethical, active religion.

– The 'distinctive' feature of Christianity, which sets it apart from all other religions, does not lie in its natural rational character but in its **redemptive character**: for everything is governed by the basic opposition of sin and grace and precisely in this way related to the 'mediator' Jesus of Nazareth.

– Its **christocentricity** is emphasized by the prominent position of christology already in the 'Introduction': in Schleiermacher, christological statements stand at the point where in orthodox dogmatics there was a discussion of Holy Scripture. The central position of the person of Jesus Christ in Christianity is indispensable for Schleiermacher!

The fundamental methodological starting-point in the consciousness of faith is maintained: Schleiermacher does not begin from the objective story of Jesus of Nazareth, but from our pious Christian '**consciousness**', the consciousness of the church community, of redemption through the person of Jesus Christ.

That brings us back to the question which we had to raise in connection with *Christmas Eve*: is the pious consciousness of the person of Jesus Christ related to a **particular**, concrete reality which thus is defined and definable, or is this particular figure included in a **universal** essence and meaning of history, and thus levelled down?

9. Christ – truly human

One difficulty about Schleiermacher's consciousness-christology was that the pious consciousness always only circles around itself, that it does not have any real object. This difficulty seems to me to be answered in *The Christian Faith*: Schleiermacher's christology is without doubt not just a postulate of the pious consciousness, is not the complex imagination of subjective faith. For we cannot overlook the fact that:

Christian consciousness, Christianity generally, is inconceivable without the historical figure of Jesus of Nazareth as its **historical origin**.

So at the centre of Christianity stands not a general notion or a moral doctrine, but a historical figure and his redemptive effect on human beings and history after him. The christocentricity of

The Christian Faith (and the picture of Christ in Schleiermacher's sermons) is thus not the result of Schleiermacher's speculation, but a consequence of the history of Jesus Christ himself and what followed from it.

In Schleiermacher the historical figure does not remain an abstract 'saving event'; rather his **history** can be **narrated**. Moreover it is no coincidence that Schleiermacher wrote a *Life of Jesus*, which depicts Jesus of Nazareth with his unshakeable consciousness of God and his concern for suffering human beings. Certainly it is idealistic, all too orientated on the Gospel of John and the Greek ideal of 'noble simplicity and silent greatness', but nevertheless it is in no way simply in conformity with the ideals of the bourgeois society of Schleiermacher's time.[27] At the same time, by taking up the criticism of the Enlightenment, but applying it in accordance with religious and not purely rational criteria, in his *The Christian Faith* Schleiermacher carried out a large-scale **demythologizing**: not only of the Old Testament narratives of an original existence of the first human couple in paradise, a primal fall and original sin, angels and devils, miracles and prophecies, but also a demythologizing of the New Testament narratives of Jesus' virgin birth, nature miracles, resurrection, ascension, and the prophecy of his return.

So there is no doubt that Schleiermacher holds firm to the **vere homo**, the 'truly man', of the classical christological confession of the Council of Chalcedon (451). But what about the **vere Deus**, the truly God, who is said to be there in Jesus?

10. Christ – also truly God?

Schleiermacher, too, did not want to go back to heretical solutions in christology. Moreover for his conception he distinguished his approach *a priori*: not only from **docetism** (towards which **supernaturalism** was now tending) on the right, which can see only a phantom existence in Jesus' human nature, but also from Nazoraeism (Ebionitism, to which **rationalism** now came close) which reduces the existence of the redeemer to the level of ordinary humanity.[28] Particularly in christology, Schleiermacher is a

'Herrnhuter of a higher order' when he attempts to transcend these oppositions.

It was a difficult task – why? Because the classical christological formula 'Jesus Christ is one (divine) person in two natures (one divine and one human)' had come under sharp criticism above all from the 'neologians' in the process of the Enlightenment. Jesus of Nazareth now appeared to many people as nothing but an ordinary man, as a more or less revolutionary Jewish improver of doctrine and the law, who to others could seem a teacher and model of moral and religious perfection. But that was too little for Schleiermacher; for him it was a quite 'meagre' '**empirical**' view of redemption! And the alternative?

Was one, like the supernaturalists, to put forward what in fact was a '**magical**' conception of redemption in which the punishment for human sin was as it were magicked away by the miraculous act of a satisfaction and a sacrifice of the Son of God, and Jesus was understood simply as the heavenly high priest mediating grace? There could be no question of that either. But what then? How was **redemption** to be interpreted meaningfully through Christ? And then above all: how was the relationship of Jesus of Nazareth to God to be described? In Schleiermacher's view the whole of Christianity stands and falls with the answer to this question.

Faithful to his starting point, here too Schleiermacher begins with the pious Christian consciousness – a 'mystical' view only in an inauthentic sense. What takes place there? Answer: in their consciousnesses, Christians can experience:

– that they are utterly dependent on the world-historical impulse which Jesus produced: Jesus is both the historical starting point and the abiding source of a new relationship with God;

– that the power of Jesus (which influences all movements of spirit, will and disposition) mediates consciousness of God in a redemptive and reconciling way;

– that in this way a new kind of personal life, indeed historical 'total life', has entered history, which is not in the grip of the consciousness of sin but – under the emanation of Christ's consciousness of God – produces a consciousness of grace.

Despite all the demythologizing, the **difference** between Schleiermacher's christology and **the Jesuology of the Enlightened**

rationalists is clear. According to Schleiermacher, it follows from an analysis of the pious Christian consciousness,

– that Christ is the active one and human beings are recipients: it is Christ who overcomes the power of sin through his grace;

– that Christ makes possible a living community with human beings and a new higher life in humankind;

– that what is decisive for this is not individual features (which are possibly dubious), but the overall impact of his ongoing personality;

– that this historical personality bears in itself a primal perfection, so that it is not only a model which human beings are to imitate but a **primal image of the consciousness of God**, which grasps and forms human beings.

So who was this Jesus Christ in his uttermost depths? The old Herrnhuter struggled passionately for the answer to this question. For a long time he had worked on new answers to old questions which were deeply religious and at the same time clear and simple. Now -- in *The Christian Faith* – he can reply: Christ is for all human beings **the same!** To what extent? 'In virtue of the identity of human nature.' Christ is **different from all human beings!** To what extent? 'By the constant potency of his God-consciousness, which was a veritable existence of God in him.'[29]

A **veritable existence of God** in Christ? Schleiermacher leaves no doubt: whereas other people have only a general religious disposition and an 'imperfect and obscure' God-consciousness, Jesus's God-consciousness was 'absolutely clear and determined each moment, to the exclusion of all else'.[30] This can be regarded 'as a continual living presence, and withal a real existence of God in him', in which at the same time his 'utter sinlessness' is given – and, as a presupposition of this, his innocence from the beginning.[31] That means that in Christ 'the being of God' is there unbroken 'as the innermost fundamental power within him from which every activity emanates and which holds every element together'[32] (to use an illustration: just as the intelligence as the basic force in human beings orders and holds together all other forces). The eternal infinite is present in Jesus' consciousness with its unconditioned power and force without annihilating it; rather, it controls this consciousness and shapes the whole of Jesus' life so that he becomes an instrument, model and primal image. And this is decisive, for without a divine dignity in the redeemer there can be no redemption, and vice versa. So the new communion of life with Christ, the beginning of new life and the renewal of the disposition which is constantly necessary, is made possible – a process which takes part utterly in grace: that is the particular concern of Schleiermacher the theologian and above all the preacher.

So has the christological question been answered in Schleiermacher? *Vere Deus?* Truly God? Yes, Jesus is formed by the divine primal ground in a way unlike any other. Certainly, God is present everywhere in the finite as **the** one who is active, but in Christ the God-consciousness is the principle which shapes the personality. His God-consciousness must be understood as a pure and authentic revelation, indeed as the true and authentic indwelling of the being of Christ in the finite. This is no supernatural miracle, and yet it is something quite unique and miraculous in this world dominated by sin. Here the believer does not postulate God's being, but becomes one with the divine which has a living influence on history with Christ – Schleiermacher's great concern since the *Speeches*.

Was all this 'orthodox'? Schleiermacher specifically states that with this interpretation of the divinity of Christ he is departing from 'that language of the Schools as used hitherto'[33] (the doctrine of the two natures). He was all the more aware of doing this since, having given lectures on almost all the writings of the New Testament, he believed that his view could be grounded in the Bible; it was grounded 'in the Pauline God was in Christ and on the Johannine the Word became flesh'[34]! So Schleiermacher understood his own Christianity 'not as an imitation of an ethical ideal, which was the approach of the Enlightenment theology of the time, nor as an obedient acceptance of incomprehensible dogmatic doctrinal statements, but as a completely inward determination by the historical Jesus and the God present in him'.[35]

But is Schleiermacher on the other hand a 'pluralist'? Schleiermacher would turn against any pluralist theology of religion which simply establishes different 'saviours' in the world and in so doing thinks that it has solved the problem of the religions' claim to truth. He was convinced that Christ 'exclusively' has the 'being of God', so that only in connection with him can it be said that 'God has become man'.[36] 'The Word became flesh' is for Schleiermacher 'the basic text of the whole of dogmatics'.[37]

11. Critical questions

Of course from a present-day perspective dogmatic theologians can ask whether in his christological statements Schleiermacher reached the 'heights' of the christological councils of the fourth and fifth centuries. But Schleiermacher would reply that he regarded these conciliar christological statements – in the perspective of the New Testament and the present – as superseded, as 'transcended'. Is not Jesus of Nazareth an authentic human person? Instead of being from eternity a second divine person who entered into human existence? Instead of a truly human person with a human will, are there then to be two natures and two wills and contradictory theories about the divine and the human in Christ? And on top of that, three persons in one divine nature? Is all this biblical, original? Is it all comprehensible and acceptable to modern men and women? There was good reason why in his *The Christian Faith* Schleiermacher put forward the programmatic thesis: 'The ecclesiastical formulae about the person of Christ need an ongoing critical treatment.'[38] Moreover in an unparalleled piece of theological thinking he developed a modern christology not only beyond the two-natures doctrine of the early church, which was obviously time-conditioned, but also beyond the meagre Jesuology of the Enlightenment.

Of course Schleiermacher's doctrine also needs 'ongoing critical treatment' – as he himself would certainly agree. And this 'ongoing critical treatment' – soon two centuries will have passed since Schleiermacher's epoch-making achievement – will have much to criticize. For me, the most important questions to ask, especially about the christology which was also central for Schleiermacher, are these:

First, in Schleiermacher's consciousness theology there is certainly room for telling the story of Jesus; after all, he himself gave lectures on the life of Jesus. To this degree he is open to a 'narrative theology'[39] (of the kind which today is simply called for in slogans). Nevertheless, there is a danger in Schleiermacher's approach and the subordinate role of the Bible in his *The Christian Faith* that our own experience of redemption will control the telling of the story of Jesus all too much, instead of constantly not only being newly inspired by the story of Jesus, but also being radically criticized and corrected by it. After all, the Christ of Christians is the abiding criterion and constant corrective of Christianity.

Secondly, the modern starting point of the human subject, from the **consciousness of the community of faith,** is to be affirmed in principle, even if one can find fault with Schleiermacher's definition of religion ('the feeling of absolute dependence') as an overextension of the results of his analysis of the consciousness. But there is a danger which needs to be taken more seriously that as a result of Schleiermacher's generally philosophical and theological remarks about religion and the definition of the essence of Christianity in his 'Introduction' a prior decision has been taken as to 'what content is left for christology if it is to be different from anthropology'.[40]

Thirdly, Schleiermacher's idealistic interpretation of reality and harmonious basic mood hardly take the **real experiences of negativity** seriously with the necessary urgency: the alienation and fragmentation of human beings; suffering, guilt and failure; and the contradictions and disasters of history – all this seems to be taken up and transcended in the unity of the divine plan of redemption. Schleiermacher also interpreted Jesus' unshakeable consciousness of God idealistically in the light of the Gospel of John, and thus largely got round and interpreted away the darkness of God and the tribulation, despite all the divine inwardness.

Fourthly, in his great systematic work Schleiermacher certainly described the prophetic, high-priestly and royal office of Jesus. But in so doing he did not give a central place to the **scandal of the cross** and the **hope of resurrection** which are fundamental to the New Testament writings. So he remained incapable of taking Jesus' abandonment by human beings and God really seriously (not to mention his flirting with the hypothesis of a pseudo-death); in contrast to the synoptic evangelists, he sees death and resurrection as a seamless transition of an ideal figure of cheerfulness and pure love from the physical to the spiritual present, which makes possible direct access to him for all those who live after him.[41]

All these are questions which have finally pushed this modern theology into the twilight: a theology of modernity which in some respects has delivered itself over too much to the spirit of modernity.

12. Nevertheless: the paradigmatic theologian of modernity

Schleiermacher died in the sixty-sixth year of his life, of inflammation of the lungs, on 12 February 1834, after celebrating the eucharist with his family. To the end he was a controversial man in his church. Just a decade earlier he had been cited three times to Berlin police headquarters for his support for a constitutional state, greater freedoms for the people, and for the students; there was a threat that he would be removed from his professorship. His very different opponents from the revival movement, conservative confessionalism and Hegel's camp to some degree pursued him even after death with their sharp repudiation.

However, his friends and supporters secured triumphs for him which he was still able to enjoy in the last years of his life – something not granted to everyone. Shortly before his death Schleiermacher was awarded an order and other honours, and in his last years he drew greater audiences than any other theologian or churchman, whether at lectures or sermons (ten volumes of sermons in the first complete edition of his work). His fearless attacks on any despotism and his concern to arouse a social concern among the upper classes (for example, shortening working hours) made him popular far beyond educated circles.

Given this influence, it is no surprise that **Schleiermacher's funeral** in February 1834 at Trinity Church in Berlin became an impressive demonstration of solidarity in which people of all classes and professions gathered together. If we follow the account of the historian Leopold von Ranke, between 20,000 and 30,000 people must have followed the coffin: 'I recall what an impression it made on me when we buried Schleiermacher, and there was weeping all down the long street from every window and from every door', an impression which is confirmed by other participants: 'Perhaps Berlin never saw such a funeral. Everyone followed the coffin and the procession wound endlessly through the streets... Generals and former ministers, the committees of the ministry and the clergy, both Catholic and Protestant, teachers from the university and the schools, students and pupils, old and young – one might even say friend and foe. It was a recognition of a spirit such as is seldom seen.'[42]

History has meanwhile often confirmed the verdict of such contemporaries. This Berlin professor of theology and academic philosopher; this interpreter of Plato and proclaimer of the gospel; this exegete, dogmatic theologian, ethicist; this critic and theologian of culture with a universal education, a passionate quest for truth and the ability to achieve public enthusiasm, was indeed a 'rare', outstanding spirit. He was an existential thinker with an amazing capacity for work, who has left behind him unmistakeable, deep traces wherever he worked. He was a many-sided scholar of the utmost precision and at the same time a brilliant writer and preacher for the cultural elite, who was convinced that the Reformation was continuing there and then. In the nineteenth century his *The Christian Faith* occupied and influenced all theologians, including the theology of his opponents.

But this Friedrich Schleiermacher, endowed with a sharp, ironic and witty spirit, continued to be remembered by his contemporaries not only for his advocacy of the truth in truthfulness but also for his concern to be a convincing Christian. Faithful to his ideal of an educated individuality, to the end of his life he was not only involved in university and academy but also in church and state, in the pulpit as well as at the lecture desk and above all in the study. He was an ardent patriot who fought for freedom, justice and reform, and at the same time an outstanding church teacher who followed his inner mission, and who also later always argued for the greatest possible independence of the church from the state (not a state church but a people's church with a synodical constitution), who against the king's will passionately attacked his liturgical reform from above and intrepidly made a stand against the king's right in internal matters and against an order of service which he had worked out personally. All in all this was a paradigmatic theologian, freely human and bound to God in a Christian way, **the** paradigmatic theologian of modernity.

As is well known, the most credible praise often comes from opponents. So let us leave the last word on Schleiermacher (like the first) to Karl Barth, who almost precisely a century after Schleiermacher's death, in the first volume of his *Church Dogmatics*, was to present a great theological alternative to Schleiermacher in the twentieth century: 'We have to do with a hero, the like of which is but seldom bestowed upon theology. Anyone who has never noticed anything of the splendour this figure radiated and still does – I am almost tempted to say, who has never succumbed to it – may honourably pass on to other and possibly better ways, but let him never raise so much as a finger against Schleiermacher. Anyone who has never loved here, and is not in a position to love again and again, may not hate here either.'[43]

Karl Barth
Theology in the Transition to Postmodernity

Chronology (according to E.Busch)

1886	10 May: born in Basel; spends his youth in Bern.
1904-08	Studies theology in Bern, Berlin, Tübingen and Marburg.
1909-11	Assistant pastor in Geneva.
1911-21	Pastor in the industrial town of Safenwil (Aargau, Switzerland).
1913	Marries Nelly von Hoffmann.
1919	*Romans* (second completely revised edition 1922).
1921	Called to be honorary Professor of Reformed Theology in Göttingen.
1925-29	Professor of Dogmatics and New Testament Theology in Münster.
1930	Begins as Professor of Systematic Theology in Bonn.
1932	Begins his (incompleted) *magnum opus Church Dogmatics*.
1934	First Confessing Synod of Barmen.
1934	'No!' to Emil Brunner.
1934	Suspended by the Nazis and forced to retire in June 1935; later ban on all Barth's works in Germany.
1935	Begins as Professor of Dogmatics in Basel.
1948	Speech to the World Council of Churches in Amsterdam.
1959	Last completed volume of the *Church Dogmatics* (IV/3).
1961-62	Last series of lectures, 'Introduction to Evangelical Theology'.
1962	First visit to the USA.
1966	Last visit to Rome.
1967	Breaks off the *Church Dogmatics* with the fragmentary volume IV/4.
1968	Death and burial in Basel.

1. A controversial Protestant in the World Council of Churches

The year is 1948. Karl Barth is sixty-two years old and – as a result of the eventful world history of the first half of the century – already has an eventful life behind him. He studied theology in Bern, Berlin, Tübingen and Marburg between 1904 and 1909; from 1909 to 1921 he was first assistant minister in Geneva and then pastor in Safenwil, in Switzerland; from 1921 to 1935 he was professor of theology in Göttingen, Münster and Bonn; all this after a single book (*The Epistle to the Romans*) which appeared in 1919 had made this Swiss provincial pastor a theologian famous throughout the whole German-speaking world. In 1935 he was driven from his Bonn chair by the Nazis, and since then had taught theology at the University of Basel, as a passionate 'Swiss voice' taking part to the end in the church struggle of German Protestantism against the barbarity of Hitlerism.

But now, after the war, in 1948, Karl Barth had been invited by his Reformed friend and fellow Reformed believer, the great Dutchman Willem Visser't Hooft, the powerful and wise spiritual director of the ecumenical movement, to take part in the **First Assembly of the World Council of Churches in Amsterdam**, which marked the foundation of the World Council of Churches (with Visser't Hooft as General Secretary). Previously Barth had taken hardly any part in the ecumenical movement. But here in Amsterdam, in conversation above all with Michael Ramsey, later to become Archbishop of Canterbury, and the Orthodox theologian Georges Florovsky, he learned that in academic theology there must also be something like an 'ecumenics', alongside 'dogmatics' and 'symbolics'. This makes it possible for an examination by competent theologians of the different churches of 'disagreements within the agreement' and 'agreements within the disagreement', so as to come a step nearer to union.

But Rome, the Pope, had refused to take part in this ecumenical gathering, as too had the Russian Orthodox Church. And what was Barth's reaction? It was typical of him. In Protestant freedom and Helvetic warmth, in his great speech he simply proposed that people should get on with the agenda. One has to hear his original words to understand how he stood, spoke and argued: 'May this freedom (for the one Lord Jesus Christ **despite** these separated eucharists) also mean that the sighing or the indignation over the refusals that we have received from the churches of **Rome** or **Moscow** occupy as little space as possible in the discussions of our first section! Why should we not simply recognize the mighty hand of God over us in these refusals! Perhaps God is giving us a sign through which he wants to take any boasting from us, as if here we could build a tower the summit of which reached to heaven. Perhaps God is showing us here how miserable our light was hitherto, as it evidently cannot even shine out into these other, yet allegedly also Christian, spheres. So perhaps God is preserving us from conversation partners with whom we could not even be a community in an imperfect way here, because – albeit for different reasons – they did not want to take part in the movement of all the churches to Jesus Christ without which Christians of different origin and nature cannot speak to one another or hear one another, let alone come together. And perhaps God is thus putting us in a very **good** place, by virtue of the fact that **Rome** and **Moscow** in particular seem to be united in wanting to have nothing to do with us. I suggest that we now praise and thank God specifically for this, that it pleases him to get in the way of our plans so clearly.'[1]

Karl Barth – an anti-Catholic rabble-rouser? That is what it might seem like to a superficial onlooker. But the polemic of published Catholic opinion at that time against an evidently anti-Catholic Barth – after all, this was the heyday of Pius XII, the last pre-conciliar Pope – was now drowned by the Catholic indignation over the revelations in Hochhuth's play *The Representative* (1962), which was to lead to street demonstrations in Basel in front of the Stadttheater.

2. A critic of Roman Catholicism

But Barth's criticism of Roman Catholicism went theologically deeper and much further back in time. In the five important years of his second professorship (after Göttingen) in Münster, 'that nest of Papists and Anabaptists':

– There Catholic dogmatics was present in the person of the Neo-Thomist Franz Diekamp, whom Barth often quoted later;
– There he studied Anselm of Canterbury and Thomas Aquinas intensively;
– There (an innovation) he invited a Catholic theologian to a seminar discussion and to personal conversations. This was the Jesuit Erich Przywara, who in an uncommonly knowledgeable and skilful way had developed a similarity of being, an **analogia entis**, between God and human beings, along the line of Augustine's, Thomas Aquinas's and Scheler's ideas of 'God in us and God over us'.

However, Przywara only confirmed Karl Barth in his conviction that while Catholic theology and the church had preserved more of the substance of Christianity than the 'Neoprotestantism' of Schleiermacher, they were flawed with the same **basic error**. They too seized God's revelation, had taken control of grace, in such a way that God could no longer be God and human beings could no longer be human beings – an issue which for him was the prime concern of 'dialectical theology'. To this extent 'Roman Catholicism' was 'A Question to the Protestant Church', as Barth entitled his controversial theological lecture of 1928,[2] because Catholicism reflected problems which were also recognizable within Protestantism. In sharp confrontation with this, Barth therefore argued for a Protestantism which had strictly to concentrate on its evangelical concern. And this means that world is world, and human beings are human beings, but God is God, and reconciliation is only in Jesus Christ!

But Catholic theology began to take note of Barth. Already in the 1920s and 1930s, first Karl Adam of Tübingen and then Erik Peterson of Bonn, and then after Erich Przywara above all Gottlieb Söhngen began to grapple with the early Barth (*Romans* and the following writings). When around 1940 German voices had to fall silent as a result of the war, French-speaking Catholic theologians could be heard: the Jesuits Louis Malevez, Henri Bouillard and the Dominican Jérôme Hamer (nor should we forget the Dutchman Johannes C. Groot). But most of these works took little note of the Barth of the monumental *Church Dogmatics*,[3] which had only been taking shape since 1940: after the *Prolegomena* (Volumes I.1-2) in 1932 and 1938, Barth's

Doctrine of God (II/1-2) appeared only in 1940/42, then his *Doctrine of Creation* (III/1-4) in the years 1945-1951. The *Doctrine of Reconciliation* (IV/1-4) and the *Doctrine of Redemption* or eschatology were to remain uncompleted. The discussion which he had by correspondence after Amsterdam with the French Jesuit Jean Daniélou – one of the main representatives of the 'nouvelle théologie' in France who was suspected of heresy, later conformed and became a cardinal – proved ultimately unproductive. 'Too much is required of both of us', Barth told him abruptly with reference to Rome's refusal to come to Amsterdam 'for us to be able to take your unconditional claim to superiority seriously and to have longed for your presence!'[4]

3. Catholic attempts at understanding

Another theologian, a pupil at the same time of Przywara and Henri de Lubac, who since 1940 had, like Barth, lived in Basel, Hans Urs von Balthasar from Lucern, was the one to write the book which for Catholic theology brought a breakthrough to a **sympathetic understanding of Barth's theology**.[5] Balthasar had left the Jesuit order because he felt called to found a 'lay order' with his spiritual friend Adrienne von Speyr. Looking back from Barth's mature work, Balthasar attempted to distinguish a 'period of dialectic' in the early Barth (*Romans*, 1919, second edition 1922), then a 'move to analogy' (*Christian Dogmatics in Outline*, 1927), which was finally extended by Barth to the full form of analogy (from *Church Dogmatics*, Volume II).

It was Balthasar who drew attention to the **artistic architecture** and intellectual and linguistic force of Barth's theology – comparable only with Schleiermacher and inspired by Schleiermacher: how creation and covenant were dovetailed on a radical christological foundation, how it arrived at a new understanding of human beings as God's partners, a new doctrine of sin and reconciliation. But Balthasar had been fascinated above all by Barth's new interpretation of predestination, which 'sublated' the Augustinian-Calvinistic dualism (part of humankind predestined to bliss, another part to hell) in a Christian universalism almost reminiscent of Origen: the Christ-centre mediates with an all-oneness of redemption. There was a **christocentricity** which was now also to make possible a new definition of the relationship between faith and knowledge, nature and grace, judgment and redemption – for Protestants and Catholics alike. But what does that mean?

In the preface to the first volume of the *Church Dogmatics* of 1932 there is the famous and notorious sentence, without any reference to Przywara: 'I regard the *analogia entis* as the invention of Antichrist, and I believe that because of it it is **impossible** ever to become a Roman Catholic, all other reasons for not doing so being to my mind short-sighted and trivial'.[6] We can understand this polemic against the analogy of being which puts God and human beings on the same level as tantamount to the Antichrist only if we recognize the **two fronts** which it is attacking.

On the right wing, Barth is primarily protesting against that Roman Catholicism which, following scholasticism and the First Vatican Council, put God and human beings on one level and thus established an interplay between human beings and God, nature and grace, reason and faith, philosophy and theology. How pernicious this 'damned Catholic **and**' was emerged for Barth above all from the Catholic mariological dogmas ('Jesus **and** Mary') and the Catholic understanding of scripture **and** tradition, of Christ **and** the infallible Pope. 'In the doctrine and worship of Mary there is disclosed the one heresy of the Roman Catholic Church which explains all the rest,'[7] wrote Barth, and his criticism of the 'Roman Catholic error'[8] which ultimately 'even declares itself identical with God's revelation' could not have been sharper.[9] But all this had to do with what in his eyes was the pernicious way in which **Catholicism put God and human beings on the same level** by its concept being (both 'are'). Barth believed that he had to protest against this in the name of a wholly other God, in the name of God as **God**.

On the left wing Barth was fighting at the same time no less against that **liberal Neoprotestantism** which, following Schleiermacher, had oriented itself completely on pious, religious human beings instead of on God and his revelation. It was no coincidence for Barth that on the basis of a 'natural theology' which levelled out to such a degree both Roman Catholicism and liberal Neoprotestantism had come to an **arrangement** in uncritical assimilation to the **ruling political systems** of their time: first with the Kaiser's empire and its war policy, and then again with National Socialism. Because of this equating of God and man, had not the Protestant 'German Christians' seen National Socialism as something like a new revelation and Adolf Hitler even as a new Luther – binding together Christianity and Germanhood – even a new Christ? Because of this analogy of being between God and human beings, had not even prominent representatives of Neoscholastic Catholic two-storey theology (Karl Adam and Michael Schmaus) found that National Socialism was to be affirmed because it wanted on the natural level what Catholic Christianity was bringing about on the supernatural level: order, unity, discipline, the Leader principle? No, here Barth could see the whole political danger of the 'Christian' natural theology which showed its true face in 1933. A stand had to be made against it because it was politically serious. The Barmen Synod of the 'Confessing Church' – in essence theologically inspired by Barth – is the most visible sign of this.

However, the irony of history is that the most important theological result of von Balthasar's book was that the whole diastasis of the analogy of being or analogy of faith which Barth stressed so strongly was seen as a **false expression of the problem**. Whatever was practised in popular Catholic piety, both Catholic theology and the Catholic church did not want simply to level out the difference between God and humankind, and could not and would not seize hold of revelation, the grace of God. Caught theologically by von Balthasar with difficult distinctions within the concept of nature, Barth finally also had to concede this. When in 1955 as a young man I returned from Rome after seven years there and – like many Catholic theologians moved by these problems – talked about this controversy with Barth in our first conversation, he proved to be a man not only of holy wrath but also winning humour: 'In theology one never knows: does he have me or do I have him?' And in connection with the much-disputed *analogia entis*, for the sake of which alone one cannot become a Catholic, he merely said, 'Now I've buried that!' And in fact after that Barth never used the expression again – though without actually pointing this out. But this has not prevented confessionally inclined Catholic and Protestant theologians who want to see the division between the churches quite personally grounded and secured in the Holy Spirit, Jesus Christ or even in God the Father rather than in pope, church and sacraments, from seeing and cherishing the *analogia entis* as what really divides the churches.

I grant without further ado that without Balthasar's book on Barth my own work on Barth would have been impossible. I learned from Balthasar that the Catholic and the Protestant can be reconciled at the very point where they are most consistently themselves. And above all I learned from him that Karl Barth, precisely because he embodied the most consistent development of Protestant theology, came closest to Catholic theology: in Protestant, evangelical fashion completely focussed on Christ as the centre and precisely in this way reaching out in a universal, catholic way – the possibility of a new **ecumenical theology.**

4. Ecumenical understanding

In connection with our portrait of Luther we heard that since the time of the Reformation and the Council of Trent the doctrine of the **justification of the sinner** has been regarded as *articulus stantis et cadentis Ecclesiae*, as the article of faith by which the church stands and falls, and thus as the fundamental obstacle to an understanding between Catholics and Protestants. It would be a considerable achievement towards doing away with the split in the church if it were possible to demonstrate a convergence, indeed a consensus, here.

My book *Justification*[10] sought to show precisely this: that in the doctrine of justification seen as a whole, a fundamental agreement could be recognized between the teaching of Karl Barth and the teaching of the Catholic church, rightly understood, and that in the light of this there was no longer any ground for a schism between Protestants and Catholics. Cunning as he was, Karl Barth cautiously wrote in his letter that went with my book: 'If what you infer from Holy Scripture, the old and new Roman Catholic theology and moreover "Denziger" and indeed the texts of the Council of Trent really **is** and is confirmed to be the teaching of your church (perhaps confirmed by a consensus over your book), **then,** having twice gone to the church of Santa Maria

Maggiore in Trent to commune with the *genius loci*, I may very well have to hasten there a third time, to make a contrite confession: *patres peccavi*, "Fathers, I have sinned".'[11] And what happened?

My book was not put on the 'Index' of forbidden books by the Roman censors, as some had hoped and some had feared. In 1958 a new Pope was elected and a new development began. Finally, in 1971, on the Mediterranean island of Malta, it proved possible for a study commission of the Lutheran World Federation and the Roman Catholic church to work out, after careful preparations, a joint document. This **Malta Document** states the consensus: 'Today there is a far-reaching consensus on the interpretation of justification. On the question of justification, Catholic theologians also emphasize that no human conditions attach to God's gift of salvation for believers. Lutheran theologians emphasize that the event of justification is not limited to individual forgiveness of sins and do not see it as a declaration of the righteousness of the sinner which remains purely external. As a foundation of Christian freedom over against legal conditions for the reception of salvation, the message of justification must constantly be expressed anew as an important explication of the centre of the gospel.'[12] So here was confirmation from Rome on the issue of the message of justification. However, Karl Barth no longer had occasion to make a pilgrimage to Trent. For three years he had no longer been among the living.

Of course the message of justification 'as a foundation of Christian freedom over against legal conditions for the reception of salvation' has radical consequences: not only for the individual but for the church, which only has meaning as a community of believers that constantly needs to live anew by God's grace, forgiveness and liberation: *ecclesia semper reformanda*!

Barth was making a programmatic statement against liberal and also Kierkegaardian individualism when he replaced the original title *Christian Dogmatics* (the false start of 1927) with **Church Dogmatics**. He was not only attacking any facile use of the word 'Christian' but above all – despite the 'laments accompanying the general course of my development' making it clear that dogmatics cannot be an absolutely 'free' science but must be 'a science bound to the sphere of the church, where alone it is possible and meaningful'.[13] So there are long ecclesiological chapters already in the Prolegomena (on church proclamation, on the hearing and the teaching church) and then in the doctrine of God and election (the election of Israel and the church), and of course above all in the three volumes of the doctrine of reconciliation. All that is said here about the gathering, building up and mission of the church through the power of the spirit of God who raises to faith, enlivens in love and calls to hope; all that is said here about the *ecclesia una sancta, catholica et apsotolica*, is the strongest development of Protestantism and the closest approach to the Catholic: a catholic and thus truly ecumenical ecclesiology concentrated on the gospel.

Ecumenical understanding on both sides became difficult only when there was talk about the **organizational structure** and **practical policy of the church**: the significance of the sacraments and above all of the theological understanding of church ministry, the ministries of priest and bishop and (of course above all) the papacy.[14] Karl Barth was fascinated by the tremendous ecumenical possibilities of the papacy, but put off by its concrete form and praxis: 'I cannot hear the voice of the Good Shepherd from this chair of Peter', he used to say. That was under Pius XII.

5. The Second Vatican Council

The pontificate of John XXIII, which lasted only five years but was epoch-making, above all the Second Vatican Council and the **double paradigm shift** that it introduced – an integration of both the Reformation and the modern paradigms into the Catholic church and theology – also moved Karl Barth deeply. It had been Barth who had challenged me, as a Catholic theologian brought up a Roman, to speak publicly about something as primally Protestant and therefore at the time suspect to Catholic ears as *Ecclesia semper reformanda*: at a lecture to 'his' university in 1959 – literally six days before the utterly surprising announcement of the Council.

Subsequently Barth took a lively interest in my programme of conciliar reform then sketched out in my book *The Council and Reunion*[15]; indeed he had even proposed its precise title. The

Council then took up what was allegedly so Protestant a statement of the need for constant reform (*Ecclesia semper in reformatione*) into its Constitution on the Church and also put it into practice: by taking up numerous concerns on the one hand of the Reformers (the revaluation of the Bible and preaching, and of the laity to the point of giving them a say in the liturgy), and on the other of modernity (freedom of faith, conscience and religion, toleration and ecumenical understanding, a new attitude to the Jews, the world religions and the secular world generally). Karl Barth began to be amazed at the movement of the Spirit which had come about at that time in the Catholic church, which seemed to contrast with a widespread fossilization in Protestantism. Moved profoundly, not simply by the human side but also by the deeply evangelical side of the council Pope, now he did not hesitate to say of John XXIII: 'Now I can hear the voice of the Good Shepherd.'

However, for all that he did not become a Catholic. In any case he had not thought of conversion to another church; his concern was the constantly new conversion of all churches to Jesus Christ. But the new situation in 1966 at any rate attracted him to make a **journey to Rome**. He called it a *peregrinatio ad limina Apostolorum*, a pilgrimage to the tomb of the apostles – ill-health had prevented him from accepting an invitation to the Council which I had conveyed to him. In Rome – after conversations with various Roman authorities – he found his generally positive impression of conciliar Catholicism confirmed: 'The church and theology there has moved to a degree that I could never have envisaged.'[16] However, Roncalli's successor, Paul VI, gave him the impression of being a man worthy of respect, indeed lovable, but somehow to be pitied; he told Barth in an almost touching way how difficult it was to bear and use the keys of Peter which had been entrusted to him by the Lord. That was still before Paul VI's fateful encyclical against 'artificial' birth control; but the aporias that would follow the council – the consequences of ongoing curial obstruction and the compromises made at the council – were already emerging.

We do not know what Karl Barth thought of the next two popes who – as an expression of both compromise and aporia – both combined the names of their predecessors, John and Paul, two such different men. A few months after his visit to Rome he finally broke off work on the *Church Dogmatics* (he had already exhausted his creative powers long before his death); all he wanted to see published was a lecture fragment of the fourth part of the doctrine of reconciliation, on ethics. It was to be his last major publication. The great thirteen-volume work remained an **unfinished symphony** like the *Summa* of Thomas Aquinas, the *magnum opus* which, as we heard, Thomas had enigmatically stopped working on some months before his death. The faith of the fathers always had to be listened to in the church, wrote Karl Barth in his last incomplete draft lecture: 'God is not a God of the dead but of the living.' 'In him they all live, from the apostles to the fathers of the day before yesterday and yesterday.' These were the last sentences that Barth, now eighty-two, was to write. The next morning, on 10 December 1968, his wife found that he had peacefully gone to sleep for ever.

In his last years Karl Barth often felt 'out of date', and then he would tell me: 'Now I would like to be as young as you again – then I would go back to the barricades.' Karl Barth again on the barricades? On the barricades of the 1970s, the 1980s? I have often asked myself in the last two decades where and how he would have gone on the barricades, what he would have done had he not been a Barthian but really a truly rejuvenated Karl Barth. And I would like to reflect a little on this question, now that I have spoken about Karl Barth's shift from confrontation with Catholic theology, through attempts to come to terms with it, finally to an ecumenical understanding with it. So we move from then to now; not, however, in arbitary hypothetical speculations, 'what ifs', but looking at the substance of Barth's theology and constructively taking it further. What now?

6. Why the paradigm of modernity has to be criticized

The first question is the question which nags at any theologian: where and how is Karl Barth to be put in the history of theology? Is he monumentally 'neo-orthodox?' (and hardly read as a whole), which is how he is classified almost all over America and often also in the Bultmann school – and written off? Or is he the unsurpassable theological innovator of the century, which is how he is glorified in Germany far beyond the Barth school – and blocked?

My comprehensive Catholic thesis against both antagonists who disqualify Barth and followers who glorify him is: Karl Barth is the **initiator** of what I would now call a **'modern' paradigm of theology**. By that I mean two things:

– I would like to make it clear to those who despise Barth that Karl Barth is really an initiator, indeed the **main initiator,** of a 'postmodern' paradigm of theology which was already dawning at that time.

– But, for uncritical admirers of Barth: Karl Barth is an initiator **and not a perfecter** of such a paradigm.

It is easy to demonstrate three things from Barth's writing and his career as it has been described in an exemplary way by Eberhard Busch 'from his letters and autobiographical texts'.[17]

First, Barth was **a decisive follower of modern theology**: originally from the middle-class world (from poetry and music through beer and student association life to the military), at a very early stage he was enthused by Schiller's idealism and Richard Wagner's Tannhäuser 'proclamation'. Soon Kant and of course Schleiermacher were the leading lights of the thought of the theological student who already in his first semester was familiarized with the historical-critical method. So he became the pupil of the great liberal masters: first Harnack (in Berlin) and then, even more importantly, Wilhelm Herrmann (in Marburg), who could combine Kant and Schleiermacher with a marked christocentricity. As editorial assistant to Martin Rade at the liberal *Christliche Welt* Barth had dealings with the intellectual products of all the eminent liberals, from Bousset and Gunkel to Troeltsch and Wernle.

But **then** Barth turned into the **sharpest critic of the modern Enlightenment paradigm** which, after a phase of strict Lutheran and Calvinist orthodoxy, had already developed in the seventeenth century, established itself in the eighteenth century and finally in the nineteenth century taken on its classical form with Schleiermacher, achieving a leading position with the liberal theology that followed him: a paradigm, as we saw, wholly orientated on humanity. Barth's ten-year experience as **pastor of Safenwil,** an increasingly industrialized Swiss farming community with all the social problems of that time, made him doubt already before the First World War the bourgeois optimism over progress and the assimilationist tendencies of culture Protestantism, and indeed made him a Socialist committed to the cause of the workers. He saw that in the oppressive crisis over preaching – empty pews, ineffective confirmation instruction – all the modern critical knowledge of the Bible was no help to him. For preaching, instruction and pastoral care he needed quite a different theological foundation, which was not primarily concerned with human beings but with God. Despite all his respect for modern liberalism, Barth sensed that historical relativism, combined with religious individualism, had increasingly evacuated Christianity.

It was the outbreak of the **First World War** in 1914 which for Barth proved a radical crisis for the modern paradigm.

– On the one hand the modern tendency of liberal theology towards assimilation had been shown up completely when ninety-three German intellectuals including almost all Barth's famous theological teachers, foremost among them Harnack and Herrmann, identified themselves in a public manifesto with the war policy of Wilhelm II and the attack on neutral Belgium.

– But on the other hand European Socialism, too, had failed in the face of the war ideology and had supported the war almost everywhere.

So Karl Barth's personal theology developed into a 'theology of crisis', which was given a highly dramatic background in 1918 with the final downfall of the German empire along with the control of the churches by local princes, with the United States in Europe, the Russian Revolution and the social unrest in Germany. Was this the collapse of an epoch – modernity with its belief in reason, science and progress – but also the birth of a new, postmodern epoch?[18]

7. Initiator of the postmodern paradigm of theology

In fact Barth became the **principal initiator of a postmodern paradigm of theology**. In the complex crisis which threatened everything it had become abundantly clear to him that Christianity cannot in any way be reduced to a historical phenomenon of its time which is to be investigated critically, and a present-day inner experience of a predominantly moral kind. In the face of the epoch-making collapse of bourgeois society and culture, its normative institutions, traditions and authorities, after the War Barth more than anyone else mobilized the critical power of faith and – in connection with *The Epistle to the Romans*[19] – along with his friends Emil Brunner, Eduard Thurneysen, Friedrich Gogarten and Rudolf Bultmann 'between the times' (the name of a new journal which they founded) called programmatically for a move to a **'theology of the Word'** (often called 'dialectical theology').

And that means that there was no going back behind Schleiermacher, but **progress forward beyond Schleiermacher:**
– away from modern anthropocentricity to a new theocentricity;
– away from a historical-psychological self-interpretation of the 'religious' person and theology in terms of history and the humanities to God's own Word attested in the Bible, to revelation, the kingdom and action of God;
– away from religious talk about the concept of God to the proclamation of the Word of God;
– away from religion and religious feeling to Christian faith;
– away from human religious needs (the modern man-God) to God who is the 'wholly other', manifest only in Jesus Christ (the 'God-man' understood biblically).

In the general political, economic, cultural, spiritual revolution after the catastrophe of the First World War the theology of Karl Barth – with Barth himself as a model of 'theological existence' – powerfully introduced the paradigm shift from the modern liberal to what we can now call in retrospect a postmodern paradigm, though at that time only pale outlines of it could be recognized. To this degree it is Barth – and not Ritschl, Harnack, Herrmann or Troeltsch – who is called the 'church father of the twentieth century'.

In the face of the crisis of the modern paradigm, Karl Barth called for and encouraged a **fundamentally new orientation of theology.** Earlier than others – in a theological critique of ideology – his theology saw through the despotic and destructive forces of modern rationality, relativized the claim of Enlightenment reason to absoluteness, and showed Enlightenment reason where it was deceiving itself; in short, earlier than others, his theology recognized the 'dialectic of the Enlightenment' and worked for an Enlightenment beyond the Enlightenment. Barth countered the liberal diffusion of Christianity into the universally human, the historical, with a new christological concentration on salvation in Christ. Over against the assimilation to social and bourgeois trends in culture Protestantism he emphasized the political and social provocation of the gospel. It remains amazing how already at that time Barth spoke out resolutely against any nationalism and imperialism, the corrupt heritage of modernity, taken over and carried to absurd extremes by totalitarian systems in our century. It is amazing how already at that time he committed himself forcefully to a policy of world peace and social justice and to a critical prophetic attitude of the church against all political systems.

Barth's fundamentally new theological involvement showed its political power in 1934 at the **Synod of Barmen**, against the Nazi pseudo-religion: in the clear confession, conceived by Barth, of Jesus Christ as the 'one Word of God' alongside which the church cannot recognize 'yet other happenings and powers, images and truths as divine revelation'.[20] Not blinded like other theologians who saw Nazi Fascist totalitarianism as the necessary great culmination of the modern development, Barth saw it more as the terrifying relic of a 'modernity' which urgently had to be transcended: the 'end of modernity', as Romano Guardini was to call it after the Second World War.

So we have not understood Barth (at any rate not the young Barth) if we brand him neo-orthodox. On the contrary, it seems to me that even today in theology we must hold to the **great intentions of Karl Barth**:

– The biblical texts are not mere documents of philological-historical research but make possible an encounter with the 'wholly other'; the utterly human testimonies of the Bible are concerned with **God's** Word, which men and women can acknowledge, know and confess.

– Men and women are thus called to more than neutral contemplation and interpretation: their penitence, conversion and faith is required, a **faith** which always remains a venture; human salvation and damnation are at stake here.

– It is the task of the church to express uncompromisingly in society, through its human words, this word of God on which men and women can always rely in trust.

Both church preaching and church dogmatics have to be utterly concentrated on **Jesus Christ,** in whom for believers not just an exemplary 'good man' has spoken and acted, but God himself; Jesus Christ is the decisive criterion of all talk of God and human beings.

That is all good, more than good. But a question must finally also be put to this theology, too. **How** are these great theological intentions to be realized in a new time? Is Barth's *Church Dogmatics,* which as a theologian he did not want to be revered, but read and taken further, already the theology that is called for in the postmodern paradigm? It seems to me that here a clear counterpoint must be set – and for that we must go back once again to the beginning of Barth's theology, the beginning of the 1920s.

8. Not the perfecter of the postmodern paradigm

In order to create the essential presuppositions for his lectures, the pastor of Safenwil who as yet had no doctorate and had now been appointed Göttingen Professor of Reformed Theology (happily the University of Münster gave him an honorary doctorate) went back to the Reformation heritage, to Calvin and the Heidelberg catechism. But that was not enough. Should we see it as chance or fate that after his first two years, in 1924, when he had to prepare his lectures on dogmatics, the newly launched professor hit upon an 'out-of-date' 'dusty' book which was to be his destiny: *The Dogmatics of the Evangelical Reformed Church* by Heinrich Heppe, from the year 1861,[21] which gave him the answers to all the dogmatic topics between heaven, earth and hell? Whose answers? Those of **old Reformed orthodoxy.**

So in Barth's first lectures on dogmatics there was a **shift** which, while not uncritical, was remarkable, since it was towards dogmas disputed in the modern world, from the Trinity, through the virgin birth and the descent into hell, to the ascension: a shift not only to old Protestant orthodoxy but also – where did this ultimately get its wisdom from? – to mediaeval scholasticism and the patristics of the early church. And what about the other brains of 'dialectical theology'? None of them went along with this move of Barth's, but all watched it, shaking their heads. However, it was not the reference back to the tradition of the early church, the Middle Ages and the Reformation in itself which was the problem (there was a good deal to be learned here) but the way in which Barth did this – simply ignoring and often defaming important results of modern exegesis, history and theology.

Of course Barth did not become an orthodox Calvinist, Lutheran confessionalist or even mediaeval scholastic as a result. His own theological approach and his own specific theological epistemology, which he further radicalized after the discontinued *Christian Dogmatics in Outline*, was too original for that. The key work here was his book on Anselm of Canterbury, *Anselm: Fides Quaerens Intellectum*.[22] What does Anselm's **credo ut intelligam** mean? For Karl Barth there is no question about that: 'I believe in order to understand.' 'Faith' has the priority in everything. Right from the beginning, according to Barth, a Christian has to take a leap into the subject-matter itself. It is not, as in Schleiermacher, a matter of first wanting to understand (the historical, philosophical, anthropological and psychological presuppositions of faith) in order then to believe. Rather, it is the opposite, first believe in order to understand by subsequent fathoming of the 'possibilities' of faith.

Barth defines faith as knowledge and affirmation of the word of Christ, but then – and this is where the problem emerges – this is very quickly identified with the church's creed, with the confession of faith which has come into being historically in a long history. This was now **Barth's approach** in the light of Anselm: on the presupposition **that** it is true that God exists, is a being in three persons, became man, there is now further reflection on how far all this is true. So now the emphatically *Church (!) Dogmatics*, published after the *Christian Dogmatics in Outline*, becomes reflection on the **creed which has been said and affirmed beforehand**. Hardly anyone can really be astonished, then, that already in the 'Prolegomena' to the Dogmatics (not what is to be said beforehand but what is to be said first), there are two hundred pages on the doctrine of the Trinity, which is not developed from the New Testament but from the church doctrine of the fourth century. This is not grounded, but made comprehensible, in a brilliantly developed conceptual dialectic – on the presupposition that it is accepted in faith. So now Karl Barth's fundamental thesis on revelation is utterly trinitarian (§8): 'God's Word is God Himself in His revelation. For God reveals Himself as the Lord and according to Scripture this signifies for the concept of revelation that God himself in unimpaired unity yet also in unimpaired distinction is Revealer, Revelation, and Revealedness',[23] or, in a biblical formulation: Father, Son and Spirit.

One can best make this procedure clear through a **comparison**: Barth's radicalized and intrinsically volatile theology of the Word is structurally reminiscent – for all the manifest differences in content – of Hegel's philosophy of the Spirit (Barth had always had a 'certain weakness' for him) in so far as this, similarly circling round itself and moving forward dialectically in three stages, presupposes the whole of truth, calls for a similar leap into the subject-matter, and presents a similar alternative:

– **Either, Hegel** would say, one raises oneself above all that is empirical and abstract to truly concrete speculative thought, and then in reflection the truth of the Spirit dawns automatically – or one does not elevate oneself to this speculative level and is then not really a philosopher.

– **Either, Barth** would say, one subjects oneself, untroubled by all historical, philosophical, anthropological and psychological difficulties, to the Word of God as it is attested in scripture and proclaimed by the church and then, indeed then, on reflection the truth of revelation will dawn of its own accord – or one does not believe and then is not really a Christian!

And for Christians – so Karl Barth now says in the *Church Dogmatics* with the utmost christological concentration but also **exclusiveness** – for Christians Jesus Christ is now the word of God made flesh, the **one**, the **only** light of life, alongside which there are **no** other lights, nor can there be, no other words of God, no revelation.

Many theologians trained by Barth (like the right-wing Hegelians of their time) see no difficulties here. One is in the circle and *a priori* thinks on the high dogmatic level that is called for. For myself, while I personally can move on this 'height' of theology myself, I cannot forget my contemporaries 'down in the valley', cannot conceal the fact that I have difficulties here and that in the light of the great Catholic tradition (which here too has largely lagged behind the Reformation tradition) I had them from the beginning. No, Barth's theology is too important for us to be able to avoid confronting its substance here.

We cannot limit ourselves to a purely immanent paraphrase of Barth, worthwhile though that may be in the interest of bringing Barth's theology alive for the present-day generation of theologians.[24] A good seventy-five years after Barth's *Romans* and a good sixty years after the first volume of his *Church Dogmatics* we cannot be content with a mere internal correction of a conventional picture of Barth while otherwise largely agreeing with him. It seems to me that criticism of Barth, too, must be more critical of Barth's theology.

So we must ask:

If **God's creation** is no longer, as the young Barth thought in his early phase, the point of contact for the grace of God falling vertically from above, and if God's creation now in the late Barth can be taken quite seriously as God's good work, so that it is now possible to write four volumes of *Church Dogmatics* about it; if all that is the case, then why should this not have consequences for a true **knowledge of God** from creation – in principle not only for Christians but for all men and women?

– If God, in terms of the **substance of theology**, beyond doubt stands at the beginning of all things and thus certainly has the primacy, why must it be **methodologically illegitimate for theology** to begin with the questions and needs of present-day people and then to ask behind them to God, on the understanding that the order of being and the order of knowing are not simply identical? Has not Barth in principle conceded this to Schleiermacher?

– If the **biblical message** is beyond question the decisive criterion of any talk of God for Christians, why should any talk of God be dependent on the Bible?

– And finally, if the **negative statements of the Bible** about the error, darkness, lie, sin of the non-Christian world are taken seriously as an invitation to conversion, why should one keep silent about, suppress or obscure the fact that the God of the Bible – also according to the testimony of the New Testament – is the God of all people and as such is near to all people, so that even non-Christians (already according to the testimony of Romans and even more so according to the testimony of Acts) can recognize the real God?

Confronted with these and similar questions, a long time ago now Karl Barth referred me to the **third volume** of his **Doctrine of Reconciliation**, then in preparation, where he discusses Jesus the light of the world. And indeed subsequently all too little note was taken of the fact that in the last completed volume of the *Church Dogmatics* (1959) there are **new theological accents**. Granted, here the old Karl Barth returns to his first and repeated harsh exclusivist thesis: Jesus Christ is 'the one, the only, light of life'. However, then (granted, with many dogmatic cautions and without open *retractationes*, as in Augustine) he concedes that now finally alongside the one light Jesus Christ there are also **'other lights'**; there are also 'other true words' alongside the one Word.[25] Granted, contrary to all empirical evidence Barth wants dogmatically to maintain that the other lights are only reflections of the one light of Jesus Christ (is the Buddha only a reflection, which only shines in the light of Jesus Christ?). Nevertheless, it is evident that in Barth's late theology a revaluation of knowledge of God from the world of creation and natural theology is in the making, a revaluation also of philosophy and human experience generally, indeed in an indirect and concealed way also a revaluation of natural law, natural religion, indeed the world religions, all of which – including the religions of grace and faith of the Indian Bhakti and Japanese Amida Buddhism[26] – Karl Barth had formerly just disqualified as forms of unbelief, indeed of idolatry and righteousness by works.[27] This revaluation also underlies the questions of the old Karl Barth to Friedrich Schleiermacher, which significantly remain 'open'.[28]

All this means that in the end the *Church Dogmatics*, which after the completion of the paradigm shift from modernity to postmodernity reached back in a second phase behind modernity (back past modern criticism to Protestant orthodoxy, scholasticism and patristics) and involuntarily led to a kind of neo-orthodoxy, that in the end this **dogmatic edifice** conceived on such a large scale, stringently constructed and carefully built, had at least in principle (though most Barthians hardly noticed) been **blown up**! Barth's 'positivism of revelation' which Dietrich Bonhoeffer criticized in his letters from a Nazi prison had fundamentally been robbed of its basis.

That may have demonstrated clearly that Karl Barth, who already at the beginning of the 1920s, after the completely revised *Epistle to the Romans*, and then again at the beginning of the 1930s, after rejecting and then completely revising the first volume of the *Dogmatics*, had said that he could and wanted to say the same thing as before but now he could no longer say it as he had once said it – this Barth, I am convinced, would say the same thing again if in the 1980s and 1990s he could return to the barricades as a young man. As he said then: 'What option had I but to begin at the beginning, saying the same thing, but in a very different way?'[29] So he might perhaps do what **Paul Tillich** also emphasized in his last lecture before his death as something greatly to be desired: he would attempt to work out a Christian theology in the context of the world religions and the world regions.[30]

Towards the end of his life – now emphasizing more the humanity of God than his divinity – Karl Barth was reconciled with his old sparring partner **Emil Brunner**, a man with whom he had broken quite unnecessarily, simply because Brunner thought that he had to speak of a 'point of contact' in human beings for God's grace (*No!*[31] was the title of Barth's work against Brunner's *Nature and Grace*,[32] published in 1934). The question is certainly not an idle one. Would not perhaps the same Karl Barth today, a rejuvenated Karl Barth, even have been reconciled with his great opponent Rudolf Bultmann, since his earlier programmatic attempt at understanding, *Rudolf Bultmann: An Attempt to Understand Him*,[33] had completely failed? Might he have become reconciled with the Bultmann who on the one hand affirmed his basic theological intentions (God as God, God's Word, proclamation and human faith) but on the other hand did not simply want to give up the important concerns of liberal theology; who therefore wanted to hold on unconditionally to the historical-critical method in exegesis and the need for demythologizing and an interpretation of scripture orientated on human understanding?

10. The abiding challenge of Rudolf Bultmann

No, today there can be no question of going over from Barth to Bultmann or conversely replacing Barth with Bultmann. That is quite wrong: both great Protestant theologians must be taken with the utmost seriousness in their own way; each has his strengths and weaknesses. And Karl Barth saw **Bultmann's weakness** clearly from that day, probably as early as 1929 in Göttingen, when Bultmann read out to him the lectures of Martin Heidegger which he had heard in Marburg and written down, to the effect that theology now had to move in an existentialist direction and also to deal with the gospel documented in the New Testament in this light. Barth did not criticize the view that scripture was to be interpreted in an 'existential' way, in terms of human existence; he did that himself in his own fashion. But he did criticize the fact that Bultmann, fettered to the early Heidegger, prescribed an **existentialist reduction** and (a criticism that Bultmann's distinguished pupil Ernst Käsemann also made):[34]
– that he bracketted out the cosmos, nature, the environment in favour of human existence;
– that he reduced real world history to human historicity, and the authentic future to human futuricity;
– that he neglected concrete society and the political dimension in his theology of being-in-the-world.

Conversely, at a very early stage Bultmann saw and noted **Barth's weaknesses:**
– that Barth liked to avoid discussions of hermeneutics, in order to go on working 'as thetically as possible';
– that after his shift to Protestant orthodoxy and to Anselm in 1930, Barth even refused to deliver a lecture on the burning topic of natural theology which he had promised to give to the 'old Marburgers', to the great annoyance and disgust of his friend

Bultmann, and thus dropped the long-expected discussion of the difference which had grown up between them in the meantime.

– that Barth argued increasingly resolutely that he could practise a 'theological exegesis', without denying historical-critical exegesis, but also without seriously bothering about it;

– that Barth also largely dropped the critical history of dogma in favour of a principle of tradition which in fact tied Christians for all times to the Hellenistic conceptualization of the relationship between Father, Son and Holy Spirit (although when he wanted to, he was capable of making conceptual corrections to the classical doctrine of the Trinity – 'mode of being' instead of 'person');

– that finally Barth, contrary to his intentions, in the Dogmatics which were so emphatically 'Church' Dogmatics, with the help of the church tradition had brought about a **conservative restructuring of pre-modern dogmatics**, large parts of which were not backed up by exegesis; in its tie to a 'past world-view' and lack of relevance to experience, this could hardly succeed in 'making the Christian proclamation so comprehensible to people today that they become aware that *tua res agitur* (it's your concern)'.[35]

So it is not wrong for writers today to speak of 'an excessive concern for a foundation' in Barth's theology, as Eberhard Jüngel does, or of a questionable 'dogmatic over-complexity' which endangers the original intent, as Karl-Josef Kuschel does.[36] Indeed in the face of the provocation of modern exegesis and the history of dogma, Karl Barth at that time (like the Swiss army in the Second World War) shut himself up in the Alpine redoubt of the orthodox dogmatics of the sixteenth/seventeenth or fourth/fifth centuries and with such a defensive strategy was prepared, for the sake of the freedom and independence of God from all human experience, if need be even to surrender the most fertile parts of the land. And how would things be today? I think that if Barth, by a miracle rejuvenated, wanted to complete in postmodern terms a theology which had begun in postmodern terms, he would not be Karl Barth if he did not once again begin from the beginning and from the regained centre and, with better strategical and hermeneutical safeguards, attempt to advance all over again.

In other words – without all this military poetry: once again he would begin from the beginning much more radically and say the same thing again quite differently. He would start from the evidence of the Bible as gained from historical criticism – not only in respect of purgatory and marian and papal dogmas, for which he criticized the Catholics harshly, but also in respect of original sin, hell and the devil, indeed in respect of christology and the Trinity; in a word, he would have attempted to work out a **responsible historical-critical dogmatics** in the light of an **exegesis with a historical-critical foundation,** in order in this way to translate the original Christian message (in accordance with Bultmann's demand, but without Bultmann's existentialist narrowing) for the future that had dawned in such a way that it was again understood as a liberating address from God. He would again speak of God in relation to human beings, even of that 'theanthropology' which the old Barth had in his sights, the Barth who in his youth had denounced anthropology as the mystery of modern theology – so applauded by Feuerbach. And here the 'historical Jesus', without whom, according to Ernst Käsemann, the 'Christ of dogma' becomes a myth that can be manipulated at will,[37] might, it seems to me, again become of the utmost importance and urgency – quite differently from his role in Barth and Bultmann – for example in respect of true human liberation in individual life, in society and in the church.

No, there is no going back: either to Schleiermacher or to Luther, to Thomas or to Augustine or to Origen. Rather, with Origen, Augustine and Thomas, with Luther and Schleiermacher, the way must be forwards, with Barth's intrepidity and resolution, concentration and consistency.

11. Towards a critical and sympathetic re-reading against the postmodern horizon

'We have no awareness of our own relativity,' Barth once critically remarked,[38] and he could say of his own work: 'I do not understand the *Church Dogmatics* as the conclusion but as the opening of a new joint discussion.'[39] Today, of course, this discussion, under changed theological and social conditions, would have to involve a **critical-sympathetic re-reading** of the *Church Dogmatics*. Such a re-reading against the post-modern horizon, for all its criticism, would have to bring the great themes and the tremendous fullness of this theology constructively into the present and treat it again in the context of the religions and regions of the world. Truly, what overflowing riches there are in this theology, in its doctrine of God, creation and reconciliation, a theology which sought to be neither Reformation nor Lutheran theology, but ecumenical theology, and the more ecumenical the more it went on! What systematic power and depth there is in the quite independent and original penetration of central theological topics like the dialectic of the divine properties, the connection between creation and covenant, time and eternity, Israel and the church, christology and anthropology, taken further in concrete terms in an ethic of freedom before God, in community, for life, within restrictions. Radical liberation theology before any theology of liberation!

And at the same time, for all its overflowing complexity, for all the wealth of material which cannot be tamed (9185 pages in the German edition of the *Church Dogmatics* alone), this theology never lost its centre. What Karl Barth could write about the 'great free objectivity' of Wolfgang Amadeus Mozart, the one musician whom he loved, here too in an inclusive way, he could have said, did say, about himself. His portraits of Mozart, both in the Church Dogmatics[40] and in his brief 1956 work on Mozart,[41] are also something like self-portraits of his theology in a nutshell. What he heard in this music he also wanted to resound in his theology. Mozart's music, he said, was 'free in a quite unusual way... free of all exaggerations, of all fundamental breaks and clashes. The sun shines, but it does not blind, consume or burn. The heaven spans the earth, but it is no burden on it, does not oppress it or swallow it up. So the earth is and remains the earth, without having to assert itself in a titanic revolt against heaven. Darkness, chaos, death and hell can be seen, but they may not for a moment gain the upper hand. Mozart makes music, knowing everything, from a mysterious centre, and so he knows and preserves the limits to right and to left, upwards and downwards... There is no light which does not also know darkness, no joy which does not also include sorrow, but conversely, there is no terror, no anger, no lament which does not have peace at a greater or lesser distance from it. So there is no laughing without weeping, but also no weeping without laughing.'[42]

Indeed, Barth's theology also comes from this **mysterious centre**, which for him was the God who shows his **gracious concern for men and women in Jesus Christ**. And because the God made visible in the crucified and risen Jesus was the centre, this theology, too, can preserve the limits, can let God be God and human beings be human beings; this theology, too, knows the darkness, the evil, the negative, the nothingness in the world, and yet at the same time is written in the great trust that the good and merciful God will keep the last word for himself. Indeed, in the theology of Karl Barth more breaks through than the demonic and tragic in the world; it too, like Mozart's music, avoids extremes, knows 'the wise confrontation and mixing of the elements', so that every No continues to be borne up by a great Yes. Those who hear this music, indeed who study this theology, 'may understand themselves to be subject to death and yet still alive, as we all are, and feel themselves called to freedom'.[43]

Epilogue

Guidelines for a Contemporary Theology

Paul, Origen, Augustine, Thomas, Luther, Schleiermacher, Barth: what each reader has learned from these great Christian thinkers, their strengths and weaknesses, their insights and limitations, will be different. I myself have learned most from studying their persons and their work. But I do not want to end by attempting a résumé, nor can I: any comprehensive comparison would be too complex. So there will now be no artificial closing septet of all too different voices, but simply a short epilogue – in academic prose: guidelines for a contemporary theology.

If one has been preoccupied all one's life with these great Christian thinkers (and with others too); if one has attempted constantly to learn something new from all of them and yet not drop any of them, the question arises: **what theology** is desirable today, what theology should one do today? I shall limit myself to three perspectives – the ethos, style and programme of theology – which have become important for my own theologizing over the course of the decades.[1]

First, it seems to me that the **ethos** of all theologizing today needs to be:

– a theology which is not opportunist and conformist but **truthful**: a thoughtful account of faith which investigates and speaks the Christian truth in truthfulness;

– a theology which is not authoritarian but **free**; a theology which pursues its task without hindrance from administrative measures and sanctions on the part of the church authorities and which expresses and publishes its well-founded convictions to the best of its knowledge and conscience;

– a theology which is not traditionalist but **critical**; a theology which knows that it is freely and truthfully obligated to the scientific ethos of truth, the methodology of the discipline and a critical examination of all its problems, methods and results;

– a theology which is not confessionalist but **ecumenical;** a theology in which each theology sees the other no longer as an opponent but as a partner, and which is concerned for understanding rather than separation – in two directions: **inwards,** for the sphere of ecumenism within Christianity and between the churches; and **outwards,** for the sphere of the world ecumene outside the churches and outside Christianity, with its different regions, religions, ideologies and sciences.

As for the **style** of theologizing, the following 'ten commandments' should apply in our time:

– No secret science for those who already believe, but **comprehensibility** also for non-believers.

– No premium on 'simple' faith or defence of a 'church' system, but uncompromising concern for the truth in a strictly **scientific approach.**

– Ideological opponents should neither be ignored nor branded as heretics, not theologically commandeered, but interpreted in the best light **in critical sympathy** and at the same time exposed to fair, relevant discussion.

– **Interdisciplinary** work is not only to be called for but to be practised: dialogue with the other sciences involved and concentration on one's own cause belong together.

– There should be no hostile opposition, nor any *laissez-faire* co-existence either, but a **togetherness in critical dialogue,** especially between theology and philosophy, theology and the sciences and humanities, and theology and literature: religion and rationality belong together, but so do religion and poetry.

– Problems of the past should not have priority, but rather the wide-ranging and complex **problems** of human beings and human society **today.**

– The norm of a Christian theology which governs all other norms cannot again be any church or theological tradition or institution, but only the gospel, the **original Christian message** itself: theology orientated on the gospel, but understood historically and critically.

– There should be no talk either in biblical archaisms and Hellenistic scholastic dogmatisms or in fashionable and theological jargon, but as far as possible in **language which can easily be understood** by modern men and women; no effort is to be spared to achieve this.

– Credible **theory** and **praxis** that can be lived out, dogmatics and ethics, personal piety and reform of the institutions, liberation in society and liberation in the church cannot be separated; rather, note must be taken of the unbreakable connection between them.

– There must be no confessionalistic ghetto mentality, but **ecumenical breadth** which takes account both of the world religions and the modern ideologies: the greatest possible tolerance of those outside the churches, of the universally religious, of the *humanum* generally on the one hand, and working out what is specifically Christian on the other, belong together.

Finally, the **programme** of a theology, a **critical ecumenical theology.** Such a theology must sustain the tensions in every new age and again **at the same time** (here, regardless of the Reformation 'alone', an 'and' is called for!) at the same time attempt to be:

– **catholic,** constantly concerned for the whole, universal church;
– and at the same time **evangelical,** strictly related to scripture, to the gospel;
– **traditional,** constantly responsible to history - **and** at the same time **contemporary,** taking up the relevant questions of the present;
– **christocentric,** resolutely and distinctly Christian;
– and at the same time **ecumenical,** orientated on the ecumene, the whole inhabited earth, all Christian churches, all religions, all regions;
– **theoretical and scientific,** concerned with doctrine, with the truth – and at the same time **practical and pastoral,** concerned with life, renewal and reform.

But enough of programmatic words! Does this programme for a contemporary theology have any prospect of being realized? Am I not perhaps the voice of one crying in the wilderness of a sometimes boring, confessionally narrow and inward-looking blind theology of the present, which seems to sense little of the breath of our seven great Christian thinkers? It is for others to judge that. But I know that I am at one with many people, not least my two Tübingen colleagues and friends, Eberhard Jüngel and Jürgen Moltmann, to whom I have dedicated this book, in criticism of a sterile, bloodless science fixated only upon itself, at one also in the ideal of a theology which is obligated to the spirit of ecumenism and the critical audience of our time.

In the more than forty years during which I have dared to do theology I have attempted to keep to the guidelines that developed over time from the process of my research and teaching which I have set out in this theological programme. And if at the age of sixty-six one is more markedly aware than previously of how limited the time remaining is, one would want at least to express the hope that younger theologians will take forward this programme critically and creatively. So *'vivant sequentes'*, 'Long live those who are to come!'

Bibliography and Notes

Literature on Paul

The basis for this chapter is H.Küng, *Judaism* (1991), London and New York 1992, 2 B, V.1-2, 'The Controversial Paul. The Sympathetic Transformation'. For research into Paul see the early important articles by R.Bultmann, K.Holl, H.Lietzmann, A.Oepke, A.Reitzenstein, A.Schlatter, A.Schweitzer, collected by K.H.Rengstorf, *Das Paulusbild in der neueren deutschen Forschung*, Darmstadt 1964. For an orientation on scholarly research, which is almost beyond surveying, cf. the account by B.Rigaux, *St Paul et ses lettres. État de la question*, Paris 1962; H.Hübner, 'Paulusforschung seit 1945. Ein kritischer Literaturbericht', in *Aufstieg und Niedergang der Römischen Welt. Geschichte und Kultur Roms im Spiegel der neueren Forschung*, ed. W.Haase and H.Temporini, II.25.4, Berlin 1987, 2649-840 (this also includes extended articles on the latest state of the interpretation of individual letters of Paul); O.Merk, 'Paulusforschung 1936-1985', *Theologische Rundschau* 53, 1988, 1-81. For an introduction to the person and work of the apostle Paul, in addition to the introductions to the New Testament, see among more recent critical works especially M.Dibelius, *Paul*, ed. W.G.Kümmel, London 1953; P.Seidensticker, *Paulus, der verfolgte Apostel Jesus Christi*, Stuttgart 1965; G.Bornkamm, *Paul* (1969), London and New York 1975; E.Käsemann, *Perspectives on Paul* (1969), London and Philadelphia 1971; O.Kuss, *Paulus. Die Rolle des Apostels in der theologischen Entwicklung der Urkirche*, Regensburg 1971; K.Stendahl, *Paul among Jews and Gentiles*, Philadelphia 1976; F.F.Bruce, *Paul, Apostle of the Free Spirit*, Exeter 1977; E.P.Sanders, *Paul and Palestinian Judaism*, London and Philadelphia 1977; id., *Paul, The Law and the Jewish People*, London and Philadelphia 1983; id., *Paul*, Oxford 1991; J.C.Beker, *Paul the Apostle. The Triumph of God in Life and Thought*, Edinburgh 1980; K.H.Schelkle, *Paulus. Leben – Briefe – Theologie*, Darmstadt 1981; G.Lüdemann, *Paul: Apostle to the Gentiles* (1980), London and Philadelphia 1984; id., *Opposition to Paul in Jewish Christianity* (1983), Minneapolis

1989; W.A.Meeks, *The First Urban Christians. The Social World of the Apostle Paul*, New Haven 1983; H.Räisänen, *Paul and the Law*, Tübingen 1983; G.Theissen, *Psychological Aspects of Pauline Theology* (1983), Edinburgh 1987; F.Watson, *Paul, Judaism and the Gentiles. A Sociological Approach*, Cambridge 1986. For Paul from the Jewish side and in Jewish-Christian dialogue, from the more recent literature see S.Sandmel, *The Genius of Paul. A Study in History*, New York 1958; H.-J.Schoeps, *Paul. The Theology of the Apostle in the Light of Jewish Religious History* (1959), London 1961; S.Ben-Chorin, *Paulus. Der Völkerapostel in jüdischer Sicht*, Munich 1970; M.Barth et al., *Paulus. Apostat oder Apostel? Jüdische und christliche Antworten*, Regensburg 1977; F.Mussner, *Tractate on the Jews* (1979), Philadelphia 1984; P.Lapide and P.Stuhlmacher, *Paulus – Rabbi und Apostel. Ein jüdisch-christlicher Dialog*, Stuttgart 1981; P. von der Osten Sacken, *Grundzüge einer Theologie im christlich-jüdischen Gespräch*, Munich 1982; id. *Evangelium und Tora. Aufsätze zu Paulus*, Munich 1987; F.W.Marquardt, *Die Gegenwart des Auferstandenen bei seinem Volk Israel. Ein dogmatisches Experiment*, Munich 1983; E.Biser et al., *Paulus – Wegbereiter des Christentums. Zur Aktualität des Völkerapostels in ökumenischer Sicht*, Munich 1984; L.Swidler – L.J.Eron – G.Sloyan – L.Dean, *Bursting the Bonds? A Jewish-Christian Dialogue on Jesus and Paul*, New York 1990; A.F.Segal, *Paul the Convert. The Apostolate and Apostasy of Saul the Pharisee*, New Haven 1990.

Notes on Paul

1. F.Nietzsche, *The Antichrist*, Complete Works, Vol. 6, London 1911, 178.
2. Ibid., 184.
3. Acts 8.3.
4. Phil.3.5f.
5. Cf. Acts 22.25-29.
6. Cf. Phil.3.5f.
7. Cf. Gal.1.13, 23; I Cor.15.9; Phil.3.6.
8. Cf. Gal.1.13f.
9. Cf. I Cor.1.17-31; Gal.3.1-14.
10. Cf. Acts 9.3-9.
11. Cf. I Cor.9.1; 15.8-10; Gal.1.15f.; Phil.3.7-11.
12. II Cor 11.23-26.

13. For belief in the resurrection see H.Küng, *Credo*, ch.IV.

14. Cf. Rom.15.9.

15. Not only the central message (the kerygma) of the crucifixion and resurrection (I Cor.15.3-8) but also the tradition of the Last Supper (I Cor.11.23-25), attitudes to marriage and divorce (I Cor.7.10f.), the instruction to provide the preacher's wherewithal to live (I Cor.9.14), the pre-eminent position of the commandment to love (I Thess.4.9; Gal.5.13; Rom.13.8-10; I Cor.13); and finally also the Davidic descent of Jesus (Rom.1.3), Christ according to the flesh from Israel (Rom.9.5), being a son of Abraham (Gal.3; Rom.4), human birth and subordination under the law (Gal.4.4), being human, humbling himself, being obedient to death (Phil.2.6-8), weakness (II Cor.13.4), poverty (II Cor.8.9), the passion (I Cor.11.23). I Cor.4.12; 13.2 and Rom.16.19 can also be added.

16. Cf. I Cor.3.11.

17. Phil.2.21: 'For all seek their own advantage and not the things of Jesus Christ.' Cf. I Cor.7.32-34, 'The things of the Lord'.

18. E.Käsemann, 'Wo sich die Wege trennen', *Deutsches Allgemeines Sonntagsblatt*, 13 April 1990.

19. S.Ben-Chorin, *Paulus. Der Völkerapostel in jüdischer Sicht*, Munich 1970, 11.

20. Ibid., 57.

21. Rom.7.12.

22. Rom.7.10; cf. 10.5; Gal.3.12.

23. Rom.2.20.

24. Rom.7.14.

25. Rom.9.4.

26. The complex problem of the law in Paul is discussed in detail and at length in H.Küng, *Judaism*, Part Three, Chapter B III, 'For the Sake of Human Beings'.

27. Rom.3.27.

28. Rom.3.31.

29. Rom.3.20; cf. Gal.3.10.

30. II Cor.3.7, 9.

31. II Cor.3.6.

32. Gal.5.1.

33. Gal.5.13.

34. Gal.2.4.

35. Rom.6.14; cf. 7.5f.

36. Cf. II Cor.3.6.

37. Cf. Gal.2; Acts 15.1-34.

38. Gal.2.11.

39. Cf. Mark 7.8; 7.4.
40. Cf. Mark 7.1-23.
41. I Cor.8.9.
42. Cf. I Cor.9.19; Gal.5.13.
43. I Cor.7.23.
44. Gal.5.13f.; cf. I Cor.13.1-13.
45. I Cor.11.7.
46. Cf. I Cor.7.1-7.
47. I Cor.14.34; the insertion extends from 14.33b to 14.36.
48. Rom.16.7.
49. Cf. Rom.16.1-2.
50. Cf. Rom.13.1-7.
51. Cf.Rom.14.1-23.
52. Rom.12.2; cf. Phil.1.10.
53. I Cor.6.12.
54. Ibid.
55. Rom.14.14; cf. Titus 1.15, 'To the pure all is pure'.
56. I Cor.6.12.
57. I Cor 10.23f.
58. I Cor.9.19.
59. I Cor.10.29.
60. Cf. I Cor.8.7-12; 10.25-30.
61. Cf. Ex.4.22.
62. Cf. Rom.9.3.
63. Cf. Rom.9.4f.
64. Cf. Rom.9.2.
65. Cf. Gal.2.14.
66. It is to the lasting credit of E.Käsemann, 'Ministry and Community in the New Testament', in *Essays on New Testament Themes*, London and Philadelphia 1964, 63-94, that he has brought to light again the significance of the charisma in criticism of the church in the twentieth century.
67. I Cor.12.3.
68. Phil.3.12-14.

Literature on Origen

The earlier literature can be found in B.Altaner, *Patrology*, London 1960, §55. Cf. also A.von Harnack, *Der kirchengeschichtliche Ertrag der exegetischen Arbeiten des Origenes*, Teil I-II, Leipzig 1918/19; id., *Geschichte der altchristlichen Literatur bis Eusebius*, second enlarged edition, Leipzig 1958, I/1, 332-405; II/2, 26-54; J.Daniélou, *Origen*, London and New York 1955; H.de Lubac, *Histoire et Esprit. L'intelligence de l'Écriture d'après Origène*, Paris 1950; id., *Recherches dans la foi. Trois études sur Origène, Saint Anselme et la philosophie chrétienne*, Paris 1979; H.von Campenhausen, *The Fathers of the Greek Church*, London 1963; H.Crouzel, *Théologie de l'Image de Dieu chez Origène*, Paris 1956; id., *Origène et la 'Connaissance mystique'*, Paris 1961; id., *Origène et la philosophie*, Paris 1962; id., *Origène*, Paris 1985; M.Harl, *Origène et la fonction révélatrice du Verbe incarné*, Paris 1958; H.Kerr, *The First Systematic Theologian. Origen of Alexandria*, Princeton, NJ 1958; R.P.C.Hanson, *Allegory and Event. A Study of the Sources and Significance of Origen's Interpretation of Scripture*, London 1959; P.Nemeshegyi, *La Paternité de Dieu chez Origène*, Tournai 1960; W.Jaeger, *Early Christianity and Greek Paideia*, Cambridge, Mass. 1961; G.Gruber, *ZOE. Wesen, Stufung und Mitteilung des wahren Lebens bei Origenes*, Düsseldorf 1963; H.Chadwick, *Early Christian Thought and the Classical Tradition. Studies in Justin, Clement and Origen*, Oxford 1966; J.Rius-Camps, *El dinamismo trinitario en la divinización de los seres racionales según Origenes*, Rome 1970; P.Kübel, *Schuld und Schicksal bei Origenes, Gnostikern und Platonikern*, Stuttgart 1973; W.Gessel, *Die Theologie des Gebetes nach 'De Oratione' von Origenes*, Paderborn 1975; P.Nautin, *Origène. Sa vie et son oeuvre*, Paris 1977; L.Lies, *Wort und Eucharistie bei Origenes. Zur Spiritualisierungstendenz des Eucharistieverständnisses*, Innsbruck 1978; id., *Origenes' Eucharistielehre im Streit der Konfessionen. Die Auslegungsgeschichte seit der Reformation*, Innsbruck 1985; U.Berner, *Origenes*, Darmstadt 1981.

Notes on Origen

1. H.Chadwick, *The Early Church*, Harmondsworth 1967, 75.
2. H.U.von Balthasar, *Origenes. Geist und Feuer. Ein Aufbau aus seiner Schriften*, Salzburg 1938, 11.
3. Cf. Eusebius, *Church History*, VI.
4. Cf. Nautin, *Origène*.
5. Cf. above all Clement of Alexandria, *Protreptikos* = Admonition to the Greeks.
6. Cf. von Campenhausen, *Fathers of the Greek Church*.
7. Cf. Matt.19.12.

8. C.Kannengiesser, 'Origen, Augustine and Paradigm Changes in Theology', in *Paradigm Change in Theology*, ed. H.Küng and D.Tracy, Edinburgh 1989, 113-29: 126.

9. Cf. Origen, *De principiis*, Preface.

10. H.Görgemanns and H.Karpp, *Origenes, Vier Bücher von der Prinzipien*, 17.

11. Origen, *De principiis*, Preface, 10.

12. Cf. id., *Contra Celsum*, V.39; *De Principiis*, I, 2, 13.

13. Cf. I Cor.15.27f.

14. Origen, *Contra Celsum*, III.28.

15. Cf. id., *De principiis*, IV.2,4-6.

16. Thus rightly (against K.L.Schmidt), A.A.T.Ehrhardt, *Politische Metaphysik von Solon bis Augustin*, II, *Die christliche Revolution*, Tübingen 1959, 204-26.

17. Kannengiesser, 'Origen, Augustine and Paradigm Changes' (n.8), 123.

18. Harnack, *History of Dogma* II, London 1900 reissued New York 1961, 380.

19. Cf. Acts 2.14-40.

20. Rom.1.3f.

21. Ignatius of Antioch, *To the Magnesians*, VI.1.

22. Id., *To the Ephesians*, VII.2.

Literature on Augustine

The earlier literature can be found in B.Altaner, *Patrology*, London 1960, §102. In addition to earlier handbooks of dogma (A. von Harnack, F.Loofs, R.Seeberg) which are still important, and more recent ones (C.Andresen, K.Beyschlag, J.Pelikan, M.Schmaus, A.Grillmeier), see the following more recent monographs and general accounts: É.Gilson, *Introduction à l'étude de saint Augustin*, Paris 1929, [4]1969; H.I.Marrou, *Saint Augustin et la fin de la culture antique*, Paris 1938, [4]1958; id., *Saint Augustin et l'Augustinisme*, Paris 1955, [8]1973; F.van der Meer, *Augustinus de Zielzorger*, Utrecht 1947; A.Zumkeller, *Das Mönchtum des heiligen Augustinus*, Würzburg 1950, [2]1968; T.J.van Bavel, *Recherches sur la christologie de saint Augustin. L'humain et le divin dans le Christ d'après saint Augustin*, Fribourg 1954; J.J.O'Meara, *The Young Augustine. The Growth of St Augustine's Mind up to his Conversion*, London 1954, [2]1980; R.W.Battenhouse (ed.), *A Companion to the Study of St*

Augustine, New York 1955; M.Löhrer, *Der Glaubensbegriff des hl.Augustinus in seinen ersten Schriften bis zu den* Confessiones, Einsiedeln 1955; A.D.R.Polman, *Het woord gods bij Augustinus*, Kampen 1955; R.Schneider, *Seele und Sein. Ontologie bei Augustin und Aristoteles*, Stuttgart 1957; G.Strauss, *Schriftgebrauch, Schrift-auslegung und Schriftbeweis bei Augustin*, Tübingen 1959; H.von Campenhausen, *The Fathers of the Latin Church*, London 1964, ch.6; C.Eichenseer, *Das Symbolum Apostolicum beim heiligen Augustinus, mit Berücksichtigung des dogmengeschichtlichen Zusammenhangs*, St Ottilien 1960: C.Andresen (ed.), *Zum Augustin-Gespräch der Gegenwart*, I-II, Darmstadt 1962/81; P.Brown, *Augustine of Hippo. A Biography*, Berkeley and London 1967; A.Mandouze, *Saint Augustin. L'aventure de la raison et de la grâce*, Paris 1968; C.Boyer, *Essais anciens et nouveaux sur la doctrine de saint Augustin*, Milan 1970; R.A.Markus, *Saeculum. History and Society in the Theology of St Augustine*, Cambridge 1970; E.Te Selle, *Augustine the Theologian*, London 1970; J.Brechtken, *Augustinus doctor caritatis. Sein Liebes-begriff im Widerspruch von Eigennutz und selbstlose Güte im Rahmen der antiken Glückseligkeits-Ethik*, Meisenheim 1975; W.Geerlings, *Christus Exemplum. Studien zur Christologie und Christusverkündigung Augustins*, Mainz 1978; W.Wieland, *Offen-barung bei Augustinus*, Mainz 1978; A.Schindler, 'Augustin', *Theolo-gische Realenzyklopädie* IV, Berlin 1979, 645-98; H.Fries, 'Augustinus', in H.Fries and G.Kretschmar (ed.), *Klassike der Theolo-gie* I, Munich 1981, 104-29.

Notes on Augustine

1. von Campenhausen, *Fathers of the Latin Church*, 183, 185.

2. Augustine, *Confessions* I.1 (1).

3. Marrou, *Saint Augustin et la fin de la culture antique*, 489-5 (for further details); the quotation comes from p.495.

4. Cf. Augustine, *Confessions* VIII, XII (28ff.).

5. Rom.13.13f.

6. Marrou, *Saint Augustin et l'Augustinisme*.

7. Augustine, *Contra epistolam Manichaei* 5 (6).

8. Id., *Sermo* 112.8.

9. Brown, *Augustine of Hippo*, 235.

10. Ibid., 240.

11. Augustine, *Confessions* X, XXXI (45).

12. Cf. id., *Sermo* 131, 10.

13. Id., *Opus imperfectum contra Julianum* II.22.

14. Cf. id., *Sermo* 151: *Contra Julianum Pelagianum*, above all book IV.

15. Cf. Augustine, *Ep.* 217 v.16; *Enchiridion* XXIII, XXIX.

16. I Cor. 4.7.

17. Augustine, *In primam epistolam Ioannis* VII, 8.

18. Cf. K.E.Børresen, *Subordination et Equivalence. Nature et rôle de la femme d'après Augustin et Thomas d'Aquin*, Oslo 1968, esp.I. 1-3.

19. Quoted in P.Brown, *The Body and Society. Men, Women and Sexual Renunciation in Early Christianity*, New York and London 1988, 424 (which is a good study of Augustine and sexuality before and after his conversion).

20. Cf. Rom.9-11.

21. Marrou, *Saint Augustin et l'Augustinisme*.

22. Augustine, *De civitate Dei* I, Preface.

23. Ibid., XXII, 30.

Literature on Thomas Aquinas

Recent literature is based on the careful researches of Neo-Thomists like J.Berthier, P.Castagnoli, H.Denifle, F.Ehrle, M.Grabmann, P.Mandonnet and A.Walz. The best historical introduction to Thomas's work is still that of M.-D.Chenu, *Introduction a l'étude de saint Thomas d'Aquin*, Paris 1950; cf. also id., *Saint Thomas d'Aquin et la théologie*, Paris 1959. The American J.A.Weisheipl's *Friar Thomas d'Aquino. His Life, Thought and Works*, New York 1974, is a thorough critical biography based on the most recent historical research. The German theologian and former Dominican O.H.Pesch has produced the most illuminating recent theological introduction against today's horizon: *Thomas von Aquin. Grenze und Grösse mittelalterlicher Theologie. Eine Einführung*, Mainz 1988, ²1989. For further important recent literature cf. J.Pieper, *Hinführung zu Thomas von Aquin. Zwölf Vorlesungen*, Munich 1958; S.Pfürtner, *Luther und Thomas im Gespräch. Unser Heil zwischen Gewissheit und Gefährdung*, Heidelberg 1961; J.B.Metz, *Christliche Anthropozentrik. Über die Denkform des Thomas von Aquin*, Munich 1962; M.Seckler, *Das Heil in der Geschichte. Geschichtstheologisches Denken bei Thomas von Aquin*, Munich 1964; E.Gilson, *Le thomisme. Introduction à la philosophie de saint Thomas d'Aquin*, Paris

1965, ⁶1983; U.Kühn, *Via caritatis. Theologie des Gesetzes bei Thomas von Aquin*, Göttingen 1963; H.Vorster, *Das Freiheitsverständnis bei Thomas von Aquin und Martin Luther*, Göttingen 1965; L.Oeing-Hanhoff (ed.), *Thomas von Aquin 1274/1974*, Munich 1974; W.Mostert, *Menschwerdung. Eine historische und dogmatische Untersuchung über das Motiv der Incarnation des Gottesohnes bei Thomas von Aquin*, Tübingen 1978; E.Schillebeeckx, 'Der Kampf an verschiedenen Fronten: Thomas von Aquin', in H.Häring and K.J.Kuschel (ed.), *Gegenentwürfe. 24 Lebensläufe für eine andere Theologie*, Munich 1988, 53-67; A.Zimmermann (ed.), *Thomas von Aquin. Werk und Wirkung im Licht neueren Forschungen*, Berlin 1988.

Notes on Thomas Aquinas

1. H.Fries, 'Augustinus', in H.Fries and G.Kretschmar (eds.), *Klassiker der Theologie* I, Munich 1981, 126.

2. Thomas Aquinas, *Summa theologiae* II-II, q.188, a.7; cf.q.185, a6, ad I.

3. OT: commentaries on Isaiah, Jeremiah, Job, Psalms; NT: commentaries on the Gospels of Matthew and John and the Pauline epistles.

4. Thomas Aquinas, *Summa contra gentiles*, I.2.

5. Cf. id., *Summa theologiae* I, q.1-26.

6. Ibid., q.27-43.

7. Id., *Summa contra gentiles*, I.2.

8. Cf. Chenu, *Thomas d'Aquin*.

9. For the circumstances of this condemnation (above all for Thomas himself) cf. Schillebeeckx, 'Kampf', 58-67; Weisheipl, *Friar Thomas*, 302-18.

10. *Codex Iuris Canonici* (1917), canon 1366, 2.

11. Cf. Thomas Aquinas, *Summa theologiae* I-II, q.109-114.

12. Cf. ibid., q.113.

13. Cf. ibid., q.110 a.1; cf. q. 116.

14. Cf. N.M.Wildiers, *Wereldbeeld en teologie*, 1972.

15. Thomas Aquinas, *Summa theologiae* I, q. 92, a, 1-4.

16. Cf. ibid., II-II, q.177, a 2.

17. Ibid., I q.92, a.1.

18. Id., *Commentary on the Sentences*, IV d.25, q 2. qla, 1. ad 4.

19. Id., *Summa theologiae* I, Supplementum q.39, a.1.

20. Id., *Summa theologiae* II-II q.177, a.2.

21. Cf. id., *Contra errores Graecorum*, Pars II, cap 32-35.
22. Cf. ibid., cap.36.
23. Cf. Pesch, *Thomas von Aquin*, 26f.
24. Cf. ibid., 34.
25. Chenu, *Thomas d'Aquin*.
26. Cf. the report and commentary on the last phase of Thomas's life from 6 December 1273 to 7 March 1274 in Weisheipl, *Friar Thomas*, 293-302.
27. Thomas Aquinas, *De potentia*, q.7, a 5 ad decimumquartum.

Literature on Martin Luther

For Martin Luther and the Reformation in Germany, in addition to important earlier works (especially H.Grisar, R.Hermann, K.Holl, J.K.Köstlin and G.Kawerau, O.Scheel), see J.Lortz, *Die Reformation in Deutschland*, I-II, Freiburg 1940; E.H.Erikson, *Young Man Luther. A Study in Psychoanalysis and History*, London 1958; H.J.Iwand, *Gesammelte Aufsätze*, I-II, Munich 1959/80; F.Lau, *Luther*, Berlin 1959; M.Lienhard, *Martin Luther. Un temps, une vie, un message*, Paris 1959, ²1991; J.Delumeau, *Naissance et affirmation de la Réforme*, Paris 1965; E.W.Zeerden, *Die Entstehung der Konfessionen. Grundlagen und Formen der Konfessionsbildung im Zeitalter der Glaubenskämpfe*, Munich 1965; id., *Konfessionsbildung. Studien zur Reformation, Gegenreformation und katholischen Reform*, Stuttgart 1985; R.Friedenthal, *Luther. Sein Leben und seine Zeit*, Munich 1967; E.Iserloh, J.Glazik and H.Jedin, *Reformation. Katholische Reform und Gegenreformation*, Freiburg 1967; R.Stupperich, *Geschichte der Reformation*, Munich 1967; H.Bornkamm, *Luther. Gestalt und Wirkungen. Gesammelte Aufsätze*, Gütersloh 1975 (which contains extensive criticism of Erikson's thesis); id., *Martin Luther in der Mitte senes Lebens. Das Jahrzehnt zwischen dem Wormser und dem Augsburger Reichstag*, ed. K.Bornkamm, Göttingen 1979; P.Chaunu, *Le temps des Réformes. Histoire religieuse et système de civilisation. La Crise de la chrétienté. L'Eclairement (1250-1550)*, Paris 1975; id., *Eglise, culture et société. Essais sur Réforme et Contre-Réforme(1517-1620)*, Paris 1981; H.A.Oberman, *Werden und Wertung der Reformation. Vom Wegestreit zu Glaubenskampf*, Tübingen 1977; id., *Luther. Mensch zwischen Gott und Teufel*, Berlin 1981; id., *Die Reformation. Von Wittenberg nach Genf*, Göttingen 1986; H.Lutz, *Reformation und Gegenreformation*,

Munich 1979; R.H.Bainton, *Here I Stand. A Life of Luther,* New York 1950; E.Iserloh, *Geschichte und Theologie der Reformation im Grundriss,* Paderborn 1980; id., *Kirche – Ereignis und Institution. Aufsätze und Vorträge II: Geschichte und Theologie der Reformation im Grundriss,* Münster 1985; B.Lohse, *Martin Luther. Eine Einführung in sein Leben und sein Werk,* Munich 1981, ²1983; M.Brecht, *Martin Luther,* I-II, Stuttgart 1981-7; W.von Loewenich, *Martin Luther. Der Mann und das Werk,* Munich 1982; O.H.Pesch, *Hinführung zu Luther,* Mainz 1982; J.M.Todd, *Luther. A Life,* London 1982; H.Junghaus (ed.), *Leben und Werk Martin Luthers von 1526 bis 1546,* I-II, Berlin 1983; H.Löwe and C.J.Roepke (eds.), *Luther und die Folgen. Beiträge zur sozialgeschichtlichen Bedeutung der lutherischen Reformation,* Munich 1983; G.Vogler (ed.), *Martin Luther. Leben, Werk, Wirkung,* Berlin 1983: R.Schwarz, *Luther,* Göttingen 1986; for Luther's life I have followed this work by the distinguished Luther scholar, which sums up his earlier researches.

Notes on Martin Luther

1. This was worked out first in an unprejudiced way on the Catholic side by Lortz, *Reformation in Deutschland,* I, 1-144. There is a recent comprehensive account in Chaunu, *Le temps des Réformes,* esp. chs.IV-V.

2. For the discussion cf. Pesch, *Einführung,* Ch. V ('The Move towards Reformation').

3. Cf. H.Denifle, *Die abendländische Schriftausleger bis Luther über justitia Dei (R 1,17) und* Justificatio, Mainz 1905.

4. In the Roman Curia the contribution was estimated at the horrendous sum of 50,000 gold ducats. Half of this was to be sent to Rome by the Fuggers, who were acting as bankers, and the other half to the Margrave Albrecht of Brandenburg – at the age of twenty-three Archbishop of Magdeburg (and Halberstadt) and then also Archbishop of Mainz – so that the Margrave could repay to the Fuggers the loan raised to pay for a dispensation which would allow him, against the regulations imposed by Rome, to hold a plurality of offices, and to do so below the minimum age.

5. Cf. H.Volz, *Martin Luthers Thesenanschlag und dessen Vorgeschichte,* Weimar 1959; E.Iserloh, 'Luthers Thesenanschlag. Tatsache oder Legende?', *Trierer Theologische Zeitschrift* 70, 1961, 303-12, expanded version, *Luther zwischen Reform und Reformation. Der Thesenanschlag fand nicht statt,* Münster ³1968; id., 'Martin Luther und der Aufbruch der

Reformation (1517-1525)', in Iserloh, Glazik and Jedin, *Reformation*, 3-114, esp. 49f.

6. Thus the Catholic Reformation historian E.Iserloh, *Geschichte und Theologie der Reformation*, 33.

7. Cf. M.Luther, *Resolutiones disputationum de indulgentiarum virtute* (1518), English translation in Luther's Works: American Edition (henceforth cited as LW), Vol.31, 77-252.

8. Cf. id., 'A Sermon on Indulgences and Grace' (1517), in *D.Martin Luthers Werke. Kritische Gesamtausgabe* (= WA), I, 239-46.

9. Cf. H.Denziger (ed.), *Enchiridion symbolorum definitionum et declarationum de rebus fidei et morum* (1854), Freiburg [31] 1960, nos.741-781.

10. Cf. M.Luther, *Appellatio D.Martini Lutheri ad concilium a Leone X, denuo repetita et innovata* (1520), in WA VII, 74-82.

11. Cf. id., *Adversus execrabilem Anichristi bullam* (1520), LW 32, 5ff.

12. Cf. id., *On Good Works* (1520), LW 32, 106ff.

13. cf. id., 'To the Christian Nobility of the German Nation', LW 44, 123-217. Cf. id., 'On the Babylonian Captivity of the Church' (1520), LW 36, 11-126.

15. Cf. id., 'The Freedom of a Christian' (1520), LW 31, 333-77; also in *Martin Luther's Basic Theological Writings*, ed. T.F.Lull, Minneapolis 1989, 585-629.

16. *Basic Theological Writings*, 596.

17. Cf. the 'Colloquy with D.Martin Luther at the Reichstag at Worms', WA VII, 814-87, esp.838; the famous statement 'Here I stand, I can do no other' is not authentic.

18. Cf. S.Pfürtner, 'The Paradigms of Thomas Aquinas and Martin Luther. Did Luther's Message of Justification mean a Paradigm Change?', in H.Küng and D.Tracy (eds.), *Paradigm Change in Theology*, Edinburgh 1989, 130-160.

19. O.H.Pesch, 'Zwanzig Jahre katholische Lutherforschung', *Lutherische Rundschau* 16, 1966, 392-406, already pointed this out over against the Loretz school (and Jedin).

20. Cf. Hans Küng, *Justification*; id., 'Katholische Besinnung auf Luthers Rechfertigunslehre heute', in *Theologie im Wandel. Festschrift zum 150-jährigen Bestehen der Katholisch-Theologischen Fakultät an der Universität Tübingen 1817-1967*, Munich 1967, 449-68.

21. That the doctrine of justification is no longer something that divides the churches was first confirmed by the agreement between the Lutheran World Federation and the Roman Secretariat for Unity, *The Gospel and the Church* (Malta Report), 1972, in H.Meyer, H.J.Urban

and L.Vischer (eds.), *Dokumente wachsender Übereinstimmung. Sämtliche Berichte und Konsenstexte interkonfessioneller Gespräche auf Weltebene 1931-1982*, Paderborn 1983, 248-71, esp.nos.26-30.

22. Cf. M.Luther, *Against the Roman Papacy, an Institution of the Devil* (1545), LW 41, 263-376.

23. Cf. H.Küng, *Judaism* (1991), London and New York 1992, Ch.I C V 2, 'Luther, too, against the Jews'.

24. M.Luther, *The Freedom of a Christian, Basic Theological Writings*, 623.

25. *Colloquy with D.Martin Luther at the Reichstag of Worms* (Luther's plea summing up his speech), WA VII, 838.

26. M.Luther, *Table Talk*, LW 54, 476.

Literature on Friedrich Schleiermacher

For Friedrich Schleiermacher cf. W.Dilthey, *Leben Schleiermachers* I, Berlin 1870, [2]1922 (ed. H.Mulert); the work was revised, extended and republished under the editorship of M.Redeker in two half-volumes, Göttingen 1966/70, using material from Dilthey's literary estate; E.Hirsch, *Geschichte der neueren evangelischen Theologie* IV, 490-82; V, 281-364, Gütersloh 1949, [2]1960; id., *Schleiermachers Christusglaube. Drei Studien*, Gütersloh 1968; Karl Barth, *Protestant Theology in the Nineteenth Century* (1952), ET London [2]1972, 452-73; P.Seifert, *Die Theologie des jungen Schleiermacher*, Gütersloh 1960; T.Schulze, 'Stand und Probleme der erziehungswissenschaftlichen Schleiermacher-Forschung in Deutschland', in *Paedagogica Historica* I, 1961, 291-326; H.-J.Birkner, *Schleiermachers christlicher Sittenlehre im Zusammenhang seines philosophisch-theologischen Systems*, Berlin 1964; id., 'Theologie und Philosophie. Einführung in Friedrich Schleiermacher', in M.Greschat (ed.), *Gestalten der Kirchengeschichte* 9,1, Stuttgart 1985, 87-115; F.Hertel, *Das theologische Denken Schleiermachers untersucht an der ersten Auflage seiner Reden 'Über die Religion'*, Zurich 1965; F.W.Kantzenbach, *Friedrich Daniel Ernst Schleiermacher in Selbstzeugnissen und Bilddokumenten*, Reinbek 1967; M.Redeker, *Friedrich Schleiermacher, Leben und Werk (1768-1834)*, Berlin 1968; H.Gerdes, *Der geschichtliche biblische Jesus oder der Christus der Philosophen. Erwägungen zur Christologie Kierkegaards, Hegels und Schleiermachers*, Berlin 1973; D.Lange, *Historischer Jesus oder mythischer Christus. Untersuchungen zu den Gegensatz zwischen*

Friedrich Schleiermacher und David Friedrich Strauss, Gütersloh 1975; id. (ed.), *Friedrich Schleiermacher 1768-1834. Theologe – Philosophe – Pädagoge*, Göttingen 1985; E.H.U.Quapp, *Barth contra Schleiermacher? 'Die Weihnachtsfeier' als Nagelprobe, mit einem Nachwort zur Interpretationsgeschichte der 'Weihnachtsfeier'*, Marburg 1978; G.Moretto, *Etica e storia in Schleiermacher*, Naples 1979; E.Schrofner, *Theologie als positive Wissenschaft. Prinzipien und Methoden der Dogmatik bei Schleiermacher*, Frankfurt 1980; U.Barth, *Christentum und Selbstbewusstsein. Versuch einer rationalen Rekonstruktion des systematischen Zusammenhanges von Schleiermachers subjektivitätstheoretischer Deutung der christlichen Religion*, Göttingen 1983; B.A.Gerrish, *A Prince of the Church. Schleiermacher and the Beginnings of Modern Theology*, Philadelphia 1984; J.O.Duke and R.F.Streetman (ed.), *Barth and Schleiermacher. Beyond the Impasses?*, Philadelphia 1988; M.Junker, *Das Urbild des Gottesbewusstseins. Zur Entwicklung der Religionstheorie und Christologie Schleiermachers von der ersten zur zweiten Auflage der Glaubenslehre*, Berlin 1990; A.Weirich, *Die Kirche in der Glaubenslehre Friedrich Schleiermachers*, Frankfurt 1990; R.D.Richardson (ed.), *Schleiermacher in Context. Papers from the 1988 International Symposium on Schleiermacher at Herrnhut, The German Democratic Republic*, Lewiston 1991.

Notes on Friedrich Schleiermacher

1. Cf. K.Barth, *Protestant Theology in the Nineteenth Century*, 425.

2. For the biographical details see M.Redeker, *Friedrich Schleiermacher*.

3. F.Schleiermacher, letter to J.G.A.Schleiermacher, 21 January 1787, in F.D.E.Schleiermacher, *Kritische Gesamtausgabe*, ed. H.-J.Birkner et al., Berlin 1980ff. (in the following notes cited as KGA), V.1, 49-52: 50.

4. J.G.A.Schleiermacher, 'Letter to F.Schleiermacher of 7 May 1790', in KGA V.1, 198f.

5. F.Schleiermacher, 'Letter to G.Reimer of 30 April 1802', in *Aus Schleiermachers Leben. In Briefen*, ed. L.Jonas and W.Dilthey, Vol.I, Berlin 1858, 309.

6. Cf. id., 'Idee zu einem Katechismus der Vernunft für edle Frauen' (fragment), in KGA I.2, 154.

7. Id., 'Der Glaube' (Fragment), in KGA I.2, 154.

8. Cf. id., *On Religion. Speeches to its Cultured Despisers* (1799), reissued with a preface by R.Otto, New York 1958.

9. R.Otto in his Introduction to *On Religion*, vii.

10. Schleiermacher, *On Religion*, 277.

11. Ibid.

12. Ibid., 101.

13. Ibid.

14. Cf. G.W.F.Hegel, Preface to Hinrichs' *Religionsphilosophie* (1822), in *Werkausgabe* XI, Frankfurt 1970, 42-67, esp.58.

15. Cf. Schleiermacher, *Monologen. Ein Neujahrsgabe* (1800), KGA I, 3, 1-61.

16. Cf. H.Küng, *The Incarnation of God. An Introduction to Hegel's Theological Thought as Prolegomena to a Future Christology* (1970), Edinburgh 1987.

17. Schleiermacher, *On Religion*, 238.

18. Ibid., 235.

19. Ibid., 246.

20. Ibid., 247.

21. Ibid.

22. Cf. ibid., *Christmas Eve. A Dialogue on the Incarnation* (1806), Richmond, Va. 1967.

23. Cf. id., *Gelegentliche Gedanken über Universitäten im deutschen Sinn. Nebst einen Anhang über eine neu zu errichtende*, Berlin 1808.

24. Cf. id., *A Brief Outline of the Study of Theology* (1811), Richmond, Va 1966.

25. Cf. id., *The Christian Faith* (1821-22, second revised edition Berlin 1830-31), English translation, Edinburgh 1928.

26. Anselm of Canterbury, *Proslogion* I; id., *De fide trinitatis et de incarnatione verbi*, II.

27. Cf. F.Schleiermacher, *Life of Jesus* (1832), Philadelphia 1975.

28. *The Christian Faith*, §22.

29. Ibid., §94, p.385.

30. Ibid., 397.

31. Ibid.

32. Ibid.

33. Ibid.

34. Ibid.

35. D.Lange, 'Neugestaltung christlicher Glaubenslehre', in id. (ed.), *Friedrich Schleiermacher*, 85-105: 101.

36. F.Schleiermacher, *The Christian Faith*, 397.

37. Cf. id., 'Über die Glaubenslehre. Zweites Sendschreiben an Lücke', in KGA I, 10, 743.

38. Id., *The Christian Faith*, §95, p.389.
39. I myself have presented one in my *On Being a Christian*.
40. Cf. M.Junker, *Das Urbild des Gottesbewusstseins. Zur Entwick-lung der Religionstheorie und Christologie Schleiermachers von der ersten zur zweiten Auflage der Glaubenslehre*, Berlin 1990, 210f.
41. Cf. Lange, *Historischer Jesus*, 170.
42. Both quotations come from Kantzenbach, *Friedrich Schleiermacher*, 146.
43. Karl Barth, *Protestant Theology in the Nineteenth Century*, 427.

Literature on Karl Barth

Important articles on Karl Barth's early period (by R.Bultmann, E.Peterson, E.Przywara, G.Söhngen) are listed in E.Jüngel, 'Karl Barth', *Theologische Realenzyklopädie* V, Berlin, 1980; cf. also James M.Robinson (ed.), *The Beginnings of Dialectical Theology*, Richmond, Va. 1968. For the period after the Second World War see J.C.Groot, *Karl Barth en het theologische kenproblem*, Heiloo 1946; J.Hâmer, *Karl Barth. L'Occasionalisme théologique de K.Barth. Etude sur sa méthode dogmatique*, Paris 1949; O.Weber, *Karl Barth's Church Dogmatics. An Introductory Report on Volume I.1 to III.4*, Philadelphia and Edinburgh 1953; H.U.von Balthasar, *The Theology of Karl Barth*, New York 1972; E.Riverso, *Intorno al pensiero di Karl Barth, colpa e giustificazione nella reazione antiimmanentistica del Römerbrief barthiano*, Padua 1951; id., *La Teologia esistenzialisi-tica di Karl Barth. Analisis, interpretazione e discussione del sistema*, Naples 1955; A.Ebneter, *Der Mensch in der Theologie Karl Barths*, Zurich 1952; H.Fries, *Bultmann, Barth und die katholische Theolo-gie*, Stuttgart 1955; B.Gherardini, *La parola di Dio nella teologia di Karl Barth*, Rome 1955; G.C.Berkouwer, *The Triumph of Grace in the Theology of Karl Barth*, Grand Rapids 1956; H.Bouillard, *Karl Barth. Parole de Dieu et Existence Humaine*, I-II/2, Paris 1957; H.Küng, *Justification. The Doctrine of Karl Barth and a Catholic Reflection* ([4]1964), London and New York 1965; E.Jüngel, *The Doctrine of the Trinity. God's Being is in Becoming*, Grand Rapids and Edinburgh 1976; id., *Barth-Studien*, Zurich 1982; id., 'Umstrit-tene Theologie. Zum 100 Geburtstag Karl Barths', *Neue Zürcher Zeitung*, 10/11 May 1986; H.Gollwitzer, *Reich Gottes und Sozial-ismus bei Karl Barth*, Munich 1972; F.-W.Marquardt, *Theologie und Sozialismus. Das Beispiel Karl Barths*, Munich 1972; E.Busch, *Karl*

Barth. His Life from Letters and Autobiographical Texts, London and Philadelphia 1976; W.Kreck, *Grundentscheidungen in Karl Barths Dogmatik. Zur Diskussion seines Verständnisses von Offenbarung und Erwählung*, Neukirchen 1978; S.W.Sykes (ed.), *Karl Barth. Studies of His Theological Method*, Oxford 1979; M.Beintker, *Die Dialektik der 'dialektischen Theologie' Karl Barths*, Munich 1987; C.Frey, *Die Theologie Karl Barths. Eine Einführung*, Frankfurt 1988; K.-J.Kuschel, *Born Before All Time? The Dispute over Christ's Origin*, London and New York 1992.

Notes on Karl Barth

1. K.Barth, 'Die Unordnung der Welt und Gottes Heilsplan', *Evangelische Theologie* 8, 1948/49, 181-8: 185.

2. Cf. id., 'Roman Catholicism: a Question to the Protestant Church', in *Theology and Church* (1928), London and New York 1962, 307-33.

3. Cf. id., *Church Dogmatics* I/1-IV/4 (1932-67), Edinburgh 1936-1968. (henceforth cited as CD).

4. Id., 'Answer to Fr Jean Daniélou', in Karl Barth. *Offene Briefe 1945-1968*, ed. D.Koch, Zurich 1984, 171-5: 174.

5. H.U.von Balthasar, *The Theology of Karl Barth*.

6. CD I/1, xiii.

7. CD I/2, 143.

8. CD I/2, 688.

9. Cf. CD I/2, 687ff.

10. Cf. H.Küng, *Justification. The Doctrine of Karl Barth and a Catholic Response*.

11. Karl Barth in his 'Letter to the Author', ibid, xviii.

12. 'Das Evangelium und die Kirche. Bericht der evangelisch-lutherisch/römisch-katholischen Studienkommission', *Herder-Korrespondenz* 25, 1971, 536-44: 539.

13. CD, I.1, xiii.

14. Cf. J.Brosseder, 'Consensus in Justification by Faith without Consensus in the Understanding of the Church? The Significance of the Dispute over Justification Today', in K.-J.Kuschel and H.Häring (eds.), *Hans Küng. New Horizons for Faith and Thought*, London and New York 1993, 138-51.

15. Cf. H.Küng, *The Council and Reunion* (US: *The Council, Reform and Reunion*, 1960), London and New York 1961.

16. Barth, *Letters 1961-1968*, Edinburgh and Grand Rapids 1981.

17. Cf. Busch, *Karl Barth*.

18. For more detail see H.Küng, *Global Responsibility* (1990), London and New York 1991, A 1, 'From Modernity to Postmodernity'.

19. Cf. K.Barth, *The Epistle to the Romans* (second edition, 1922), Oxford 1933.

20. 'The Barmen Declaration', in *Creeds of the Churches*, ed. John H.Leith, Atlanta, Ga ³1982, 520.

21. Cf. H.Heppe, *Dogmatics*, London 1950 (with a preface by Karl Barth).

22. Cf. K.Barth, *Anselm: Fides quarens intellectum (1931)*, London and Richmond, Va 1960.

23. CD I/1, 295.

24. Cf. F.-W.Marquardt – D.Schellong – M.Weinrich (eds), *Karl Barth: Der Störenfried?*, Munich 1986.

25. CD IV/3, 38-164.

26. CD I/2, 280-97.

27. CD I.2, 300-25.

28. Cf. K.Barth, postscript to *Schleiermacher-Auswahl*, ed. H.Bölli, Munich 1968.

30. Cf. P.Tillich, 'The Significance of the History of Religions for the Systematic Theologian', in *The Future of Religions: Memorial Volume for Paul Tillich*, ed. J.C.Brauer, New York and London 1966, 80-94.

31. Cf. K.Barth, *Nein! Antwort an Emil Brunner* (1934, the English translation is entitled *Natural Theology*, London 1946).

32. Cf. E.Brunner, *Natur und Gnade. Zum Gespräch mit Karl Barth*, Zurich 1934 (included in *Natural Theology*, see n.31).

33. Cf. K.Barth, 'Rudolf Bultmann. An Attempt to Understand Him' (1952), in *Kerygma and Myth* II, London 1962, 83-162.

34. Cf.E.Käsemann, 'Those who Hunger and Thirst for Righteousness', in id., *Jesus Means Freedom*, London and Philadelphia 1969, 130-43.

35. Bultmann to Barth, 11-15 November 1952, in *Barth-Bultmann Letters, 1922-1966*, Edinburgh and Grand Rapids 1982.

36. Cf. K.-J.Kuschel, *Born Before All Time? The Dispute over Christ's Origin* (1990), London and New York 1992, 123. In his fine article ' "Jesus Christ is the Decisive Criterion": Beyond Barth and Hegel to a Christology "From Below"', in *Hans Küng. New Horizons for Faith and Thought* (n.14), 171-97, Kuschel has shown how much in my theology I have kept the substance of Barth's basic concern (despite all the differences in method and content).

37. Cf. E.Käsemann, 'Blind Alleys in the "Jesus of History" Controversy', in *New Testament Questions of Today*, London and Philadelphia 1969, 23-65. For a reply cf. R.Bultmann, 'Antwort an Ernst Käsemann',

in id., *Glauben und Verstehen. Gesammelte Aufsätze* IV, Tübingen 1965, 90-8.

38. K.Barth, *Die Woche*, 1963, no.4.

39. Id., *The Christian Century*, 1963, 1, 7ff.

40. CD III/3, 298f.

41. Id., *Wolfgang Amadeus Mozart 1765/1956* (1956), Grand Rapids 1986.

42. Ibid., 53f. (I have preferred my own translation.)

43. Ibid., 54f.

Notes on the Epilogue

1. I develop the following fundamental statements in connection with my books *On Being a Christian* and *Does God Exist*. Cf. H.Küng, *Theology for the Third Millennium* (1987), San Francisco and London 1991, 202ff.